THE LIFE OF
STS. MAXIMUS & DOMETIUS

MONASTERY, HYMNOGRAPHY & ICONOGRAPHY

THE LIFE OF
STS. MAXIMUS
& DOMETIUS

MONASTERY, HYMNOGRAPHY & ICONOGRAPHY

Translation and Introduction by
Shady Kiryakos Nessim

ST SHENOUDA PRESS
SYDNEY, AUSTRALIA
2022

THE LIFE OF STS MAXIMUS AND DOMETIUS
Translated by Shady Kiryakos Nessim

The English text is a translation of the Bohairic *Life* found in manuscript *vat.copt.67* (Vatican library). Extract translations from the Sahidic and Arabic versions are also included.

COPYRIGHT © 2022
St. Shenouda Press

All rights reserved. Except for brief quotations in critical publications or reviews, no part of this book may be reproduced in any manner without prior written permission from the publisher.

ST SHENOUDA PRESS
8419 Putty Rd,
Putty, NSW, 2330
Sydney, Australia

www.stshenoudapress.com

ISBN 13: 978-0-6451395-2-5

All scripture quotations, unless otherwise indicated, are taken from the New King James Version®. Copyright © 1982 by Thomas Nelson, Inc. Used by permission. All rights reserved.

About the author:
Shady Kiryakos Nessim is an Associate Lecturer in Liturgical Studies and Ancient Languages at St Athanasius College, University of Divinity in Melbourne, Australia. He is currently a doctoral student at the Catholic University of America.

Cover Design:
Dionysia Tanios
@dionysiandesigns

Contents

Preface	1
Notes on the *Life*	3
The *Life* of Saints Maximus and Dometius	15
Extracts from the Sahidic Version	51
Extracts from the Arabic Version	61
The Monastery of al-Baramūs	69
Liturgical Hymns	79
Iconography of Saints Maximus and Dometius	99
Appendix 1: Manuscripts Consulted	109
Appendix 2: Transcription of the Bohairic Life	113
Bibliography	145
Index	149

Abbreviations and Notes on Translation

Patrologia Greaca = *PG*
Patrologia Orientalis = *PO*
Bulletin de la Société d'Archéologie Copte = *BSAC*
Coptic Encyclopedia = *CE*
Life of Maximus and Dometius = *Life*
Ⲟⲩⲁⲗⲉⲛⲧⲓⲛⲟⲥ translated as "Valentinian"
ⲡⲟⲩⲣⲟ translated as "Emperor"
ⲙⲁⲛ̀ϣⲱⲡⲓ lit. place of dwelling. Translated as "cell"
Asqīṭ Makārīyūs lit. Scete of Macarius. Translated as "desert of Macarius"

PREFACE

Presented in this modest book is the *Life of Saints Maximus and Dometius*, two Roman brothers to which the famous Monastery of al-Baramūs in Wādī al-Naṭrūn is dedicated to. Included also is an overview of the monastery, its foundation, naming, and iconography. This book an English translation of the 13th-century Bohairic manuscript that is currently housed in the Vatican Library. The hymns presented are from Coptic liturgical books, and for the purpose of accuracy, have been re-translated from the original Coptic or Arabic where necessary. English translations for excerpts of the Sahidic and Arabic versions are to be found following the translation of the Bohairic.

Until the turn of the 20th century, little was known about the two holy fathers because an Arabic translation of their life-story from the Coptic existed only in manuscripts of monastic libraries. One only knew about these saints from the Synaxarium (a shorter account of a saint's life that is read in the liturgy), hymns and expositions, and iconography. There was the first printed translation of the Sahidic life in 1916, the Bohairic in 1977, and finally the Arabic edition in 1989 by the monks from the Monastery of al-Baramūs.

In this book, we learn of two Roman imperial (Greek East) foreigners who become influential figures that inspire the namesake and foundation of the Monastery of al-Baramūs in the Wilderness of Scete. The *Life* details their longing for the monastic life, their ascetic struggle, and their God-inspired miracles. Young men who are moved by their example, flee the world to bear their name: "*al-Baramūsī*". Even hymns, icons, and festivities have developed in their name to preserve their memory. It is no surprise then that we should call them foreigners, not only because they were foreigners to Egypt, but because they considered themselves strangers to the whole world, citizens in heaven. Every encounter Abba Macarius had with them, we cannot help but ponder at how he silently observes their peculiarity, watching them pray, quietly admiring their prayerful countenance.

Certainly, Abba Macarius is the key figure whom we should acknowledge as the foundation for their legacy by preserving their memory through oral stories. He said of them, "Woe is me! For I never became a monk. These are true monks, for in a short time of tribulation they quickly found the place." (#87)

Notes on the *Life*

Throughout the Life, there are a number of figures whose identity may cause some confusion. We will investigate the cases of Pshoi of Constantinople, Emperor Valentinian I, and Abba Arsenius the Great. A brief introduction to various versions, namely the Apophthegmata Patrum, Sahidic, Bohairic and Arabic versions will also be introduced.

a) Pshoi of Constantinople

The *Life* of the holy brothers Maximus and Dometius was made known by one long document attributed to a certain Pshoi who professes to be a native of Constantinople and ended his days in the Wilderness of Scete (Wādī al-Naṭrūn) as a disciple of the great Abba Macarius (†390). Pshoi claims to have received the personal testimony of Abba Macarius regarding these two saints and seems to employ his monastic position (perhaps as a scholar and scribe?) to endorse and verify their biography. Moreover, there is some confusion concerning who this Pshoi really is, and Buzi has already provided two hypotheses:[1] 1) Pshoi of Constantinople and Abba Pshoi of Scete (†417) are the same person; 2) that they are different persons, and the name was

---

[1] Paola Buzi, "The Life of Maximus and Domitius: Considerations for a Reconstruction of the Cultural Life of Western Lower Egypt in the late Coptic age", in *Augustinianum II* (2001): 521-544.

invented to give authority to the work. Pshoi of Scete or Abba Pshoi (Pishoy or Paisios), is known by the Coptic Church as Bishoy the beloved of Christ (ⲡⲓⲙⲉⲛⲣⲓⲧ ⲛ̀ⲧⲉ ⲡⲭ̅ⲥ̅) and is often painted carrying Christ on his shoulder or washing the feet of Christ. The first hypothesis is unlikely because Pshoi of Scete became a monk under the hand of Abba Pambo and lived under his spiritual guidance, not Abba Macarius as the *Life* indicated.[2] The second also cannot be true, since it is evident that the author used the name of Abba Macarius to verify the text. However, we must acknowledge that it was not unusual for foreigners to seek the monastic life in Egypt, and such was the case with Abba Arsenius who was also from Constantinople. It remains difficult to establish the true identity of Pshoi, author of the *Life*.

b) Emperor Valentinian I

Another confusion is seen in the person of Valentinian who is recognised as the father of the two saints. Anthony Alcock has identified him as Valentinian II (reigned 375 to 392) based on the Sahidic version who, according to this version, was succeeded by Theodosius I (reigned 379 to 395). Historically, Valentinian II was a co-ruler with Theodosius I and the latter was the successor of Valens (364 to 378)[3]. Theodosius ruled the Eastern Roman Province and Valentinian II ruled the West. If we are to follow the account in the Bohairic, Emperor Valentinian I would be the most likely figure named as the father of Sts Maximus and Dometius. And since the mention of Valentinian is associated with Emperor Jovian in the Bohairic, it is safe to

---

2 Leo Papadopulos, trans., *Saint Paisios the Great*, (New York: Holy Trinity Monastery, 1998).
3 He was the younger brother of Emperor Valentinian I.

say that their upbringing takes place in the Eastern Provinces where Valentinian I reigned. The *Life* reads:

> *Under the reign of Valentinian, the son and servant of God, Emperor Jovian, who destroyed all the temples of impure idols and who tore what remained of its walls, so that there was a great peace to the churches of God on earth, and Valentinian was called the new Constantine. (#8)*

Some of the Arabic versions have even confused Valens as the father of the two saints by naming him *Lāwen*.[4] However, despite the confusions between the different recessions, it is possible to know the identity of their father by an estimation of the time periods provided to us from the *Life* and from what is known by the historical sources.

The Sahidic text tells us that they had left for their monastic calling one year before their father died,[5] leaving us with the date 374 if the text means Valentinian I, and 391 if the text is referring to Valentinian II. But it cannot be the latter since Abba Macarius' death was in 391 and the two brothers had already died before him. Moreover, Fr Ṣamū'īl Ṭāwaḍrūs al-Suryānī identifies the year 384 as the year in which Sts Maximus and Dometius departed.[6] Considering that these dates are accurate, we can conclude that:

1. Maximus and Dometius had left for the desert on the year 374.
2. Valentinian I (364-375) is, in fact, the recognised father.

---

4 Edward Granville Browne, *A hand-list of the Muḥammadan manuscripts: including all those written in the Arabic character, preserved in the library of the University of Cambridge*, (University Press, 1900), 280.
5 This is mentioned in the Sahidic text. See, *(B) How Theodosius became emperor.*
6 Fr Ṣamū'īl Ṭāwaḍrūs al-Suryānī, *al-ādyurah al-maṣriyah al-'āmerah*, (Cairo, 1968), 183.

3. Their monastic life was no longer than 10 years. We are able to identify at least the first six years spent in Syria under Abba Agabus (#17) and the remaining with Abba Macarius.

c) Abba Arsenius the Great

The case of Abba Arsenius also raises a question: Was Abba Arsenius the Great (†445) really the tutor of these brothers as al-Maqrīzī stated?[7] His name is not mentioned in either of the Coptic versions, the Arabic version,[8] or the Synaxarium.[9] Evelyn White suggests that Pshoi of Constantinople could be Abba Arsenius,[10] but other than having Arsenius and Pshoi as natives of Constantinople, there is little evidence to suggest this. Moreover, the entry of Abba Arsenius in the *Apophthegmata Patrum* says that he was appointed by Theodosius I to tutor his children, Honorius and Arcarius[11] and does not mention the two saints being tutored. The account by al-Maqrīzī is most unlikely, since he also says that they became monks under the hands of Abba Arsenius, whereas all the available sources only mention Abba Agabus and Abba Macarius who become their spiritual fathers. Furthermore, it is unlikely that they even encountered each other in the desert because we know he went to the monastery in circa 394, ten years after the two brothers departed.[12]

---

[7] Taqī al-Dīn al-Maqrīzī, *al-Mawaiz wa al-I'tibar fi al-Khitat wa al-Athar*, vol.2 (Cairo: Government Press, 1892), 508-509.
[8] E Amélineau, *Monuments pour servir à l'histoire de d'Égypte chrétienne: histoire des monastères de la Basse-Égypte; vies des saints Paul, Antoine, Macaire, Maxime et Domèce Jean Le Main, etc*, (1894): 262-315.
[9] Iacobus Forget, ed., *Synaxarium Alexandrinum Tomus I* (1905), 216-219.
[10] Evelyn-White, *The monasteries of the Wadi Natrûn*, 98 n.7, and 101.
[11] Benedicta Ward, *The sayings of the desert fathers: The alphabetical collection (rev. ed.)*, (Kalamazoo: Cistercian Publications, 1984), 9.
[12] Ward, *The sayings of the desert fathers*, 9.

d) The Apophthegmata Patrum

The *Apophthegmata Patrum* is the oldest account of these two saints,[13] and can be compared with section 58-68 of the Bohairic in this edition. The Bohairic is elongated with a different sequence and mostly includes the authors' commentary on the account. The oldest known apophthegm is in Greek and reads:

> *Abba Bitimius[14] related that Abba Macarius said this: 'When I was living at Scetis, two young strangers came down there. One had a beard, the other was beginning to grow one. They came towards me saying, "Where is Abba Macarius' cell?" I said to them, "What do you want with him?" They replied, "We have heard tell of him and of Scetis and we have come to see him." I said to them, "I am he." Then they bowed low to me and said, "We want to live here." Seeing that they were delicate and had been brought up in comfort, I said to them, "You cannot live here." The elder said, "If we cannot live here, we will go somewhere else." Then I said to myself, "Why chase them away and be a stumbling block to them? Suffering will make them go away of their own accord." So I said to them, "Come and make yourselves a cell, if you can." They said, "Show us a place, and we will make one."*
>
> *The old man gave them an axe, a basket full of bread and salt, and showed them a lump of rock, saying, "Cut out some stones here, and bring wood from the marsh, make a roof, and live here." He added, "I thought they would choose to go away,*

---

13 Ward, *The sayings of the desert fathers,* 134.
14 He is not mentioned in the Bohairic.

because of the hardship. But they asked me what work they should do here." I replied, "Rope-making." And I took some leaves from the marsh and showed them the rudiments of weaving and how to handle the reeds. I said to them, "Make some baskets, give them to the keepers, and they will bring you bread." Then I went away. But they, with patience, did all that I had told them and for three years they did not come to see me. Now I wrestled with my thoughts, thinking, "What is their way of life? Why do they not come to ask me about their thoughts? Those who live far off come to see me, but those who live quite close do not come. They do not go to anyone else either; they only go to church, in silence, to receive the oblation." I prayed to God, fasting the whole week, that he would show me their way of life. At the end of the week, I got up and went to visit them, to see how they were.

When I knocked, they opened the door and greeted me in silence. Having prayed, I sat down. The elder made a sign to the younger to go out and he sat plaiting the rope, without saying anything. At the ninth hour, he knocked, and the younger one returned and made a little soup and set the table at a sign of his elder brother. He put three small loaves on it and stood in silence. As for me, I said, "Rise, and let us eat." We got up to eat and he brought a small water-bottle and we drank. When the evening came, they said to me, "Are you going away?" I replied, "No, I will sleep here." They spread a mat for me on one side, another for themselves in the opposite corner.

They took off their girdles and cowls and lay down together on the mat. When they were settled, I prayed God that he would show me their way of life. Then the roof opened, and it became as light as day, but they did not see the light. When they thought I was asleep, the elder tapped the younger on the side and they got up, put on their girdles again and stretched their hands towards heaven. I could see them, but they could not see me. I saw the demons coming like flies upon the younger one, some sitting on his mouth and others on his eyes. I saw the angel of the Lord circling round about him with a fiery sword, chasing the demons far from him. But they could not come near the elder one. When early dawn came, they lay down and I made as though I had just woken up and they did the same. The elder simply said to me, "Shall we recite the twelve psalms?" and I said to him, "Yes." The younger one chanted five psalms in groups of six verses and an alleluia and at each verse a tongue of flame came out of his mouth and ascended to heaven.

Likewise, with the elder, when he opened his mouth to chant it was like a column of fire which came forth and ascended to heaven; in my turn, I recited a little by heart. As I went out, I said, "Pray for me." But they bowed without saying a word. So, I learned that the first was a perfect man, but the enemy was still fighting against the younger. A few days later the elder brother fell asleep and three days afterwards, his younger brother died too.' When the fathers came to see Abba Macarius, he used to take them to their cell, and say, 'Come and see the place of martyrdom of the young strangers.'

This apophthegm begs the question as to whether there was a Greek *Life* that existed before the Sahidic, or whether it was originally written in Sahidic[15] as an extended version of the apophthegm. The only explicit indication of a Greek version is given to us from the concluding remark of the Arabic version: "[this] was copied from Greek into Arabic. Praise be to …".[16] Nothing is known about a Greek *Life*, other than the Greek apophthegm that was provided above.[17] Furthermore, the same Greek apophthegm exists in the Sahidic *Apophthegmata Patrum*.[18] It is probably the case that the original Sahidic *Life* was composed and expanded from the Greek apophthegm.

e) The Sahidic version

The *Life* comes from two copies in both Coptic dialects. The Sahidic text dates to the 10th/11th century and is found in the Pierpont Morgan Library, codex 40. It is published and translated into French by Henri Munier,[19] and into English by Anthony Alcock.[20] Unfortunately, the text lacks a beginning which are about ten leaves that deal with their years as youth. The text begins with the prostitute of Latakia (See, *Sahidic Extracts (A)*). The parchment codex that contains the Sahidic text found in Hamuli (in the surroundings of the modern village of Hamuli, in Fayum oasis) were found in the remains of the monastery of St Michael which, in 1910, brought to light a quantity of Coptic codices, most of which were purchased one year later by

---

15 This is the belief of Munier. See Henri Munier, "Une relation copte sa'îdique de la vie des saints Maxime et Domèce", 94.

16 Pirone, "Vita dei Santi Massimo e Domezio nelle Fonti Arabe, 249-388.

17 *PG 65* (1864), 237-238; see also, F. Nau in *PO 5* (1910), 750-751.

18 M. Chaîne, *Le manuscrit de la version copte Apophthegmata Patrum*, (Cairo, 1960), 71-72.

19 Henri Munier, "Une relation copte sa'îdique de la vie des saints Maxime et Domèce", *BIFAO* (1917): 94-140. See also the photographs of the manuscript in Henri Hyvernat, *Bybliothecae Pierpont Morgan codices coptici, Photographice Expressi, Codices M584, Tomvs XL* (Romae, 1922), 35-96.

20 It is freely available on his academia page.

Pierpont Morgan.[21] The title of this version is very long, which Buzi[22] suggests is evidence of a later work copied from an older transmission that no longer exists. The title reads:

> *The story of the life of the Roman saints Maximus and Dometius, sons of Valentinus, emperor of the Romans, who completed a good life full of all virtues and who, in it, also fulfilled all the commands of the gospels. One died on the 14th of the month of Tuba, the other on the 17th of the same month. It was narrated by Abba Pshoi of Constantinople, the first deacon who lived with Abba Macarius, man of God, and Abba Isidoros. He died a deacon. Abba Moses the Ethiopian was appointed in his place. Pshoi wrote the life of the saints on a papyrus scroll. He left it in the church as a benefit and a memorial, for all readers, of a beautiful way of life in accordance with God and in virtue, for he had met with them for some days while they were still alive when he came to Scetis. When Scetis had been laid waste by Mastikoi, Abba Isidoros took it with him to Alexandria to the Xenon. He spoke about the life of those saints and about his great zeal for them. It then remained there until the time of Abba Khael, the most holy archbishop of Alexandria. It was brought to light by a deacon names Eustathios, who had found it in a large storage box of old parchment books written in quires, when he was looking for books that might have deteriorated over*

---

21 Twenty-eight folios are divided between Cairo, Strasbourg, and Port Said. See Leo Depuydt, *Catalogue of Coptic manuscripts in the Pierpont Morgan Library Vol.I* (Peeters, 1993), 333.

22 Paola Buzi, "The Life of Maximus and Domitius: Considerations for a Reconstruction of the Cultural Life of Western Lower Egypt in the late Coptic age", 521-544.

time, for he was a servant of God. He then met a monk living in the Ennaton, who was from Scetis, and gave it to him. This is the way in which the life of those perfect saints of God was revealed. For the glory of our Lord Jesus Christ. In God's peace. Amen.

f) The Bohairic version

This version is preserved in a 13th-century Bohairic manuscript (see, Appendix 1.2 and 2) now located in the Vatican Library and known as *vat. copt. 67*. Amélineau published a French edition in 1894.[23] An English translation and transcription of the Bohairic manuscript is provided in the two chapters that follow.[24] A comparison of the Sahidic and Bohairic versions shows us that they are analogous, with the Sahidic version being more precise. Portions of the Sahidic text have been removed in the Bohairic version, such as the prostitute in Latakia, Emperor Theodosius' enthronement, the healing of the blind calf, and Dometius' encounter with the serpent. Since the first half of the Sahidic is missing, the Bohairic provides an indication of what the Sahidic may have contained. Whether the lost part of the Sahidic bears any similarities is only speculation, but from what is extant in the Bohairic, it is most likely the case that this lost portion was more or less the same.

---

23 E Amélineau, *Monuments pour servir à l'histoire de d'Égypte chrétienne: histoire des monastères de la Basse-Égypte; vies des saints Paul, Antoine, Macaire, Maxime et Domèce Jean Le Main, etc,* (1894): 262-315.

24 I have included the Coptic transcription here and distinguished them by numbered paragraphs that align with the English for two reasons: First, for easy access to the readers if they wish to provide better or a more accurate translation. And, secondly, so that this text could be used with my students studying Coptic language at St Athanasius College who spend some time engaging with and translating snippets of similar texts.

g) The Arabic version

For the Arabic *sīrah*, B. Pirone completed a critical edition of the text and published it in 1988.[25] It is more or less similar to the Sahidic and reflects all the same stories. The only major difference is the story that is placed after *Miracle #9: The Antiochene merchant,* which is an added part about the saints' mother learning of their new life and her venture to visit them. It is a significantly extended version of *#41* of the Bohairic text. The scribe seems to be confused with the emperor as he omitted the name of Theodosius and replaced it with the father of the saints instead, sparking the family crisis that exists in the Arabic version. Therefore, the story of Theodosius, the empress and daughter, becomes the saints' father (Valentinian), their mother and their sister.

The account reveals a passionate and loving mother who cannot live without the close proximity of her sons. On the one hand, she compares seeing them again to the Genesis story of Jacob when he had seen his son Joseph for the first time after 22 years, and on the other, the struggle to accept the reality of a monk's life that requires a complete rejection of the world, even their own family. It is a text written to emphasise the typical emotional conflict known to parents who go through the difficulty of accepting their children's choice to join the monastic life.[26] The scribe may have added this segment with the intention to inform and comfort parent-readers who are in this same position. The text is included in *Extracts from the Arabic Version*.

---

25 Pirone, "Vita dei Santi Massimo e Domezio nelle Fonti Arabe", 225 and 388.
26 Evidently seen today when men or women join the monastery.

The *Life* of Saints Maximus and Dometius According to the Bohairic Text

Prologue

1. The *Life* of the Roman saints, Maximus and Dometius, sons of Valentinian the emperor of the Romans. They completed their life filled with all virtue after having kept all the commandments of the holy Gospels. One of them, Maximus, rested on the 14th day of the month *Tōbi*,[27] and the other, Dometius, on the 17th day of the same month.

2. It was narrated by Pshoi, a man from Constantinople and archdeacon[28] who lived in Scete near Abba Macarius, the man of God, and next to Abba Isidore, who had been replaced by Moses the Black after departing as a deacon.[29] Abba Pshoi wrote the lives of these two saints to remember them. He placed it in the church for the benefit of whoever desired to live a life according to God.

Panegyric

3. Come all today! O my holy fathers and God-bearers! Assemble with me attentively, so that I may tell you the virtues, the miracles, and the wonders of these holy Romans, Maximus and Dometius, the sons of Valentinian the God-loving emperor.

4. It happened in the time of Abba Macarius, the holy spirit-bearer and man of God, who was the head and the first of Scete, who was the first vine of this tree of the Lord of Sabaoth known as Scete, so that he may establish there the fruits of true repentance according to God.

---

27 ⲧⲱⲂⲓ (*Tōbi* also read from the Arabic as *Tubah*)

28 ⲡⲓϣⲟⲣⲡ ⲛ̄ⲇⲓⲁⲕⲱⲛ (lit. the first deacon)

29 It is interesting to note that Abba Isidore here is given the title deacon, and not priest. John Cassian is one of the earliest sources to identify him as an abbot of one the four monastic communities in Scete. See Ward, *The sayings of the desert fathers*, 96.

5. O blessed Mountain of Scete! The mountain on which God and His angels dwell! O mountain that remits sins! O mountain that leads sinners to see God! O spiritual mountain which makes this entire place filled with perfumes by the prayers of the saints who dwell in it! O holy mountain of the Natrun which has become a spiritual natron that washes away the defilements of the soul![30] How can I speak about the glory that has been bestowed on you? O pure mountain of salt, from which much salt of the rational earth has come out of according to the testimony of our Saviour, which is the seasoning of the souls that were spoiled by iniquities! O holy Mountain of Scete, the place of unity between the angels and men, living together.

6. For I speak briefly about this mountain! This which changed the thieves who plundered[31] and those who performed other evil works became prophets and eloquent speakers of God, the Creator! For the interpretation of ⲱⲓϩⲏⲧ is the place of union for those who seek God with all their heart. Those whom God the Word has gathered from the four corners of the earth through the holy words of the holy Gospel which says, "He who loves himself, must deny himself, take up his cross and follow Me."[32] For by this He implanted in them the passion of His holy cross through His servant Abba Macarius, who is an example of[33] it in all faithfulness, that by the strength of the holy cross they may fight against all the power of the adversary in the desert. But in order not to defer in this speech and so as not to neglect the discourse of the subject[34] that we first proposed, I

---

30 He is using a play on the word ϩⲟⲥⲉⲙ to identify the place and also as the mineral used as a disinfectant.
31 This may be a reference to Abba Moses the black.
32 Matthew 16:24
33 ⲧⲩⲡⲟⲥ (Can also mean an 'type of').
34 ϩⲩⲡⲟⲑⲉⲥⲓⲥ (lit. Hypothesis)

will turn to the matter of my speech, and I will speak according to what the Holy Spirit will reveal to me.

Fleeing Their Imperial Life

7. It so happened when I heard Abba Macarius, the man of God, talking with the other elders, that he said to them, "Come, let us look at the martyrdom of the young foreigners, and the work of necessity to me for the zeal of God, that I unveil to you the courage of these blessed ones and their virtuous way of life.

8. Under the reign of Valentinian, the son and servant of God Emperor Jovian,[35] who destroyed all the temples of impure idols and tore what remained of its walls, so that there was a great peace to the churches of God on earth, and Valentinian was called the new Constantine.

9. Moreover, he honourably brought up his sons Maximus and Dometius, as well as their little sister, in all piety and good instruction, with psalms, fasting, prayers at night and in the day in continual meditations, so that the palace during those days was like a monastery of monks. He encouraged them to perform all ascetical practices, from the littlest to the greatest, as do the monks. It was to the extent that these saints were called by everyone from their childhood "elders" because of their good work and their blessedness as servants of God.

10. When the blessed Maximus and Dometius had grown up and had advanced in good works according to God, they sought after the angelic life, that is to say that of the monks, and they began to discuss with each other saying, "How can we flee so that we can become monks?" So, the younger one said to the older, "Let us excuse ourselves from our father and tell him that

---

35 Jovian was Roman emperor from June 363 to February 364. Jovian was petitioned by bishops over doctrinal issues concerning Christianity and by September 363, he had re-established Christianity as the state religion.

we will travel to Nicaea to pray in the place of our holy fathers, the bishops. If he gives us permission to go to the place where we want to go, we will get there." When they had agreed on their plan, they went to their father, and he freely let them go.

11. Now, there was a holy priest living in the place of the 318 bishops whose name was John, a monk. Emperors would come on several occasions to ask for his advice, as well as the bishops of this place. When these blessed ones found a suitable day, they put on good clothes, mounted their horses, and journeyed as though they were going to Nicaea to pray in the place of our holy fathers the bishops.

12. When they had arrived at Nicaea, they found the holy priest John, whom we just mentioned, and he received them with meekness and honour. They told him of their monastic inclinations. But he, by the grace of God, tested their thoughts in order to know what they desired before responding with any word whatsoever. When he saw the genuineness of their decision in God, he greatly rejoiced and encouraged them. They begged if they could stay near him, but he did not want to endure it and said, "I am fearful because of your father the emperor. I will not do this deed, but since you are leaving to become monks, arise and go to Syria. I heard about an anchorite in that place who lives on a rock near the sea, and it is he whose fame has filled all of Syria and Palestine. His name is Agabus, and he is a man from Tarsus in Cilicia. He resembles Paul by his faith and his deeds. If you like the suggestion, go to his place."

Meeting Abba Agabus

13. When they heard this, they rejoiced greatly. He prayed over them and dismissed them in peace. They withdrew from him in great joy and did not embark on returning to their city to see their father, but they went directly to Syria. As they had inquired about the blessed Agabus, they became informed of his place. When they had found him, he received them with great joy, and they told him of all their deeds.

14. Now, when the God-bearing elder saw their love for God, he immediately laid on them the holy habit[36] of the monks of Syria, because the monks of this place do not wear a scapular[37], but they wear a black garment, for that is the habit in Syria.

15. Therefore, I teach you according to the manner that these saints told me: "When the saintly elder Agabus was about to rest, we questioned him, saying, 'Tell us a word, our holy father, so that we can live by it.' He said to us, 'I saw myself this night standing over this rock which is south of us. I saw a monk standing in front of me. He was a tall man, dressed in clothes that had black bands and a hood on his head with crosses on it. He had in his hand a cross. Seeing him, I feared, but he approached me, greeted me, and said to me, 'Do you know who I am?' I replied to him, 'No, my father.' He said to me, 'I am Macarius, the Egyptian. I have come to welcome your children and take them with me to Egypt.' I replied to him, 'You cannot take them.' He said to me, 'No, but I inform you that after three days you will depart and go to the Lord, and the emperor will send for his children to return them to Constantinople. Therefore, beware, order them to go down to Egypt so that they may dwell with me, for the Lord has appointed them to me as sons. Behold, this is what I tell you.'"

16. And when he said these things to me, he vanished. Now, I inform you that it has been many days since I have heard the

---

36 ⲥⲕⲉⲙⲁ refers to monastic clothing and practice.
37 ⲙⲁⲣⲟⲛⲁϩ I am unsure about this word. ⲟⲛⲁϩ signifies the forearms or upper limb. The Arabic equivalent would be *dirāʿ*, which is often translated to 'breast plate' or 'chainmail'. Monks were known to weare sleeveless robes, so this could be referring to an aristocrats longsleeve shirt.

good news of this man Abba Macarius, and so I say to you, if the emperor finds out where you are, he will not allow you to stay here. Therefore, after the end of my life, go down to Egypt, and dwell with the holy Abba Macarius, until the Lord visits you."

17. When the elder Agabus had said this, he departed in peace. They dwelled with him for six years, and his spirit was doubled on them like the spirit of Elijah was doubled over Elisha in former times.

18. Come, therefore, while I tell you of the signs, wonders, and the gifts of healing that God performed through their holy hands. For thus their fame spread over all of Palestine and all the region of Pisidia[38] regarding their healing of the sick in the name of our Lord Jesus Christ. For there were crowds who had unclean spirits in them. When the spirits heard the names of these saints, they came out of them, and also the sick were immediately healed by the grace of our Saviour.

Miracle #1: The man with a curious spirit healed

19. Listen to this great wonder which was done by them. A man was brought to them from Asqelon[39] in whom there was a curious spirit. While he was far from the cell of these saints, he cried out with a loud voice, saying, "O, what violence do I suffer from you, Macarius the man of Egypt, the anchorite! We left the desert of Egypt to you, and you have come here again. Behold, your prayers make me suffer right here, for you have given a hand to these Romans." And when he said this, the unclean spirit went out from the man, and whoever heard of it glorified God.

---

38 ⲡⲓⲥⲓⲧⲓⲁ is a city in the ancient world of Asia Minor, which is present day Turkey.
39 ⲁⲥⲕⲁⲗⲱⲛ is an ancient city on the coastal plain of Palestine

Miracle #2: The large beast tamed

20. On the path that leads to Iconium, there was a hollow in the mountain whereby a large beast[40] would destroy crowds of men walking in this path. When the inhabitants of Iconium saw the destruction that occurred, they went to these blessed ones and informed them of the harm inflicted on them by this evil beast. Then the blessed Maximus wrote a small letter, saying, "In the name of Lord of the Sabaoth, the God of Abba Macarius and of Abba Agabus our father - men who are Christ-bearers - and the Word of the Father, if one carries this little letter at the entrance of your den, you, beast, will go out closing your mouth, laid down in the middle of the path, without moving from this place until the birds of sky eat your flesh." And when they had taken this letter, they gave it to a man mounted on a horse. They went and placed the letter at the entrance to the cave of the beast, and immediately fled.

21. O the great wonder which happened at this time! For at that moment the wicked beast immediately came out of his cave and laid down under the heaven in the middle of the path, at the sight of everyone, so that even those who were far came a day's journey to see it. It could not move from its place at all, and they threw stones at it and glorified God who works wonders through his saints.

Miracle #3: The leprous man healed

22. A man came from Lystra to see the wonder that had taken place. His whole body was leprous. And when he had gone to the saints, he recognised them by their great faith, and was immediately cleansed of leprosy. Everyone glorified our Lord Jesus Christ because of the healings which He carried out by the hands of these blessed ones.

---

40 ⲟⲩⲛⲓϣϯ ⲛ̇ⲇⲣⲁⲕⲱⲛ (lit. A large dragon)

Miracle #4: The man with inverted face healed

23. Someone was brought to them from Magdala[41] of Pisidia whose face had been inverted by the force of a demon for three years. And when these saints saw him, they were greatly saddened at the condition of his face. So, they took a little water, they sanctified it in the name of our Lord Jesus Christ, they poured the water on him, and at that moment, his face was rectified. O these great gifts which the Son of God worked with these sons of the king! For truly, those who love God, He works with them all good work!

24. Please, let no one be an unbeliever of the things I say, because I too, the worthless Pshoi, as I was still in Constantinople, even before knowing where Scete was, learned from merchants of the healings that these saints performed in the name of our Lord Jesus Christ, God the Word. I went to Syria, still a pragmatist, in order to see with my own eyes what I had heard, so that my heart was persuaded, saying in my mind: The sight of the eyes is as good as the hearing of the ear. Because from the day I saw their good works, I decided to become a monk, but I did not have the strength to do so until the moment when God came to my aid, that he pulled me out of the worries of this world and took me to Scete. And what I had heard in Syria and in Scete, I now write in this book. Now, therefore, so as not to delay the discourse in this way by confirming the truth so that I forget the great gifts, we will again return to the unperishable gifts that Christ our God worked by these sons of the king, who had put on Christ like Paul and Timothy, whereby God worked in them also.

---

41 Ⲙⲁⲕⲇⲁⲗⲁⲛ was an ancient city on the shore of the Sea of Galilee.

Miracle #5: The possessed priest from Gabala healed

25. There was also a priest in Gabala[42], the city of the Gabaleans, whose name was Zachariah. A spirit posessed him, summoning him with wonders by demons, so that he caused all Gabaleans to be lead astray. And when the bishop of Gabala saw the harm that was happening in the diocese, he took with him other priests, and he went to these saints. He informed them of all that had happened. When they heard these things from the bishop, they were very saddened to the heart, and they said to him, "How did you not bring him with you?" He said to them, "He is not listening to me, O holy fathers." The bishop spoke and said to them, "I implore you, my holy fathers, that you send for him, that he should immediately come."

26. The holy Maximus, having taken a paper, wrote thus, saying: "I, the weak Maximus, the servant of Christ, write with my hand, by the power of the Lord of the Sabaoth, God of the apostles, of the prophets, of Abba Macarius the Egyptian, the one whom our father Agabus saw in vision. I write to Zachariah: 'If it is the teaching of the apostles that you teach this, then hold to it in this manner. But, if it is that of the demons and if you are disobedient to your bishop who teaches you your salvation, then we command this demon, in the name of Jesus the true Word of God, may this demon come upon you, may he torment you and may all know the error in which you find yourself.'" So, he wrote the name of Abba Macarius on the exterior of the letter, gave it to the bishop and confided in him. O the marvel of what is accomplished at the time when the bishop gave him the letter saying, "The anchorites greet you!"

27. Glory to you, Christ, the Word of God, and to the power that You manifest out of those who are Your followers and who serve Your holy name! For the demon who was corrupting souls

---

[42] Γαββαλων also known as Jableh, is a city in present day Syria.

did not let him read the letter, rather, immediately tackled him, knocked him down to the ground in the midst of those who were standing. He made him suffer by uttering cries, and he barked like a dog, so that the whole town of Gabala gathered around him to see him, marvelling at what had happened to him who a few moments before was praising himself. He remained in this torment for ten days. Then, they brought him to the saints, bound in shackles. But they, when they saw his suffering, were greatly saddened. They took a little water, sanctified it, and poured it on him in the name of Christ. Immediately he was saved from that demon. He stayed with the saints three days and they taught him the way of salvation. They dismissed him in peace, and he gave glory to God.

28. In all these healings which were performed by these blessed ones, they were not exalted in heart at all and were not proud, nor did they speak a word to any man using authority, but they humbled themselves below all mankind, as if they had been despicable, making themselves unworthy, saying at all times, "The grace of God is enough. As for us, we are weak and sinful."

Miracle #7: The sinful priest repents

29. There was a priest in Seleucia of Isauria. When he had just committed impure deeds, he would go and stand at the altar of God after he had fallen with a Samaritan woman. While he persisted in these actions, God wanted to reveal what this priest was doing to all Isauria, so that the others would know and be afraid. On the day when St Ignatius is commemorated, the priest committed the sin, and then he went to church again to worship. When he finished reading the Gospel and the other prayers, he approached the altar in order to worship without any fear. Moments later, an angel of the Lord struck him with a very violent blow, so that the skin of his body swelled like wineskin, and immediately he fell to the earth, and became like a corpse. They took him up, brought him to his house in great distress.

30. Ten days later, his whole body became ulcerated so that worms came out. Being in much pain, he cried out day and night in a stinging voice because of the disease that was devouring him. He would weep, confessing in everyone's presence all the impurities he had committed. So, he was placed on a bed by men who carried him and put him at the feet of the holy servants of the Most-high God.

31. When he was placed in their presence, they were wholeheartedly saddened. They saw his condition and said to him, "What have you done that this should happen to you?" But he replied to them, "Forgive me, my holy fathers. Christ has revealed to you my actions first." They said to him, "Do you know Christ is good, and he sees the works you do?" He said, "Yes, my lords and fathers. He gave me this lesson in goodness."

32. Then the blessed athletes of Christ Jesus - knowing that God does not want anyone to die tarnished by his sins, but rather he wants them all to turn to him in true repentance - took a little water, sanctified it with the sign of the cross and sprinkled it over him saying, "O Lord Jesus Christ, the true medicine of our souls and of our bodies. He who does not wish on any of those who have strayed to perish, and who will let them all return to His spiritual fold through repentance. May his soul be saved, for it is You who will heal us all through the prayers of Agabus our father and of Your servant Abba Macarius." When they had poured the water on him and left him for two days near those who were praying over him, the ulcers cleared up and he was healed. The saints dismissed him in peace, saying, "Since you have lamented, sin no more, lest the wrath of God take hold of you again, and you severely die." And whenever he was reminded of the saints, he would give glory to God at all times because of the healing which he had acquired through the prayers of these saints.

Miracle #8: Two Greek philosophers repent

33. By chance, there were two Greek philosophers in Athens who had heard about the healings which took place because of these saints and by the power of Christ Jesus. They accused them, saying, "Who are those who are said to cast out demons from men, when they pray on them in the name of Christ? Are these not the gods of the Athenians?" These idolaters therefore arose in a spirit of deceit and wanted to test these saints. They contracted their hands and bound them with bands in the manner of a maimed person, and they closed their eyes in the manner of the blind, saying, "Since they are prophets and they hunt demons, they will know our work." Another man was taken with them, as though he was leading the way for them. And when they arrived at the place of the saints, the man leading them knocked at the entrance.

34. The holy Dometius answered them, saying, "What do you want from this place?" And they replied to him, "We came to you, saints of God, to entreat to you, so that you will have mercy on us and that you pray over us, that we should be healed. For we are paralysed and blind. Here, you see, this man led us and brought us to this place." The holy Dometius said to them in simplicity, "May the Lord Jesus Christ heal you and do to you as you have requested." Immediately, they became paralysed and blind. Their hands crippled and they became maimed. Immediately they shouted with a loud voice saying, "O men of God, have mercy on us, for we have come to this place to test you."

35. Instantly they threw themselves on the floor before the feet of these holy ones with great faith saying, "We beg you, have mercy on us, help us and we will become Christians from today, and we will be servants of Christ." And the holy Maximus said to them, "Do you now believe the truth?" They replied, "Yes, we believe with all our hearts that Jesus is the Son of God and that there is none other than Him." When the servants of Christ heard these words from them, they prayed over a little oil and gave it to them saying, "Go to the place of the holy Leontius and wash yourself in his well. Anoint yourselves with this little oil, and we believe that you will be redeemed."

36. And they did as the saints said to them, and they were healed by the power of Christ. Immediately they were baptised in the name of the Father, the Son and the Holy Spirit and became Christians in this place. They preached the wonder which had befallen them in Athens, the city of the Athenians. Since that day, multitudes of them have become Christians, glorifying God the incarnate Word. And, if I counted the number of healing gifts that God performed by the hands of these saints, there would not be enough time for me to speak.

Miracle #9: The Antiochene merchant

37. There was a merchant from the city of Antioch, who went from time to time to these blessed ones to receive their blessing and to take their handiwork, for they made ropes. As a result of his faith in these saints, he wrote down their names on the ropes and arranged them in a cross to the middle of the sail of the boat to sail in the ocean. The boat had arrived in Constantinople with its merchandise to be sold there because the port of the city is located inside its city walls.

38. When the emperor knew that the waves were violent, he ordered the boats to be placed inside the city because of the brutality of the waves of the sea. There were bells hanging in the entrance, and the chains were removed. The boats were positioned to enter the port, and there were officials of the emperor and soldiers who stood to inspect the boats that were approaching. The official was alert and saw the sail of the boat which we have already mentioned lying on the floor as the sailors tied it. He saw the names of the blessed Maximus and Dometius written on the ropes of the sail. When he had read the names, he ordered the sailors to be brought to him. He said to them, "What are these names written on your sail?" They replied to him, "They are holy men of God who live in our city." The officials said to them, "Does this boat belong to them?" They replied to him, "No, but we have their names on our sail because of their holy prayers, so that they may offer us help with our boat and our travels." He said to them, "Do you know their good place in which they dwell?" They replied to him, "Yes, our lord, they live in Syria."

39. Then the official ordered that the sailors should be tied up and brought to the emperor. As for the official, he preceded them in order to inform the emperor, and the emperor said to bring them into his presence. The name of this emperor was Theodosius. Theodosius was originally from Egypt and the chief general of the horses of Emperor Valentinian, I mean, the father of these saints. Valentinian saw that Theodosius was a courageous man, and appointed him to take charge of all the stables where the horses of his kingdom were being trained.

40. When Emperor Valentinian had rested, following the true and unfathomable judgments of God and unanimously by the whole senate, Emperor Theodosius the general was proposed to sit in place of Valentinian, the father of the blessed Maximus and Dometius, according to what is written in the history of the Church. But when the pious Emperor Theodosius saw the sailors chained, he had them released, saying, "These are my companions. Do not leave them bound lest Christ should be angry with me." And the God-serving Emperor said to them gently, "Who are these men of God whom you know?" They replied, "Our lord, Maximus is one, Dometius is the other." Then he said to them, "What do they look like?" They replied and told him, "One is a grown man who has a beard. The other is a short man with long hair and a small beard." Then the emperor ordered three pieces of gold be given to each sailor and then dismissed them in peace.

Emperor Theodosius and the Roman brothers

41. Then the emperor called a palace eunuch named Marcellus, who was a man courageous in his actions like a lion. He gave him a mighty horse and sent him to Syria, in order to have confirmation of it before announcing it to the empress. And after a few days the eunuch returned to the emperor saying, "The emperor's children, the brothers, send their greetings." And Emperor Theodosius rejoiced after hearing this and told the empress and all of his family. There was great joy in the palace that day.

42. A few days later, the emperor sent their mother and their sister to Syria, so that they could see them and set their heart to rest. The saints encouraged their mother and sister that their heart may be relieved and dismissed them in peace. From that day on, the people of Constantinople made their way to these saints. Day and night, the roads brought to them whoever was unwell from all sorts of illnesses and those who had unclean spirits. Those who had come to these blessed ones were prayed on, and were healed by the grace of God our Saviour.

43. Then Emperor Theodosius himself came to them to take their blessing, counsel, and learn of their good works that he may deal generously for his kingdom and for the Church of God. In this, they greatly strengthened[43] him in all firmness to

---

43 ⲁⲩⲧⲁϫⲣⲟϥ ⲛ̄ⲕⲁⲗⲱⲥ (lit. They thoroughly strengthened him).

keep the faith of Nicaea and to place the children of the Church whom he respected in all honour.

44. Moreover, when these blessed ones had established themselves and acquired a reputation throughout Syria, the pious Emperor Theodosius himself came to them seeking their advice and enjoying their teaching and blessing, as if recognising that they belonged to the empire. For truly the visits became profitable and greatly instructive to him, and, in short, through them he acquired a great Godly-love and an honour towards the churches of God, and it was all through the instructions of these blessed ones. And not only him, but also his children, Arcadius and Honorius, whom he brought up in this piety by the teaching and the virtuous advice of these saints. So also was Theodosius the Younger.[44]

Maximus and Dometius travel to Egypt

45. After this, the archbishop of Constantinople rested. It was undoubtedly because of this that God led these saints to Scete, just like the patriarch Jacob who went down to Egypt because of the famine, until the inhabitants increased and filled the face of the earth.[45] So also was it with these blessed ones, Maximus and Dometius, sons of the emperor. I will not cease to name them sons of the emperor until each one knows their dignity, their angelic life, and their way of life, for they loved Christ more than the entire glory of this world and have followed Him with all their heart.

46. For this reason, truly, Jesus Christ also gave them glory, so that He moved their heart to go to the holy Mountain of Scete in order to die there and that a church be built in their name. For

---

44 The grandson of Theodosius. Most notably associated with the Theodosian Codex.

45 Genesis 46

they had established their foundations on the immovable rock, Christ, who has become a harbour of salvation for everyone who will turn to God for the forgiveness of their sins. Truly, the Paradise of God rejoices for the salvation of the souls of sinners in this place, and Scete will not cease to be a harbour of salvation for ever and ever. But let us return to the reason these blessed saints went to Scete.

47. When they were looking to consecrate someone archbishop over the royal city, all the people together went to Theodosius, asking him to make Maximus the archbishop in the place of the one who had rested. Then Emperor Theodosius rejoiced greatly in this regard, and immediately sent for an official and twenty-five soldiers. He wrote to the governor of Syria that he might apprehend the saints and watch over them until the bishops of the provinces assembled.

48. When they reached the governor and gave the letter from the emperor, the governor rejoiced and said to them, "Let us eat today, for you have exhausted yourselves on the way. Tomorrow we will bring them by the will of God." By divine providence, when the governor's wife heard this, she knew that perhaps the emperor would take these blessed ones to Constantinople. She became greatly distressed, for she had great faith in them. She immediately sent her son and one of her eunuchs to them in the night. They warned the saints saying, "Look, the emperor has ordered to have you brought to Constantinople. So, you may want to escape."

49. When the saints heard these words, they hastened immediately and left the monastery saying, "This is the time whereby God is calling us to the place of Abba Macarius." They found an elderly shepherd and he took them to his shelter and hid them there.

50. On the following day the official and his escort arrived at the monastery, looking for the saints. They did not find them, and they became extremely upset. The governor then ordered a thorough search to be made for them everywhere in Syria and Palestine. For this reason, the saints remained in hiding for a number of days and they did not show up at all because everyone knew them, from the inhabitants of Syria to its surroundings. They later arose by the direction of God, removed their monastic garments, took a sack, and put on lay garments and tied turbans on their heads so that they would not be recognised. They went out, each carrying a small sack and wearing lay garments to look like Syrians. They continued to walk, praying to God, "God of our father Abba Macarius, You will show us the way and bring us to him in peace."

51. They walked for two days on the banks of the river. The younger said to his elder brother firmly, "My brother, be strong by the will of our Lord Jesus Christ, the true God, and the prayers of our father Macarius, whom Abba Agabus our blessed father saw in the vision saying to him, 'Order your sons and let them come to Egypt and be with me.' We believe that his prayers will guide us to his place in Alexandria. Let us therefore walk along the coast of the sea with endurance until we reach Alexandria. Did you not listen to the trader when he said, 'sail over the coast of the sea until we reach Alexandria'?" but Maximus replied, "Yes, but where are we to stop and drink?" His younger brother said in joy and hope, "My brother and my master, do you not believe that the Lord Jesus has the power to move these mountains, rocks, and harbours of water?" His brother said, "Yes, my Lord. I believe that He can do all these things. Forgive me, my brother, for I have sinned as a man."

52. After these words, they walked in peace and gladness of heart, rejoicing, and blessing the Saviour, and they continued to encourage each other incessantly. It was God who led Israel in the wilderness and on the sea, and the same who also guided these saints. If they were thirsty, they would go to the sea to drink fresh water there, and they did not wonder to ask whether it was sweet or bitter.

53. When they were walking, they arrived at a steep rock, so that they had to climb using their hands and feet. There are more which these blessed ones endured on these high rocks. In fact, they did not know where they were going, but the joy they felt and their hope in Christ that was in their hearts made these tribulations insignificant. As these blessed ones, who had walked nine days, said to me, they felt great pain in their feet because they were of a delicate build and not accustomed to these conditions. They said, "We settled on a high rock, and we were unable to walk, so we laid down, stretched out on the high rock."

54. Observe the courage of these warriors and athletes of Christ, who were martyred without shedding blood by the multitude of sufferings which they endured. They spent another five days lying on that rock, without eating, or drinking, lying like corpses. But God saves those who at all times hope in Him and rescues them from all their tribulations. It is He who remembered Daniel when He saved him from the mouths of the lions.[46] He saved Jonah from the belly of the whale.[47] He saved Susanna from the one who pronounced the sentence of death on her.[48] He also saved His Roman servants from the mouths of wild beasts in that place and flesh-eating birds on the seashore.

55. The God of powers who turned Enoch from seeing death.[49] He too sent the chariots of fire and snatched Elijah up

---
46 Daniel 6
47 Jonah 1-4
48 Daniel 13
49 Genesis 5: 21-24

to heaven.[50] He sent His angel and transported Habakkuk by air without harm to Babylon above the lions' den to bring Daniel food. And He returned him to Judea instantly, although Judea was a three-month journey from Babylon.[51] It was He also who sent His angel and transported the saints without difficulty to Scete and placed them on a high rock, south of which is the wetland. For in this place a sign from God manifested. When it happened, the servant of God, Abba Macarius, called it the "Rock of the Belly's Hollow".[52]

Maximus and Dometius meet Macarius

56. Pay full attention and listen to the miracle that happened to these blessed ones, as they recounted to me. For God brought these blessed ones to Scete during the night. They saw a man who was radiating light before them, taking their hand, and leading them in the air until he brought them to the rock we mentioned previously.

57. They said, "When we rose in the morning by the strength which Christ had manifest in us, we found ourselves on the rock of Scete. When we looked over the hillside, we saw wetland and a few date palms. At the sight of the desert, we were amazed, and our hearts were at peace. We reflected over what had happened to us, because in the evening before, we were sleeping exhausted on the shore of the sea with its waves, and today we are in a serene place, sheltered with a view of the date palms and water wells and other such sights.

58. After some time, as we looked in each direction, at the fifth hour we saw a man leading a camel in the wetland to the south

---

50 2 Kings 2
51 Daniel 14:33-36
52 ⲧⲡⲉⲧⲣⲁ ⲛ̀ⲕⲟⲩⲛⲛⲉϫⲓ ϣⲁ ⲉϧⲟⲩⲛ ⲉⲫⲟⲟⲩ. He may be referring to a known cave during their time.

of us. We rejoiced greatly and came down on to the rock. We went to him and asked where we were. He saw from our clothes that we were foreigners with turbans bound around our heads. He became afraid and was about to let his animals loose until we prostrated ourselves before him so that he may feel at ease. We approached and asked him, but he did not know our language and we did not know his. Finally, he said to us, 'Come and I will take you to the place of Abba Macarius.' When we heard the name of Abba Macarius, we were reassured and rejoiced, so we followed him, thanking God, and blessing Him that He had shown us the way to the place of His servant.

59. When we reached the place of the prophet of God, he received us with compassion and asked us why we had come. We replied, 'We have heard of your virtues and of Scete. We have come to be under your guidance and become monks with you.' He continued to look at us prudently. Then he said, 'You will not be able to remain here because the desert is exhausting.' We prostrated ourselves before him saying, 'If we cannot stay in this place, we will go to another. But for the sake of God, do not reject us, our good father.' He replied, 'Good. If it has to be like this, come and I will tell you about the place where you will labour.' He then led us to a rock and taught us how to build a cave and about the rest of the manual work according to the rule of Scete."

60. All these things these blessed ones told me had happened to them. Now, I am a native of Constantinople, like them. Continually, the saints kept making me promise with the sanction, "Say nothing of what we have told you while we are still alive."[53] Indeed, if I had not already known them, they would not have spoken to me. But I knew them, and they too knew me.

---

53 Cf. Mark 7:37; Matthew 8:4

Their manual labour and ascetical habit

61. The prophet of the Lord, Abba Macarius led the young prophets and brought them to the rock, showed them the place where stone should be mined, and gave them tunnelling tools. He showed them the beginning of basket making because they were not skilled at weaving. He also gave them other instructions and returned to his cell in peace. But these saints took off their worldly Syrian garments and put on the habit of the monks in that place. They started to speak to each other, "Look, be careful and do not let anyone know our name or that we were formerly monks, because this place is near the emperor and near Syria."

62. They always took all care not to speak with any man or to visit anyone outside their own cell and the church. Their food was at all times bread and salt. From the time they joined the monastic life, they tasted neither meat, wine nor fish. They fasted for two days at a time and spent much time in prayer. They used to recite their psalms six by six verses with a sign of the cross, according to the custom of the Syrians.

63. They lived in Scete and saw no man except for an old watchman, who would take the handiwork of those in the Natrun and brought them small amounts of bread. The same man also served Abba Macarius because he had known him from the beginning, going to him on many occasions and receiving his blessing.

64. When the saints would go to church, they never raised their eyes at all to see the face of anyone but kept them lowered until they came to their cave silently and attentively. For truly, if you see them in this state, you will say, "God really lives with these men." And if you wish to know this more accurately, it is just as He dwelled with Elijah and John. Similarly, the fire of the Holy Spirit was in them, burning all the destructive power of the spirits of wickedness that are constantly and shamelessly at war with everyone.

65. It is not I who says this, but the spirit-bearing Macarius. He then said, "I went to visit them three years later to find out how they were. And when evening fell, they said to me, 'Are you leaving, our father?' I said to them, 'No. I am sleeping here'. They put out for me a small mat on the ground in the corner of the cave, while they stayed on the other side and slept in one space. They took a belt and a cloak and put them before me on the ground and then they were silent."

66. They did this for a certain reason: the garb was Syrian, and they did not have a girdle, but they wore only black clothes. And when the saints had seen their spirit-bearing Abba Macarius wearing the girdle and garment, they too wished to imitate their father and clothe themselves like him. This is why they brought a girdle and garment to him. They did this that he might pray over them so that they might put them on when they got up. At that moment Abba Macarius knew this through the prophetic spirit that was in him, and he prayed over them.

67. He (Macarius) said, "I prayed to God that their way of working might be revealed to me. The ceiling opened and there was a light like that of the day. But they did not see that I can see the light, as they thought I was sleeping. The older then signalled to the younger and they arose, and they girdled themselves. I, of course, saw them, but they did not see me. They stretched out their hands to the heaven. I saw demons surround them like flies. Some had come over his eyes and mouth. And I saw an angel of the Lord, holding in his hand a fiery-flaming sword, shielding, and chasing the demons away, and they did not dare to even approach the older one.

68. As morning was about to appear, they laid down on the ground again, sleeping, and I too pretended to be in deep sleep.

And the older one said to me this single word, 'Do you want us to say the twelve psalms?' I said to them, 'Yes'. And the younger one said six psalms, six by six verses and one alleluia. With each verse that came out of his mouth a flame of fire went up to heaven. In the same way, as the elder brother opened his mouth to chant, a great fire came from his mouth and went up to heaven.

69. And I too, say with a sincere heart, when I saw their condition, their good work, and their great fervour for God, I benefited much from them, and as I was leaving, I said, 'Pray for me.' And they begged me to give them the habit. And so, I calmed their heart, and agreed to their request. I put it on them, and I left them in peace."

70. Behold, we have heard the great Abba Macarius telling us explicitly that the blessed ones are worthy of the grace of the Holy Spirit, the Paraclete, like fire. For truly if I begin to speak of all the things that that great one told me and the things I saw with my own eyes, the discourse will become very long. For this reason, I have omitted the excess. For the sake of those of little faith, that they may not think that the truth is a lie, I will reduce a lot to a little and I will impose a limit to the discourse.

Miracle #10: Healing the camel and the old man's eye

71. The old man of whom we have spoken as the servant of these saints was a very God-loving man. He had great faith in them. This man was forcibly discharged of his camels by a soldier. He grabbed the old man, stretched out his hand, and struck him on his right cheek. The old man turned the other cheek to him, to fulfil the injunction of the Gospel.[54] The tyrannical soldier repeated his attack and struck the old man's face with the thing in his hand and took out his left eye. The old man gave

---

54 Matthew 5:38–42 and Luke 6:27–31

thanks to God that he had been worthy to lose his eye for the injunction of the Gospel of our Lord Jesus Christ.

72. It once happened that he took the small baskets of the blessed ones to Egypt and prepared for them some bread as he normally did. He was a man of Jepro Menesina[55] in the district called Andropolis[56] in the region of Pinoub.[57] After he prepared the small amount of bread for the saints, he took the camel and went to Scete. Having reached the wetland, he walked for some time with his camel and came to a place that was full of excrement and, by a conspiracy of the enemy who hates all that is good, the camel slipped and fell, and broke his two feet, only having the skin remaining intact.

73. When this happened, the old man wept bitterly and was in heartfelt distress. He tore his garments and put dirt on his head, for the camel did not belong to him. Again, he thanked God saying, "I thank You, my Lord Jesus Christ, God of the saints." He then went into a cave and left the camel rested on the ground. When he met the saints, he told them what had happened, weeping profusely. They did not know what exactly had happened. But when they saw him weeping woefully, they walked with him.

74. When they reached the place that was still a little way off from the camel, the old man wept when he saw it. They stood and prayed to God. As they went over to the camel, it became afraid and bellowed. It put its face on the ground, as if worshipping the saints. They said to the camel, "Do not be

---

55 I think this is now modern day Shoubra?
56 ⲁⲡⲃⲁⲧ is identified as modern Kherbeta in present Egypt.
57 Although there is no evidence to where this location was, there is a hypothesis as to its vicinity given in: Sylvain Dhennin, "(Per-) Inbou, Per-Noubet et Onouphis. Une question de toponymie", (2016): 49-68.

afraid, but arise and stand through the power of the One who rose from the dead, Jesus Christ, the God of the Christians."

75. Having said that, they raised their eyes to heaven saying, "God of our father Abba Macarius, listen to us." At that moment, the camel suddenly jumped up. It stood on its feet as though it had never fallen and suffered an injury. The elder kissed the saints saying, "Blessed be the Lord Jesus Christ, the One who is in you!"

76. While they were walking together to their cell, the holy Dometius saw the face of the old man full of dirt because of the time when he had put it on his head when the camel fell from him. The holy Dometius took the corner of his cloak to wipe the face of the old man. Because of his great faith, and the miracle that had happened through the power of the holy saints, the old man took the blessed one by the hand to be blessed by him and put it on his injured eye. When the hand touched his eye, he was able to see straightaway.

77. The old watchman who was the camel driver appreciated what had happened, namely that not only had they healed the camel, but also that he himself had his vision restored as soon as he had placed the saints' hand on his eye. So, he greatly glorified God for the gift he had received. He was instructed not to say anything to anyone: "Do not think that this cure happened to you because of us, for we are sinners. It happened because of the victorious power of Christ."

78. After he had set out the small amount of bread for them, he returned to his work in the Natrun. When his companions saw him with his eye open, they were astonished and asked him how he was able to see. He told them that he had been cured by the servants of God and disciples of Abba Macarius. All who heard glorified God.

Macarius, On the extent of their holiness

79. For I myself, when I heard this story after they had died, asked the great Abba Macarius to confirm it saying, "My holy father, I have heard about the saints that they opened the eyes of the blind. Is this true or not?" He replied, "Indeed, it is true." And I said to him in astonishment, "Really, it is a great work!" He answered me and said, "It is not a great work. It was according to the power of the grace they received from God. For they were worthy of the grace that was in Elijah and John. Christ having given the order of his apostles to them because they did not seek the glory of this perishable world.

80. For this reason, they were like a fiery flame that burns brightly, and so also was the breath that came from their mouth a burning fire. When they opened their mouth to pray, the flame came from their mouth like bright lightning up to heaven. Now, my son, believe all that you have heard about them." I kissed his holy hand, glorifying God, who performs wonders in those who do His will.

Repose of Maximus

81. Then after this, it pleased God, the lover of mankind to give rest to His servants, and transport them out of this perishable world and its torments which last but a fragment of time, and to introduce them into the place of eternal rest, filled with joy and gladness. The place of which pain, sorrow and lament have fled away.

82. In the holy day of Epiphany, which is a feast in the month of Tōbi, the blessed Maximus was bedridden. He had become ill with a vicious fever that seized him. So, as he was getting worse in sickness, he said, "Do me a favour[58] and call my father Abba

---

58 ⲁⲣⲓ ϯⲁⲅⲁⲡⲏ (lit. make for me charity)

Macarius." So, I went and called him. Then, when it was sunset, he said to us, "What time is it?" We informed him, "It is the end of the day." He replied to us, "A little more, and I will go to the place of rest."

83. As it was getting dark, our father Abba Macarius said, "Light the lamp." And we lit it up. Then the mind[59] of the blessed Abba Maximus was taken to heaven, and he began to speak, "Send Your light and Your truth, my God, that they may guide me, for I believe that You will make straight my way and save me from the powers of darkness of the air, which are the spirits. Prepare my paths in Your way, my God,[60] that I might come to You without hindrance. Be a powerful hope for me, Jesus my God, for You are my light and my salvation. Whom shall I fear?"[61]

84. He then fell silent for a short time. And again, he said, "Arise, let us go from here. Look! The apostles, they have come with the prophets to take me from this place." He then fell silent. After a little while, Abba Macarius saw the chorus of saints who had followed him. Suddenly Abba Macarius stood up. He continued to stare in awe.

85. When I saw the lamp extinguished, I said to the elder, Abba Macarius, "Do you want us to light the lamp, my father? He said, "No, leave it as it is." I begged him, saying, "Do me a favour, my lord and father, and rest on this blanket for a while." He replied, "Be quiet, my son. This is not the time for speaking but rather it is for silence."

---

59 ⲛⲟⲩⲥ. Often refers to a part of the human soul or the eye of the soul. It comes from Greek philosophy and is seen in Paul's letters. cf. Eph 4:23 - be renewed in the spirit of your minds.
60 Psalm 85:13
61 Psalm 27:1

86. The blessed Maximus then spoke with one of the saints, asking him the name of the saints around him. We did not understand what he said. But the spirit-bearer told us that he had been told the name of those saints. And as his soul was enjoying the coming of the saints, it immediately sprang with joy out of the body. And this is how this blessed one died, in peace, having found his rest with all the saints on the 14th of Tōbi.

Repose of Dometius

87. When we buried his holy remains, his blessed brother Dometius laid down and became ill. He had been taken by a severe fever. When the great Abba Macarius saw this, he said to me, "Stay here, my son, and attend to him so that you may receive his blessing." I kissed his feet, saying, "Pray for me, my holy father."

88. On the following day, Dometius' fever became worse. On the evening of the 3rd day, I saw him in pain. I said to him, "Do you want me to call our father Abba Macarius." He said, "Yes." So, I went and called him. As I was walking along with Abba Macarius on the path, he stood for a long time, looking at this side of the cave. He then turned to the east. I thought to myself that perhaps he might be praying, but he was looking at the chorus of saints processing before the soul of the blessed Dometius. He was looking up to heaven, sighing, weeping, and beating his chest, saying, "Woe is me! For I never became a monk. These are true monks, for in a short time of tribulation they quickly found the place."

89. When I saw him weeping, I was in awe and said, "What is wrong, O my holy father?" and he said to me, "Come, my son, the blessed Dometius has gone to his rest." When we entered the cave, we found him leaning against the wall, with his two hands stretched out to heaven. And this is how he died, on the 17th of Tōbi. We took his holy body and laid it on the ground. As we looked at him, Abba Macarius testified to Abba Isidore, "The ranks that had come for the soul of the elder, have also come for the soul of his brother to also be with them."

90. So now, we have told you how these blessed ones completed their course and their angelic life. They loved the strict life, the discipline, and the transient hardship. They were long-suffering and struggled well because they ran the race of courage and stretched themselves at the finish, as the apostle said,[62] in order to dwell with the One they yearned for, Jesus Christ, the true agonothetes,[63] after having rejected the temporal glory of this world and its insignificant, vacuous, and perishable pleasures. They continued to reject the world as a prison.

Grasp the name of Christ

91. It happened once, while I was speaking with them, that I said to them, "If you were in Constantinople, my fathers, you would indeed now find yourselves emperors." They turned to me and said to me gently, "Where is your mind, O brother, that you say such a word? Perhaps it is in the place about which you have just spoken? We have already told you many times, our brother Pshoi, whether you stay with us or in your own small cell, grasp the blessed name of Jesus Christ without letting go of it. Indeed, if this holy name were in your heart, you would not have said what you said just now. So, pay close attention, our beloved brother. Do not neglect this name of salvation but keep it in your heart steadfastly and say it when you are suffering. For if you neglect it, then we will certainly die in our transgressions.

---

62 2 Timothy 4:7

63 In ancient Greece, an *agonothetes* was the judge or superintendent of one of the Panhellenic Games.

92. So let us not love bold speech, playful language, and empty words, for these are things that destroy the entire fruit of the monk, as we came to know while we were still in Syria, as humanity made us high-spirited, that is, we were prevented from thinking of our sins. Exile, knowing silence and tribulation are tools of our people. Tribulation gives birth to prayer in purity. Prayer gives birth to the fear and love of God, and these things give birth to weeping. Weeping purifies our sins, because no rank or wealth or supremacy is revered by God, but a pure soul is what He seeks. His sacrifice and His offering is our salvation." As for me, I received their words with a joyful heart, and repented, saying, "Forgive me, my fathers, and pray for me."

Naming the Monastery of al-Baramūs

93. A year after the death of these saints, the desert began to become very famous everywhere, whether in the desert of Pernouj[64] or in the monasteries scattered around Egypt. In short, the desert became a widespread area. A large church was constructed, and Isidore ordained a presbyter. And I too, the unworthy, was made deacon. The great Abba Macarius called out from within the church and said, "Call this place the Roman Quarter."

---

64 Ⲡⲉⲣⲛⲟⲩⲭ is a town in Damanhur

94. The three great elders of Pernoudj who were with us, Abba Pamo,[65] Abba Pihor[66] and Abba Hatre,[67] said to Abba Macarius, "Do you not know their name, O blessed father?" He said to them, "Yes, but is not fitting to use the name of one and not the other in this place. They both completed an equal contest and so we have named both by calling their monastery the Romans." Thus, he had their names written on the diptych, "Our Romans Fathers", as he was ordered by God.

95. We have confirmation of this in the testimony of Abba Paphnutius,[68] the disciple of Abba Macarius who succeeded him as father of Scete. He then said, "When we built the church, God ordered our father through the Cherubim of light: 'Call this place the Roman Quarter. And you, follow me and I will show you the place that will be called after you.'

96. Then the Cherubim went before him and brought him to the Southern Bend of the marsh in the place of the spring. He stood on the rock to the west. He promised him that place,

---

65 More commonly known as Pambo. He was born about A.D. 303, and was one of the first to join Amoun in Nitria. He was an Egyptian and illiterate, until taught the Scriptures as a monk and ordained priest, in 340. He was invited by Bishop Athanasius to go to Alexandria. With Macarius and Isidore he was counted by Jerome as one of the masters of the desert. Melania met him when she visited Egypt. He died about A.D. 373.

66 Also known as Abba Hor or Pior, an early settler in Nitria, lived at first with Antony the Great. He was a priest and became a solitary in Scetis.

67 More commonly known as Abba Hedra. He was one of the bishops of Aswan in the fourth century. Abba Hedra lived in the time of Saint Poeman, whose disciple he became. After eight years spent with him, he asked to live as a hermit in the desert. He lived in a cave and applied himself to the study of the life of Saint Antony. The present-day Monastery of Saint Symeon is in fact Dayr Anba Hedra.

68 Paphnutius, born early in the fourth century was influenced by Antony the Great and became a disciple of Abba Isidore and of Abba Macarius. He was trained first in a cenobitic monastery, then became a solitary. He was called 'the Buffalo 'for his love of solitude. When St John Cassian visited Egypt, he was head of the four monasteries of the desert.

saying, "This is the place that will be named after you. It is also the place which you will build and will be given in perpetuity to the Romans, because they are the ones who left their body in this holy desert as first fruits of your labours in the vineyard of the Lord of Sabaoth, which is the revered family of monks, the people who perform the will of God. The people who transfer the worthiness of God to mankind because of their practices, of their prayers, of the tears which they shed day and night without ceasing because of sinners, in order that they turn to God with all their heart, that He forgives His creation according to His mercies.

Epilogue

97. I therefore beseech you, my holy fathers, not to doubt what we have said about these saints. But accept to yourselves in love these words of our blessed fathers, especially those of our great spirit-bearing father Abba Macarius the man who carries God and whom God loved because of his purity. For, it is written that if elders go to that great one, he receives them in his cell, saying, "Come and see the shrine of these young strangers so that you too may make progress in their virtues and be worthy of the portion and the lot belonging to them in the kingdom of our Lord Jesus Christ."

98. Look at how the great Abba Macarius spoke of them as martyrs when he had gone to his cave with the elders in order to faithfully pray. For they were martyred by their own choice, without shedding blood, by their contempt toward this perishable kingdom of their worldly father for the sake of the kingdom of God and its goodness. And because they renounced the memory of the palace and its elegances of different kinds. The oppressions which they endured on the painful paths of the sea and the danger of the reptiles in this place, until God guided them by His help, walking before them, until He led them to the Mountain of Scete of the holy Abba Macarius where they completed their lives. This is why I said that they were martyrs without a sword.

99. For by allowing ourselves to remember the teaching of our holy fathers, we will convert from worldly customs and receive the form of light in the ways of our blessed fathers, as we leave behind us the things of the past and give ourselves to others in true humility and love, walking with unerring footsteps and performing the laws of Christ and the evangelical commandments of monasticism that lead us directly to God, attaining all that is good in paradise.

100. For our fathers made the small cell belonging to our holy fathers like a church for themselves, to which they would go from time to time and pray in faith. Large numbers of the sick, whether in Scete or the Mountain of Pernouj, when they came to their tomb to pray, would be cured by the grace of God and the prayers of His servants of our Lord Jesus Christ, who heals those who are sick; whether an illness of the body, or of the soul, through the prayers of our holy fathers the Romans, Maximus and Dometius. The saviour of everyone is our Lord, our God, and our saviour Jesus Christ. This is He to whom is due all glory, all honour, all adoration that is befitting to the Father with Him and the life-giving Holy Spirit, who is of the same essence with Him, now, and at all times, even to the ages of all ages. Amen.

Extracts from the Sahidic Version

WHAT SURVIVES FROM THE SAHIDIC VERSION IS THE OLDER AND more concise account of the Life. This translation is based on the text edited by Henri Munier[69] and the English translation of Anthony Alcock.[70] There are five accounts that do not exist in the Bohairic version:

A) *The prostitute in Latakia;*

B) *How Theodosius became Emperor;*

C) *Healing the blind calf;*

D) *Dometius and the two serpents;*

E) *The vision of Abba Macarius concerning St Maximus*

---

69 Henri Munier, *Une relation copte sa'idique de la vie des saints Maxime et Domèce*, (Imprimérie de l'Institut Français d'Archéologie Orientale, 1917).
70 It is not published anywhere, but he has made this freely available on his Academia profile (2016).

A) The Prostitute in Latakia

The beginning of it is lost in the Sahidic version.

[…]⁷¹ they being told of that poor woman that they would pray for her. When they heard of the impiety that she had committed, became distressed about the corruption of her soul, and said to her parents, "We will not pray for her unless she confesses what she has done before everyone, for she is not worthy to be prayed for as she has made God angry. Her parents told the saints that she had confessed what she had done before the entire town. The servants of Christ Jesus took some water, sanctified it, prayed over it and gave it to her parents, saying, "Pour this over her in the name of Our Lord Jesus Christ and we believe that she will be healed." They took the waters in great faith, poured them over her and she was healed that day, fulfilling Scripture, "I am living, said the Lord. I do not want the death of the sinner as much as that you should turn from the path of evil and live."⁷² That woman spent the rest of her days in seemliness and wisdom, giving glory to the God of these saints. Listen to this other miracle and true cure of our servants of Christ Jesus, as if he were in the hands of the apostles.

---

71 The beginning found in the Arabic reads: And I also saw there a wonderous miracle that was frightening. There was a woman from the city of Latakia who had committed many evils. From her adultery, she became pregnant with a boy and plotted to kill him in the womb. The devil conspired with her with through some sorcery and gave her a chalice to drink from it until the baby was to come out of her womb. But God is gentle with all people according to their virtue. As she was trying to look for the boy, her intestines gushed out before her with the placenta that is connected to the boy. And she was carried to her house and remained lying in her bed of death for several days. All who were in Latakia heard her screams. So, the people said to her parents, "Go look for and plead to those saintly monks, and they will release her." Thus, they went to them and told them all about her aborted child. See, Pirone, "Vita dei Santi Massimo e Domezio nelle Fonti Arabe Edizione, traduzione e note", 286-287.
72 Ezekiel 33: 11

B) How Theodosius became Emperor

This section is only preserved in the Sahidic and is the account which identifies Valentinian I as the father of the saints, although it was most probably Valentinian II as we have discussed in the chapter: "Notes on the Life". It omitted from both the Bohairic and the Arabic.[73]

I will reassure those listening. Theodosius the emperor was an Egyptian by birth, originally a stable boy of Valentinian, that is, the father of the saints. When he saw that Theodosius was a strong man, he gave him charge of all the stables, the training places of the horses of the empire. These blessed ones rejected the world while their father Valentinian still had one year to live.

Then, as he was about to die, he assembled the whole senate and said to them, "I am about depart the way of all the world. See, therefore, do not let any Arian sit on the throne of my fathers. But be strong enough to keep the holy faith of Nicaea." The senators replied and said, "Where are we to find an orthodox man worthy of this great honour of the empire? Your sons have gone, and we do not know where they are. Will your daughter be able to administer the empire?" The emperor then said, "Perhaps my sons have been abducted by barbarians. Now, I have no-one, great or small, who will sit on my throne in my place, but if I die, bring Theodosius to the palace and marry him to my daughter and install him on the imperial throne that he might be emperor after me in my place."

The senators and the imperial archons all answered, "You have ordered us, emperor, and we will do as you say." After his speech he dismissed the senate and called two senior generals of his, Sergius and Anastasius, who were very important figures and

---

73 In the Arabic, any mention of Theodosius was rendered as "al-malik" (emperor) to refer to the saints' father.

greatly respected by him. The emperor said to them, "When I die, the archons of the city will perhaps not agree with the appointment of Theodosius, as I have ordered. If it happens that you reach the point of deploying the army against them, do not let anyone sit on my throne after me but Theodosius." The generals replied, "God willing, our lord emperor. If all the Byzantines (Romans) gather together against us, they will not be able to overturn the order which you have entrusted to us."

After the senators had finished their meeting with the emperor, they left him in peace. There was a great nobleman at Constantinople of the household of Julian the Lawless,[74] who firmly believed that he would occupy the throne after the death of Valentinian. When the emperor died and he heard that Theodosius had been appointed in his place, he became very angry. After the death of the emperor the senators gathered around the nobleman asking him to give his opinion whether he agreed with them or not. They said to him, "Whom do you want to be emperor?" He replied, looking at them and knowing that he was being tested, "Truly, it is not my concern that Theodosius the general should be made emperor. The privilege is yours." At that moment they cried aloud in a single heavenly voice three times, "Worthy, worthy, worthy! Augustus Theodosius!" And this is how he was appointed to the imperial throne.

---

74 Commonly known as Julian the Apostate. He was Roman emperor from 361 to 363.

C) Healing the Blind Calf

It happened on the day of the Feast of the Theotokos in *Paōni*,[75] that I went to them to receive their blessing. I found them just about to leave to draw water. I went with them. When we reached the *Anaboullos*[76] and were within a short distance of it, we found a hartebeest[77] there with its calf that was blind. When she saw us, she ran away. When her calf was about to do the same, he fell into a pit of salt water. He was in distress in the pit, floating on and drowning in the water. When I saw the creature in this way, I could not contain myself but started to laugh. I looked at the saints with their faces cast down and meditating. I went and got the calf and brought it to the *Anaballous* and said to the saints, "My holy fathers, come and see. This calf is blind." They said, "Blessed be God."

I brought it to them, as I told them about it. The blessed Maximus made the sign of the cross on the eyes of the calf, in awe at God's creation saying, "My Lord Jesus Christ, you are blessed and the miracles you perform." When he said this, the eyes of the calf opened. He said to me, "Let him go. For he is not blind." I released him and he hurried away leaping on the hillside searching for his mother. I was greatly amazed, glorifying God and His saints.

---

75 The Arabic version says: "On the 16th day of June, and it is the commemoration of all the saints". Pirone, "Vita dei Santi Massimo e Domezio nelle Fonti Arabe (Edizione, traduzione e note, 319.
76 The salt wetland is called Anaboulos or the big rock to the south of which is the outpouring of water.
77 A type of antelope.

D) Dometius and the Two Serpents

Let us once again tell you of this amazing incident of the new Daniel. It happened once as I was walking with the blessed Dometius. We were bringing palm leaves from the marsh, and, on my way, I found a small pile of dates, with two large serpents among them fighting each other, one of them having eaten half of the other. When I saw them, I fled in fear. Saint Dometius said to me, "Why are you running away like this?" I said to him, "My father, I have just seen serpents." He replied to me, "Whether Satan appears as a serpent or a lion, do you take flight quickly and without self-restraint?" I prostrated myself saying, "Forgive me, father. Come and see, each one is devouring the other."

When he came to the place where they were, he saw them as I had told him. He was very distressed at their violent behaviour towards each other. He went to them and said, "Look at the hostility of these others, each one wishing to devour his brother." He then took them in his two hands and seized the one being devoured by the other and dragged it from the belly and expelled it that it might go away and seized the other by the neck and hurled it away, so that they would not be able to find each other again. I stood there stupefied like one in distress. I was astonished to see how he dealt with the serpents.

E) The Vision of Abba Macarius Concerning St Maximus

"Those to the right", he said, "were John the Baptist and the holy apostles. Those to the left, were Moses the Lawgiver, Elijah, and Elisha and the twelve minor prophets." "I saw", he said, "King David and Constantine the Roman Emperor, standing next to each other with crowns on their head and an angel of light standing by them with a sword of fire in his hand." If any energies of the spirits appeared, he pursued them.

And this is what I saw him doing in the air, as he led the saints. The saints were gathered around the saint, looking to the command from God. He therefore said, as his soul was about to be taken, "I saw John the Baptist, with a gleaming garment, he spread it out and took the two corners and signalled to Moses, and he took the other side. The saints then all stood up. I saw Paul the apostle signalling to the emperor Constantine, saying, 'Extend to him the free faith.' He handed him a sealed book; the name of Nicaea written on it. I saw the entire chorus of the saints, giving strength to the soul of the saint and saying, 'Do not be afraid, but be strong.'" The soul then leapt into the bosom of John and Moses, and the rest of the saints followed him, chanting, "I have heard their sweet voice. I have never heard a voice so sweet."

Extracts from the Arabic Version

The Arabic version is more similar to the Sahidic and includes more or less the same miracle stories. The text from the Arabic sīrah that is entirely new is the account that is titled here: The weeping empress.[78]

The Weeping Empress

The patrician[79] to whom he had entrusted this task[80] had left immediately. And when he was in the city, he asked for information as to the whereabouts of the two brothers' cell, and they directed him to it. When he arrived at their place, he knocked on the door and they went out to him and asked them to pray for him. He saw their appearance and noted their cell and did not let them know the reason to which he had come.

He continued to accompany them for two days, then left them and returned to the emperor. Once he had arrived, the emperor asked him about the matter. The patrician told him all of that he had seen. He described their cell to him and even made him aware of everything he had personally noticed about them. The emperor responded, "These are really my children!" and he wept greatly. He then honoured the messenger, left him, and entered into the empress's chamber to tell her of the matter because she had no knowledge of it from the beginning.

When she heard, she became severely distressed to the point where she felt she was going to die. She cried, "Why had not the messenger who went there take them and bring them here?! How could he have gone and returned without them accompanying him, and after having discovered who they really were?! If it had been others, we would not have felt obliged to

---

78 This section spans from 77-98 as numbered in the edition of Pirone on pages 358-363.
79 *al-baṭrīq* (Greek πατρίκιος) an honorary title given to eunuchs in Roman courts.
80 To find the brothers.

have them brought here!" And the emperor replied, "O woman, they are boys who have renounced the glory of the world and have sought after the life that is to come. If we bother them on this journey and force them to come here, they will lose their souls. Now is the time to endure and persist in order that they reach their purpose and salvation by the grace of God."

But the empress replied, "From this moment onward, I will not find peace if I do not see them." And he said, "It is not possible to make them come here so that their souls do not perish, and we do not become regretful." But the woman replied, "Then let me go to them. Since it is not possible to make them come here, I will go to them." The emperor answered her, "And I will not prevent you from leaving. Indeed, if at the moment it was also possible for me to set out, we would both leave. And yet I am aware that leaving together would not be acceptable for them. However, if you wish to go, then be on your way."

And immediately the lady empress prepared herself. She took with her a good number of soldiers, and her daughter also, and left until they arrived at the place. The two holy brothers learned of the arrival of the soldiers and of the lady empress.

They were surprised and said, "They probably are intending to go to the holy house to prostrate there." And yet they did not know who she was or why she had come. Without the brothers noticing, the soldiers used every means at their disposal in order to know the place where the two monastic brothers were. So, when they went to them, the soldiers said, "The lady empress comes on purpose and asks to meet you and to receive your blessing."

This made them feel very remorseful, and they said, "Perhaps this is a trial from the devil with which he intends to pester us to lose our souls." And while they were in this manner, the empress and her daughter arrived and forced the brothers to meet them, even as they were still unaware of who she was. They went out with their heads facing the ground, not lifting it up or looking at anyone.

When the lady arrived, she approached and looked at them. She could not stand. Instead, she fell from the horse, setting foot on the ground and prostrated herself before them, shouting their names. When they saw her and recognised her, they struck their heads against the earth, while she and her daughter instantly fainted, as though they were dead, so much so that the servants believed they were really dead.

They remained in this state for a long time and when they woke up, the woman said to them, "My children, what is this that you have done? If you have gained your souls, you have made me perish!" And they began to cry, she and her daughter and most of those around her, even the two saints.

They wept for a few hours, then they said to her, "Follow us, that we may enter the church to pray." She therefore went with them, accompanied by her daughter and the servants, leaving all the people who were with her camped outdoors, and continued to walk with them praising: "Today Christ is pleased with me, since He has allowed me to see the joy of my eyes and the fruit of my heart. Today, Christ is pleased with me since He has given me back the light of my eyes. Today, Christ is pleased with me since I saw the joy of my heart alive. Today, I am like Jacob the patriarch,[81] for God restored his son Joseph to him. After many years, Jacob saw his son while he was the servant of the Pharoah, king of Egypt.[82] So, I also, saw the fruit of my heart, servants of the King of heaven and of the earth.

---

81 Arabic, *yaʿqūb al-ʾab*
82 Genesis 46

How could I ever repay the grace of God, I a sinner, who does not deserve such blessed fruit to have come from me? Glory to You, O my God, and my King! The two sons that You have given me You have introduced into the company of Your sincere friends, and You have manifested Your power in them, so that they could accomplish wonders like Your holy apostles James and John, sons of Zebedee. O Lord, let them share with these saints. For this, they have abandoned the world, its pleasure and its kingdom and have sought your good pleasure. Guard them against the snares of the enemy and grant me their prayers and their supplications."

They replied, "We, together with the saints, will pray and remember you at all times. We will not fail to mention you and our father, so that God may grant you salvation for your souls and fortitude toward us."

Thus, they spoke to her with compassion, and she and her daughter went back to their cell, and stayed with them for a few more days, asking them to go with her to the city and to greet their father. But they said to her, "This is not possible." She responded, "I have struggled a lot to come here, and it is therefore impossible for me to return without you being with me. Indeed, I had thought to have you brought to me from the moment I heard about you. But the emperor said to me that you will not accept this. I have therefore come here to achieve my purpose, which is to see you, and you yours, which is to be left in peace. Now, however, there is no way I can leave without you. Get up, then, and think about it. I will build you a monastery where you can stay all alone. I want nothing else than to be close to you."

But they answered her, "We have long been dead to this world, and we crave nothing of its vain seductions. If you really love us and respect our place, leave us as we are. For the world, and all its lustful desires will vanish,[83] and everything you see and possess will perish, and it will all seem like a dream. Even if we do not want to separate from you, you know well what the Gospel says, 'Whoever loves a father or a mother or a woman or brother or sister more than Me is not worthy of Me.'[84] We have no authority to violate the Gospel, but you are able to because of the inclination of your nature. Therefore, make it known within yourself, that you have not found us and that we will continue to live as we have done until today. You will not hear from us anymore. It will be better this way, both for us and for you. But if you force us to go back, you will lose our souls and be found guilty by God. That is, if Christ does not take our souls before we even go back! This we would ask Him, and He (glory be to Him!) will certainly not reject our plea. Therefore, you would have achieved nothing. You will experience an ever-increasing heartbreak in this life, and you will carry the sin in which you would incur in the presence of Christ, our Lord."

They remained with her, teaching through the words of scripture and comforting her, until, after much difficulty, she gave up and they managed to persuade her to make her way back without them. Then she consented during the long nights that she had stayed with them to entreat Christ the Lord and to turn to Him with an ardent heart and with tears so that He would make it easy for her heart to separate from them in order that she would not allow the devil to entice them and allow them to do as they wish. The Lord who saves thus accepted her plea and made it easy for her to separate from them.

So, when she decided to set out, weeping and with an afflicted heart, they went out with her to wish her and her father well. They prayed that God may grant him victory over his enemies

---

83 1 John 2:17
84 Matthew 10:37

and inspire within him and her patience from seeing them. And they asked and appealed to her that she would plead for them, saying, "By your petitions, we become what we are by the purity of your womb and by your sincere intentions towards us."

They prayed for her, and she departed from them, arriving to her city in peace. She informed the emperor of what she had seen and learned. She made him aware of the solitude they wanted, and how they did not consent to return with her. And he said to her, "I had known this from the beginning. I even told you that they returning here here would not be acceptable for them."

The empress then informed him of the invocation that the brothers raised to God for him, and so he replied, "Let us leave them, they are a treasure with Christ for us, and let us gain their prayers. All that we are in is only short-lived and a confused dream. They, on the other hand, have gained the eternal kingdom, which is better than the kingdom of this temporary world."

The Monastery of al-Baramūs
(Dayr al-Baramūs)

In the Wādī al-Naṭrūn (also known as 'the Wilderness of Scete'), one of the most famous monastic establishments in Egypt is the Monastery of al-Baramūs. It is also called the Monastery of the Romans.[85] In fact, it is said to be the place where Abba Macarius the Great settled in 340 (or as early as 330) when he was first initiated into the monastic life. The monastery is roughly an hour drive from Cairo.

Two monasteries rest there under the name of the Virgin Mary: The Monastery of the Syrians (*Dayr al-Suryān*) and the Monastery of the Romans (Dayr al-Baramūs). Within al-Baramūs are two sites of significance; the old Baramūs which was excavated by a team of archaeologists lead by Karel Innemme in 1995,[86] and the modern Baramūs which stands today. The

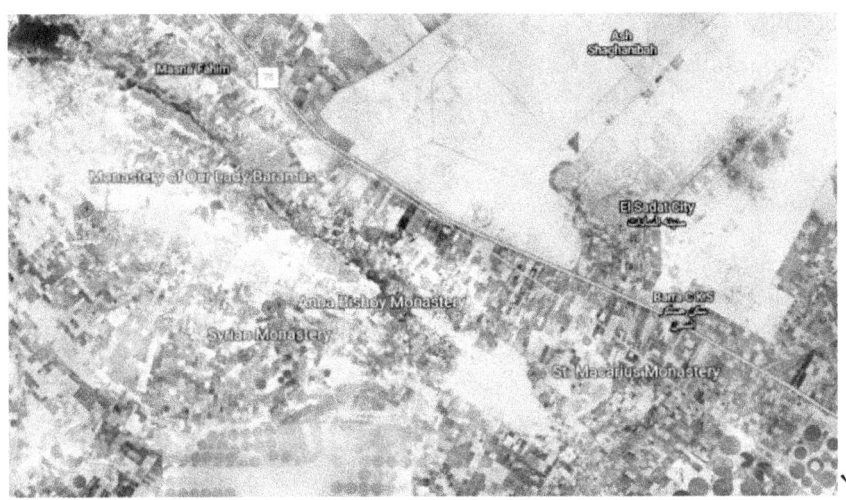

Figure 1. Google Earth view of the four monasteries of the Wādī al-Naṭrūn.

---

85 "Roman" or the Arabic "*al-rūm*" (singular) often means the Greek.

86 Karel C Innemée, "Deir al-Baramūs, excavations at the so-called site of Moses the Black, 1994-1999", *BSAC 39* (2000): 123-135; Karel C Innemme, "Excavations at the site of Deir Al-Baramūs 2002-2005", *BSAC 44* (2005): 55-68.

monastery is home to five chapels.[87] The oldest, dating to the 6th century, bears the name of the Virgin Mary and contains the relics of St Moses the Black (†405). The second chapel is dedicated to St Theodore of the General (†306), the third to St George of Melta[88] (†303), the fourth to St John the Baptist, and the fifth to Archangel Michael located in the fortress.

a) Construction and naming

The old Baramūs monastery is commonly known as the Monastery of St Moses the Black because he lived there after the departure of Sts Maximus and Dometius. By the 15th century, this monastery was ruined and left unoccupied.[89] Recent excavations found this ruined monastery to be in fact the first Monastery of al-Baramūs established in the 4th century, and from the textual evidence that we have, we can say that the old Baramūs Monastery was established by Abba Macarius the Great (†392).[90] It has the oldest archaeological remains in that region that date to the 4th century which means that the old

---

[87] A sixth chapel had also existed under the names of Abba Apollo and Abba Abib. This chapel was built by a famous Copt of the 18th century who spent much of his life building and restoring churches. While Yūsāb, bishop of the Coptic Church in Jerusalem, was on retreat at the Monastery of al-Baramūs, the monks asked him to build a chapel under the name of Abba Apollo and Abib. After its construction was completed, Bishop Yūsāb consecrated it on the third Sunday of Lent in the year 1489AM (1773AD). It is said that the monks prayed all their services there, and due to overuse and structural instabilities the walls began to crack, and the monks saw that it was too dangerous to continue praying in it. In the year 1881, the monks decided to seal the doors. This chapel no longer exists. See, Fr Ṣamū'īl Ṭāwaḍrūs al-Suryānī, *al-'adyūrah al-maṣriyah al-'āmerah*, 186-7.

[88] Also known as St George the Cappadocian. There is an icon of him housed in the altar of his chapel in al-Baramūs that was painted in 1193 AM (1477AD) by Simʿān al-Nāsiġ (Simeon the Scribe).

[89] Fr Ṣamū'īl Ṭāwaḍrūs al-Suryānī, *al-'adyūrah al-maṣriyah al-'āmerah*, 183; Innemee, "Excavations at Deir el Baramūs", 15-18.

[90] Karel Innemee, "Excavations at Deir el Baramūs", in *Grafma Newsletter* (1 1997 & 2 1998): 15-18.

Baramūs monastery is the oldest church that exists in the Wādī al-Naṭrūn.[91]

The modern Monastery of al-Baramūs was founded next to the old Baramūs as a "twin monastery" was in fact established in the 6th century as a result of a theological controversy between Julian, bishop Halicarnassus (†518) and St Severus, Patriarch of Antioch (†ca. 465-583) on the corruptibility or incorruptibility of Christ before the resurrection. Those who followed St Severus, founded another four monasteries as "counterparts" (see figure 1):[92]

1. The modern Monastery of al-Baramūs was the counter monastic establishment of the old Baramūs.

2. The Monastery of the Virgin of Anba Pshoi known now as the Monastery of al-Suryān is the counter monastic settlement of the old monastery of St Pshoi.

3. A counter monastery for St John the Little which survived until approximately the 14th century.

4. And a counter monastery for Dayr Abū Maqār, which no longer exists.

All four of the monasteries in Wadi al-Naturn were victim to six raids that occurred in 407, 410, 444, 507, 817 and the last in the 11th century. One of the threatening periods in particular came from the Black Death of the 14th century, which was followed by a period of famine. Each time the communities were attacked, the monastic buildings were damaged, the churches plundered and the monks either slain or carried off as captives.[93]

---

91 Gawdat Gabra, *Coptic Monasteries: Egypt's Monastic Art and Architecture*, (Oxford University Press, 2002), 38-42.
92 Ibid.
93 An example of this is seen by the 49 Martyrs of Scete who were massacred in 444 and are now commemorated by the Copts on 26th of *Tōbi*. See, H.G. Evelyn

The Muslim historian Taqī al-Dīn al-Maqrīzī (1364–1442) confirms that in his time only 12 monks still lived in the crumbling remains of al-Baramūs. He wrote:[94]

> *The Monastery of the Virgin Baramūs, dedicated to the name of the Virgin Mary; there are some monks. Opposite to it stands the monastery of Moses or Abu Moses the Black also called the Baramūs; this monastery is dedicated to the Virgin of Baramūs, so that Baramūs is the name of the monastery. A story is told of it as follows: Maximus and Dometius were sons of the emperor of the Romans, and had a teacher called Arsenius. The teacher took himself from the land of the Romans to Egypt, crossed this desert of Scete, adopted the monastic life, and remained there till he died. He was an excellent man, and both the aforesaid sons of the emperor came to him during his life and became monks at his hands. When they died, their father sent and the church of Baramūs was built in their names.*

With respect to the name of "al-Baramūs", there are a few traditions that exist. One is that the Arabic name "Baramūs" derives from the Coptic "ⲡⲁⲣⲟⲙⲉⲟⲥ" or "ⲡⲓⲣⲟⲙⲉⲟⲥ" which means "that of /the Romans". The other relates to Abba Arsenius the Great (†445) who was known as the tutor to Arcadius and Honorius, the sons of Emperor Theodosius I in Constantinople. Like Sts Maximus and Dometius, Abba Arsenius became a Roman living in the Egyptian desert of Scete and later its abbot. When the monastery was destroyed in 407 by the Berbers and

---

White, *The monasteries of the Wâdi'n Natrûn vol. II the History of the Monasteries of Nitria and Scetis,* (Arno Press, 1973), 164–167; and, Archbishop Basilios, "Forty-Nine Martyrs of Scetis", *CE 4.*
94 Taqī al-Dīn al-Maqrīzī, *al-Mawaiz wa al-I'tibar fi al-Khitat wa al-Athar,* vol.2 (Cairo: Government Press, 1892), 508-509.

the Bedouins, Abba Arsenius returned to rebuild it.[95] Therefore, the hypothesis that the name "al-Baramūs" has some relation to Abba Arsenius is plausible and carries some weight. However, the tradition most attested to is the monastery's association with the Roman saints Maximus and Dometius which we can see in the *Life* and also in liturgical texts. Of these, the Coptic doxology for the two brothers reads: ⲉⲛⲉⲣϣⲁⲓ ϧⲉⲛ ⲧⲟⲩⲉⲕⲕⲗⲏⲥⲓⲁ ⲉⲛϫⲱⲕ ⲙ̄ⲡⲟⲩⲉⲣⲫⲙⲉⲩⲓ̀ ⲉ̀ⲃⲟⲗ ⲉⲛϯⲱ̀ⲟⲩ ⲛ̄ϯⲧ̀ⲣⲓⲁⲥ ⲙ̀ⲡⲓⲉ̀ϩⲟⲟⲩ ⲛⲉⲙ ⲡⲓⲉ̀ϫⲱⲣϩ (English: We are celebrating **in their church**, we are completing their commemoration, and we are glorifying the Trinity, by day and by night).

From their *Life* we gather that it was Abba Macarius who ordered the building of a church in their memory. The church was given the name "Cell of the Romans" by Abba Paphnutius (Abba Macarius' successor) and at another time Abba Macarius is also naming the place:

> *In short, the desert became a widespread area, a large church was constructed, and Isidore ordained a presbyter. And I too, the unworthy, was made deacon. The great Abba Macarius called out from within the church and said, "Call this place the Roman Quarter. (#93)*

The *Life* also mentions that the location of the church (whereby the monastery was constructed around), was ordered by God

---

95 See, White, *The monasteries of the Wâdi'n Natrûn vol. II the History of the Monasteries of Nitria and Scetis*, 122-124; and, Tim Vivian, "The world is too much with us: The sayings of Arsenius in the Alphabetical Apophthegmata Patrum. A new translation with comments", *The American Benedictine review 70*, no. 2 (2019): 163-192.

and completed by a Cherub. Abba Paphnutius is cited in their biography to have said:

> *When we built the church, God ordered our father through the Cherubim of light: 'Call this place the Roman Quarter. And you, follow me and I will show you the place that will be named after you.'*

> *Then the Cherubim took him to the Southern bend of the wetland in the place of the spring. He stood on the rock to the west. He promised him that place, saying, "This is the place that will be named after you. It is also the place which you will build and will be given in perpetuity to the Romans, because they are the ones who left their body in this holy desert as first fruits of your labours in the vineyard of the Lord Sabaoth, which is the revered family of monks… (#95, 96)*

The *Life* includes another reference to the construction of the church after their name:

> *For this reason, truly, Jesus Christ also gave them glory, so that He moved their heart to go to the holy Mountain of Scete in order to die there and that a church be built in their name. For they had established their foundations on the immovable rock, Christ, which has become a harbour of salvation for everyone who will turn to God for the forgiveness of their sins. Truly, the Paradise of God rejoices for the salvation of the souls of sinners in this place, and Scete will not cease to be a harbour of salvation for ever and ever. (#46)*

From this we see that their cell was turned into a shrine and place of prayer. Soon after, and like many other monastic establishments, a monastery was constructed in memory of the two brothers and all those who were inspired to follow in their footsteps joined the monastery to form an ascetic community.

Liturgical Hymns

Liturgical Hymns 81

HYMNS AND EXPOSITIONS ARE ONE OF THE MANY WAYS THE Coptic Church express their love for the saints. Clergy and deacons were known to string hymns that commemorate a saint's virtuous life in the church setting. For the Monastery of al-Baramūs, hymns and melodies were written by the monks for the communal veneration of the two brothers of whom they have discipled themselves under. To our knowledge, there are no Greek or Sahidic hymns that are known for Sts Maximus and Dometius.[96] Rather, we have original hymns written in Bohairic that consist of: a doxology, two antiphonaries, and two Psalis. A melody is later composed in Arabic.

The Arabic Synaxarium of Mikhail of Malij (†13th century) assigns 17th *Tōbi* as the commemoration of the brothers Sts Maximus and Dometius, sons of the Emperor Valentinian and disciples of the great Abba Macarius of Scetis.[97] The more recent editions of the Synaxarium has the 14th of *Tōbi* as the commemoration of only the departure of St Maximus.[98] Their entry in the Synaxarium follows the Arabic version of their *Life* which is evident by the story of their mother and sister visiting Sts Maximus and Dometius begging them to return to the palace (see, *Extracts from the Arabic Version*).

Moreover, the *Life* does not include any eucharistic features other than their church attendance. But Abba Macarius is recorded to have been the person to include their names in the diptych (#93).[99] The only other liturgical inference is to the canonical

---

[96] The Sahidic Difnār do not include an entry for them. See, Mickel Helmy, ed., *al-difnār: al-āntīfūnāriyūn al-ṣaʿīdī*, (Cairo: Alexandria School, 2018).

[97] *PO Tome 11* (1915): Mois de Toubeh et d'Amchir, 609-614.

[98] *Coptic Synaxarium*, (Chicago: St George Coptic Orthodox Church, 1995), 180-181.

[99] See, al-Qummuṣ ʿAbd al-Massīḥ Ṣalīb al-Masʿūdī al-Baramūsī, *kitāb al-ḫūlāǧī al-muqaddas,* (Cairo, 1902). It is preserved in the Basillian, Gregorian, and

hours which is apparent by the usage of the twelve psalms. The account reads:

> *They used to recite their psalms six by six verses with a sign of the cross, according to the custom of the Syrians. (#61)*

Another citation to the canonical hours occurs during matins:

> *As morning was about to appear, they laid down on the ground again, sleeping, and I too pretended to be in deep sleep. And the older one said to me this single word, "Do you want us to say the twelve psalms?" I said to them, "Yes". And the younger one said six psalms, six by six verses and one alleluia. (#68)*

What we see here is the typical psalm singing found among Egyptian monastics in 4th-century Scete. Generally, if there are two people gathered, then the twelve psalms are distributed among the two, and prayed. In this account there are three monks gathered together. Perhaps it was because Abba Macarius was considered the abbot, and so he was presiding over the small synaxis which explains why the psalms were not distributed among the three instead. Furthermore, the psalmody here that is attributed to the Syrian rite is similar to that of the rite according to Scete and is known to us by St John Cassian (†435)[100] who provided the order as two daily prayers which occur during matins (1st hour) and after the daily meal (9th hour). Although, the Syrian rite referred to here is actually the rite of Scete, the author of the *Life* is perhaps considering two details when making this conclusion: 1) that they spent much time as Syrian monks, and 2) that this rite was perhaps different to the 12/13th-

---

Cyrillian liturgy as, "...and our lords and holy fathers, the Romans, Maximus and Dometius", see pp. 356, 520-521, and 600.
100 *Institutes* 2. 5-11.

century monastic practice in Scete. If we are to take Cassian's account, then their daily routine would have consisted of twelve psalms prayed in this order:

- Seated: Psalm read slowly by a soloist, standing.
- Standing: Silent prayer with arms extended.
- Prostrated: Praying all the while.
- Standing: Silent prayer with arms extended; done by the presider.
- 12th psalm is an alleluia followed by Glory be to the Father (Doxa Patri).
- Two scriptural lessons to conclude the service.

a) The Doxology of Sts Maximus and Dometius

Doxologies are the liturgical veneration of the saints chanted during matins and vespers of everyday.[101] This doxology[102] appears in modern editions of the euchologion. Below is a revised translation:

Doxology of Maximus and Dometius	
Coptic	English trans.
ⲚⲒⲪⲰⲤⲦⲎⲢ ⲚⲦⲈ ϮⲘⲈⲐⲘⲎⲒ ⲞⲨⲞϨ ⲚⲒⲚⲒϢϮ ⲚⲀⲢⲬⲎⲄⲞⲤ ⲚⲦⲈ ⲦⲈⲚⲤⲨⲚⲞⲆⲒⲀ ⲈⲐⲞⲨⲀⲂ ⲘⲀⲌⲒⲘⲞⲤ ⲚⲈⲘ ⲆⲞⲘⲈⲦⲒⲞⲤ	The luminaries of truth and the great leaders of our holy community[104] are Maximus and Dometius.

---

101 Aelred Cody, "Doxology", *CE 3*.
102 Yassa 'Abd al-Massīḥ, "Doxologies in the Coptic Church", *BSAC 4* (1938) 97-113; "Doxologies of the Coptic Church", *BSAC 5* (1939) 175-191; "Doxologies in the Coptic Church, Unedited Bohairic Doxologies II (Tûbahan-Nasî)", *BSAC 11* (1946-1947) 95-158.
104 This is a clear indication that the monks in the monastery of al-Baramūs were the authors of this doxology.

ⲛⲁⲓ ⲉ̀ⲧⲁⲥⲑⲟⲩⲱⲧⲉⲛ ϧⲉⲛ ⲛⲟⲩⲣⲁⲛ ⲛ̀ϫⲉ ϯⲧⲣⲓⲁⲥ ⲛ̀ⲣⲉϥⲧⲁⲛϧⲟ ⲑⲣⲉⲛⲙⲟϣⲓ ⲛ̀ⲥⲁ ⲛⲟⲩϣⲉⲛⲧⲁⲧⲥⲓ ⲛ̀ⲧⲉⲛⲉⲣⲫⲟⲣⲓⲛ ⲙ̀ⲡⲟⲩⲥ̀ⲭⲏⲙⲁ<?> ⲉⲑⲟⲩⲁⲃ	These whom the life-giving Trinity have gathered in their name that we should follow in their footsteps and be clothed by their holy habit.
ⲁⲩϯ ⲉ̀ⲧⲟⲧⲉⲛ ⲛ̀ⲛⲓⲱϣ ⲉⲧⲥ̀ϧⲏⲟⲩⲧ ϧⲉⲛ ⲡⲓⲉ̀ⲩⲁⲅⲅⲉⲗⲓⲟⲛ ⲉⲧⲉ ⲑⲁⲓ ⲧⲉ ϯⲙⲉⲧⲙⲁⲓⲥⲟⲛ ⲡ̀ϫⲱⲕ ⲉ̀ⲃⲟⲗ ⲛ̀ⲛⲓⲁⲣⲉⲧⲏ ⲧⲏⲣⲟⲩ	They handed to us the promises written in the Gospel, which is brotherly love, the perfection of all virtues.
ⲉⲛⲉⲣϣⲁⲓ ϧⲉⲛ ⲧⲟⲩⲉ̀ⲕⲕⲗⲏⲥⲓⲁ ⲉⲛϫⲱⲕ ⲙ̀ⲡⲟⲩⲉⲣⲫⲙⲉⲩⲓ̀ ⲉ̀ⲃⲟⲗ ⲉⲛϯⲱ̀ⲟⲩ ⲛ̀ϯⲧⲣⲓⲁⲥ ⲙ̀ⲡⲓⲉ̀ϩⲟⲟⲩ ⲛⲉⲙ ⲡⲓⲉ̀ϫⲱⲣϩ	We are celebrating in their church, completing their commemoration, glorifying the Trinity by day and by night.
ⲭⲉⲣⲉ ⲛⲱⲧⲉⲛ ⲱ̀ ⲛⲓⲇⲓⲕⲉⲟⲥ ⲭⲉⲣⲉ ⲛⲓⲡ̅ⲛ̅ⲁ̅ⲧⲟⲫⲟⲣⲟⲥ ⲭⲉⲣⲉ ⲛⲉⲛⲓⲟϯ ⲉⲑⲟⲩⲁⲃ ⲛ̀ⲣⲱⲙⲉⲟⲥ ⲙⲁⲍⲓⲙⲟⲥ ⲛⲉⲙ ⲇⲟⲙⲉⲧⲓⲟⲥ	Hail to you, O righteous ones! Hail, spirit-bearers! Hail, our holy Roman fathers, Maximus and Dometius.
ⲧⲱⲃϩ ⲙ̀ⲡⲟ̅ⲥ̅ ⲉ̀ϩ̀ⲣⲏⲓ ⲉϫⲱⲛ ⲛⲉⲛⲓⲟϯ ⲉⲑⲟⲩⲁⲃ ⲛ̀ⲣⲱⲙⲉⲟⲥ ⲙⲁⲍⲓⲙⲟⲥ ⲛⲉⲙ ⲇⲟⲙⲉⲧⲓⲟⲥ ⲛ̀ⲧⲉϥ ⲭⲁ ⲛⲉⲛⲛⲟⲃⲓ ⲛⲁⲛ ⲉ̀ⲃⲟⲗ	Pray to the Lord on our behalf, our holy Roman fathers, Maximus and Dometius, that He may forgive us our sins.

b) Antiphonarium (Difnār): 14ᵗʰ & 17ᵗʰ of *Tōbi*[103]

The Antiphonarium is a liturgical book also known as the *Difnār*.[104] It contains praises offered after the midnight praises (*tasbeḥah*) and is chanted during the commemoration of

---

103 Interesting to note is the presence of a commemoration in the 14ᵗʰ of *Tōbi* in the Antiphonarium, and no commemoration given in the Synaxarium prior to the late 20ᵗʰ century. Cf. *PO Tome 11* (1915): Mois de Toubeh et d'Amchir, 609-614 and *Coptic Synaxarium*, (Chicago: St George Coptic Orthodox Church, 1995), 180-181.
104 Emile Maher Ishaq, "Difnar", *CE 3*.

any given saint. In its essence, the Antiphonarium serves as a Synaxarium in song. In some monasteries today the Antiphonrium is chanted beneath the icon of the commemorated saint. One can only imagine a group of monks standing beneath the 13th-century wall painting at the Monastery of al-Baramūs (see Figure 4) chanting these hymns. It is hardly ever chanted in what is known as 'cathedral worship' i.e., churches in the city. There are two tunes for the Antiphonary, the *adam* and the *watos/batos*.[105]

The reader should note the apparent literary style used throughout the chant. A contrast between the worldly life and the heavenly life becomes an overarching premise that was aimed to remind monks of their own surrenders and the splendour they would receive in the life thereafter. More apparent in the *batos* Antiphonary of the 17th of *Tōbi*, is the contrast observed between each stanza. One recalls the worldly thrones, crowns, and vestments that they had forsaken, and the other reinforces the gifts of the heavenly kingdom, that the two saints "became kings with Jesus Christ forever."

The Antiphonary follows a similar acrostic pattern that is seen in many of the Psali's of the Coptic Church which are intended to help memorise the verses. At times, we see that the first letter of a word is altered to fit the acrostic method of the hymn by employing letters with similar phonetics. For example, ⲍⲉ is meant to read ⲇⲉ (meaning 'but') where the ⲇ is replaced by the ⲍ to remain consistent with its ascending alphabetic order. The same instance is seen with ⲩⲗⲟⲥ and ⳁⲱⲑⲏⲣ where in the instance of the former, there is a change in the way the word is spelled from ⲩⲗⲟⲥ to ⲏⲗⲉⲱⲥ, while keeping the same sound.

---

[105] These are taken from the first word of the Monday Theotokia ⲁⲇⲁⲙ ⲉⲧⲓ ⲉϥⲟⲓ ⲛ̀ⲙ̀ⲕⲁϩ̀ⲛ̀ϩⲏⲧ (Adam was saddened...) and the Thursday Theotokia ⲡⲓⲃⲁⲧⲟⲥ ⲉⲧⲁ ⲙⲱⲩⲥⲏⲥ (The bush which Moses...) of the midnight praises.

The latter ϯⲱⲧⲏⲣ combines the article ⲡ and the consonant ⲥ which together form the sound ϯ.

With translation, the current English editions that are printed or digitised are a translation of a translation i.e., they are translated from Coptic to Arabic, then Arabic to English. Provided here is a translation from an 18th-century manuscript belonging to Wādī al-Naṭrūn and now housed in the Vatican Library (see Appendix 1.1). Fr O'Leary De Lacy transcribed this text and published it in 1928.[106] The Antiphonary is identical to that of the *adam* and *watos* Psali in the 1913 edition by Fr Fīlūtạ̄'us al-Maqqārī[107] with the addition of one extra strophe in the *adam* Psali that helps us identify the author of this hymn as Yūḥanna 'ibn Matta (John the son of Matthew):

ⲱ ⲡⲉⲛϭⲟⲥ ⲓⲏⲥ ⲡⲭⲥ ⲁⲣⲓⲫⲙⲉⲩⲓ ⲙ̄ⲡⲓⲉⲗⲁⲭⲓⲥⲧⲟⲥ ⲓⲱⲥ ⲡϣⲏⲣⲓ ⲙ̄ⲙⲁⲧⲑⲉⲟⲛ ⲛⲉⲙ ⲛ̄ⲑⲉⲡⲓ ⲛ̄ⲛⲓⲭⲣⲓⲥⲧⲓⲁⲛⲟⲥ	O our Lord Jesus Christ, remember the wretched John, the son of Matthew, with the all the Christians.

In the Arabic translation, there are several strophes which were evidently misread or misunderstood and therefore bore a different meaning from the original Coptic. A clear case of this is with the word ⲛⲓⲥ̀ⲧⲣⲁⲧⲏⲗⲁⲧⲏⲥ ⲛ̄ⲧⲁⲫⲙⲏⲓ was rendered as 'the true Israelites' instead of 'the true/faithful soldiers' or the interrogative pronouns such as ⲛⲓⲙ or ⲟⲩⲏⲣ that were rendered as statements instead of question form. For this reason, a revised translation is provided here for an accurate reading.

---

106 O'Leary De Lacy, "The Difnar (Antiphonarium) of the Coptic Church/2 Second four months, Tubeh, Amshir, Barmahat and Barmuda/from the Vatican Codex Copt. Borgia 59; edited by De Lacy O'Leary" (1928).

107 See Fīlūtạ̄'us al-Maqqārī, *al-'ibṣāliyāt w-al-ṭurūḥāt w-al-wāṭos w-al-adām*, (Cairo, 1913), 415-426.

14ᵗʰ *Tōbi* - Adam Exposition

ϯⲁⲗⲓ ⲛ̄ϩⲟⲥ ⲁⲇⲁⲙ (Psali in the Adam Tune)

Coptic	English trans.
ⲁⲗⲏⲑⲱⲥ ⲟⲩⲛⲓϣϯ ⲡⲉ ⲡⲓⲱⲟⲩ ⲛⲉⲙ ⲡ̄ⲧⲁⲓⲟ̀ ⲛ̀ⲛⲉⲛⲓⲟϯ ⲛ̀ⲣⲱⲙⲉⲟⲥ ⲛⲉⲛϣⲏⲣⲓ ⲙ̀ⲡⲟⲩⲣⲟ	Truly great is the glory and honour of our Roman fathers, the sons of the emperor.
ⲃⲟⲛ ⲛⲓⲃⲉⲛ ⲉⲑⲟⲩⲱϣ ⲉ̀ϣⲉⲙϣⲓ ⲙ̀ⲫϯ ⲙⲁⲣⲟⲩⲭⲟϩ ⲉ̀ⲡⲟⲩⲃⲓⲟⲥ ⲛⲉⲙ ⲧⲟⲩ ⲁ̀ⲛⲁⲥⲧ̀ⲣⲟⲫⲏ	All those who desire to worship God may envy their life and their manner of living.
ⲅⲉ ⲅⲁⲣ ⲁⲗⲏⲑⲱⲥ ⲁⲩⲉⲣⲕⲁⲧⲁⲫⲣⲟⲛⲓⲛ ⲙ̀ⲡⲱⲟⲩ ⲛ̀ⲧⲉ ⲡⲁⲓⲕⲟⲥⲙⲟⲥ ⲉⲑⲛⲁⲥⲓⲛⲓ ⲛ̀ⲭⲱⲗⲉⲙ	For truly they rejected the glory of this quickly passing world.
ⲇⲓⲕⲉⲟⲥ ⲁⲗⲏⲑⲱⲥ ⲁⲩⲕⲱϯ ⲛ̀ⲥⲁ ⲫϯ ⲉⲃⲟⲗ ϧⲉⲛ ⲡⲟⲩϩⲏⲧ ⲧⲏⲣϥ ⲓⲥϫⲉⲛ ⲧⲟⲩⲙⲉⲧⲕⲟⲩϫⲁⲓ	Truly righteous are they who sought after God with all their heart from their youth.
ⲉⲣⲉ ⲛⲓⲙ ⲛⲁϣⲥⲁϫⲓ ⲛ̀ⲛⲓⲁⲥⲕⲩⲥⲓⲥ ⲛⲉⲙ ⲛⲟⲩⲡⲟⲗⲏⲧⲓⲁ ⲉ̀ⲧⲟⲩⲓⲣⲓ ⲙ̀ⲙⲱⲟⲩ	Who can speak of [their] asceticism and the way of life which they did?
ⲍⲉ ⲥⲱⲧⲡ ⲉⲙⲁϣⲱ ⲛ̀ϫⲉ ⲡⲟⲩⲃⲓⲟⲥ ⲛ̀ⲁⲅⲅⲉⲗⲓⲕⲟⲛ ⲟⲩⲟϩ ⲉϥⲟⲓ ϣ̀ⲫⲏⲣⲓ	For highly elect is their angelic and wonderous life.
ⲏⲇⲉⲟⲥ ⲁⲗⲏⲑⲱⲥ ⲁⲩⲙⲉⲛⲣⲏϯ ⲛⲏⲥⲩⲁ ⲛⲉⲙ ⲛⲓⲡ̀ⲣⲟⲥⲉⲩⲭⲏ ⲙ̀ⲫⲣⲏϯ ⲛ̀ⲏⲗⲓⲁⲥ	Truly pleasant was their love for fasting and prayer, like Elijah.
ⲑⲁⲓ ⲅⲁⲣ ⲁⲗⲏⲑⲱⲥ ⲧⲉ ⲧⲟⲩ ⲉ̀ⲡⲓⲑⲩⲙⲓⲁ ⲉⲩⲕⲱϯ ⲛ̀ⲥⲁ ⲡⲓⲱⲣϥ ⲛⲉⲙ ϯϩⲥⲩⲭⲓⲁ	For this was indeed their desire, to seek after solitude and tranquillity.

Coptic	English trans.
Ⲓⲏⲥ ⲡⲉⲛⲥⲱⲧⲏⲣ ⲛⲁϥϣⲟⲡ ⲛⲉⲙⲱⲟⲩ ⲡⲉ ϧⲉⲛ ⲛⲟⲩϩⲃⲟⲩⲓ̀ ⲧⲏⲣⲟⲩ ⲉ̀ⲧⲟⲩⲣⲁ ⲙ̀ⲙⲱⲟⲩ	Jesus, our Saviour was with them in all their deeds.
Ⲕⲁⲗⲱⲥ ⲁⲗⲏⲑⲱⲥ ⲁϥϣⲁⲓ ⲛⲁⲛ ⲙ̀ⲫⲟⲟⲩ ⲛ̀ϫⲉ ⲡⲉⲣⲫⲙⲉⲩⲓ ⲛ̀ⲛⲉⲛⲓⲟϯ ⲛ̀ⲣⲱⲙⲉⲟⲥ	Truly splendid [is] the feast of our fathers today, namely, the commemoration of our Roman fathers.
Ⲗⲁⲗⲓⲁ ⲛⲓⲃⲉⲛ ⲛ̀ⲧⲉ ⲛⲓⲁⲅⲅⲉⲗⲟⲥ ϩⲩⲙⲛⲟⲥ ⲛⲓⲃⲉⲛ ⲉⲧⲥⲱⲧⲡ ⲛ̀ⲉ̀ⲡⲟⲩⲣⲁⲛⲓⲟⲛ	Everyone joyfully sings of all the angelic hymns which are chosen from heaven.
Ⲙⲁⲝⲓⲙⲟⲥ ⲡⲓⲛⲓϣϯ ⲛⲉⲙ Ⲇⲟⲙⲉⲧⲓⲟⲥ ⲛⲁⲩⲃⲉⲃⲓ ⲙ̀ⲙⲱⲟⲩ ⲉ̀ⲡ̀ϣⲱⲓ ϧⲉⲛ ⲡⲟⲩϩⲏⲧ	Maximus the great and Dometius poured out their heart toward heaven.
Ϩⲓⲧⲉⲛ ⲛⲓⲉⲩⲭⲏ...	Through the prayers...

17th *Tōbi* - Adam Exposition

Ϯⲁⲗⲓ ⲛ̀ⲏⲭⲟⲥ ⲁⲇⲁⲙ (Psali in the Adam Tune)

Coptic	English trans.
Ⲙⲁⲝⲓⲙⲟⲥ ⲡⲓⲛⲓϣϯ ⲛⲉⲙ Ⲇⲟⲙⲉⲧⲓⲟⲥ ⲁⲩⲣⲁⲛⲁϥ ⲙ̀ⲫϯ ⲁⲩⲓⲣⲓ ⲙ̀ⲡⲉϥⲟⲩⲱϣ	Maximus the great and Dometius, they pleased God and they did His will.
Ⲛⲓϣ̀ⲫⲏⲣⲓ ⲉⲧⲁⲩⲁⲓⲧⲟⲩ ϧⲉⲛ ⲫ̀ⲣⲁⲛ ⲙ̀ⲡⲭ̅ⲥ̅ ⲛⲉⲙ ⲛⲓϩ̀ⲙⲟⲧ ⲛ̀ⲧⲁⲗϭⲟ ϩⲁ ⲛⲁⲧϭⲓⲡⲓ ⲙ̀ⲙⲱⲟⲩ	The wonders which they performed in the name of Christ and the gifts of healing are countless.
Ϩⲩⲛⲟⲥ ⲁⲗⲏⲑⲱⲥ ϧⲉⲛ ⲟⲩⲙⲉⲧϣⲉⲙⲙⲟ ⲉⲑⲃⲉ ⲫ̀ⲣⲁⲛ ⲙ̀ⲡⲭ̅ⲥ̅ ⲉⲧⲁϥϣⲉⲙⲙⲟ ⲉⲑⲃⲏⲧⲉⲛ	They were truly supported in their sojourn concerning the name of Christ, who Himself became a sojourner for us.

ⲟⲩⲏⲣ ⲡⲉ ⲡⲓϩⲓⲥⲓ ⲉⲧⲁⲩϥⲁⲓ ϩⲁⲣⲟϥ ϧⲉⲛ ⲛⲓⲙⲱⲓⲧ ⲙ̀ⲙⲟϣⲓ ⲉⲑⲃⲉ ⲓⲏⲥ ⲡⲭⲥ	How many were the toils which they had endured along the way for Jesus Christ?
ⲡ̀ⲱⲟⲩ ⲧⲏⲣϥ ⲙ̀ⲡⲓⲕⲟⲥⲙⲟⲥ ⲛⲉⲙ ⲧⲉϥϩⲩⲇⲟⲛⲏ ⲛⲉⲙ ϯⲙⲉⲧⲣⲁⲙⲁⲟ ⲁⲩϣⲓⲛϣⲟ ⲙ̀ⲙⲱⲟⲩ	All the glory of the world, its pleasures, and riches, they despised.
ⲣⲱϥ ⲛ̀ⲟⲩⲟⲛ ⲛⲓⲃⲉⲛ ⲥⲉ ⲧⲁⲓⲟ ⲙ̀ⲙⲱⲟⲩ ϫⲉ ⲁⲩⲕⲱϯ ⲛ̀ⲥⲁ ⲫϯ ⲉⲃⲟⲗ ϧⲉⲛ ⲡⲟⲩϩⲏⲧ ⲧⲏⲣϥ	The mouths of all honoured them for they sought God with all their heart.
ⲥⲉⲉⲣⲙⲉⲗⲉⲧⲁⲛ ϧⲉⲛ ⲛⲓⲅ̀ⲣⲁⲫⲏ ⲉ̀ⲑⲩ ⲛⲉⲙ ϯⲉⲛⲟⲙⲟⲥⲓⲁ̀ ⲛ̀ⲧⲉ ⲫⲣⲁⲛ ⲙ̀ⲡⲭⲥ	They pondered over the holy books and recited the name of Christ.
ⲧⲟⲩϩⲉⲗⲡⲓⲥ ⲉⲧⲧⲁϫⲣⲏⲟⲩⲧ ⲛⲉⲙ ⲧⲟⲩⲁ̀ⲅⲁⲡⲏ ⲙ̀ⲙⲏⲓ ⲉϧⲟⲩⲛ ⲉ̀ⲁⲃⲃⲁ ⲅⲁⲃⲟⲥ ⲉⲧⲉ ⲡⲟⲩϣⲟⲣⲡ ⲛ̀ⲓⲱⲧ	Their hope was firm and so was their love toward Abba Agabus who was their first father.
ⲩⲇⲉⲟⲥ ⲁⲩⲉⲣⲉⲧⲓⲛ ⲟⲩⲟϩ ⲟⲛ ⲁⲩϭⲓ ⲁⲩⲕⲱϯ ⲁⲩϫⲓⲙⲓ ⲁⲩⲕⲱⲗϩ ⲁⲩⲟⲩⲱⲛ ⲛ̀ⲱⲟⲩ	For they sought and found, they asked and received, they knocked, and it was opened for them.
ⲫϯ ⲡⲉⲛⲥⲱⲧⲏⲣ ⲁϥϭⲓ ⲙⲱⲓⲧ ϩⲁϫⲱⲟⲩ ⲛ̀ⲛⲉⲛⲓⲟϯ ⲉ̀ⲑⲩ ϣⲁ ⲡ̀ⲧⲱⲟⲩ ⲛ̀ⲁⲃⲃⲁ ⲙⲁⲕⲁⲣⲓ	God our Saviour guided them to the holy mountain of our father Abba Macarius.
ⲭⲉⲣⲉ ⲛⲱⲧⲉⲛ ⲛⲓⲟ̀ⲙⲏⲓ ⲛⲉⲛⲓⲟϯ ⲛ̀ⲣⲱⲙⲉⲟⲥ ⲟⲩⲟϩ ⲛⲓϣⲟⲣⲡ ⲛ̀ϣ̀ⲫⲏⲣⲓ ⲛ̀ⲧⲉ ⲁⲃⲃⲁ ⲙⲁⲕⲁⲣⲓ	Hail to you! Our righteous Roman fathers, the first children of Abba Macarius.
ϯⲱⲧⲏⲣ ⲱϣ ⲉⲃⲟⲗ ϧⲉⲛ ⲡⲉϥⲣⲱϥ ⲛ̀ⲛⲟⲩϯ ϫⲉ ⲁⲙⲱⲓⲛⲓ ϩⲁⲣⲟⲓ ⲛⲏ ⲉⲧⲥ̀ⲙⲁⲣⲱⲟⲩⲧ ⲛ̀ⲧⲏⲓ	The Saviour promised with His divine mouth, "come to me, O blessed [of my Father, inherit the kingdom that is prepared for you]."

ⲱⲟⲩⲛⲓⲁⲧⲉⲛ ⲑⲏⲛⲟⲩ ⲛⲉⲛⲓⲟϯ ⲛ̀ⲣⲱⲙⲉⲟⲥ ϫⲉ ⲁ̀ ⲫϯ ⲛ̀ⲧⲉ ⲧ̀ⲫⲉ ϯ ⲛ̀ϩⲁⲛⲧⲁⲓⲟ ⲛⲱⲧⲉⲛ	Blessed are you, our Roman fathers for the God of heaven has honoured you.
ϩⲓⲧⲉⲛ ⲛⲓⲉⲩⲭⲏ…	Through the prayers…
ⲛ̀ⲑⲱⲟⲩ ⲋ︦ ⲏ̄ ⲃⲁⲧⲟⲥ (Another in the Batos Tune)	
ⲁⲗⲏⲑⲱⲥ ⲟⲩⲛⲓϣϯ ⲡⲉ ⲡ̅ⲧⲁⲓⲟ̀ ⲛ̀ⲧⲉ ⲛⲉⲛⲓⲟϯ ⲛ̀ⲣⲱⲙⲉⲟⲥ ⲙⲁⲝⲓⲙⲟⲥ ⲛⲉⲙ ⲇⲟⲙⲉⲧⲓⲟⲥ ⲛⲉⲛϣⲏⲣⲓ ⲙ̀ⲡⲟⲩⲣⲟ ⲉ̀ⲧⲁⲩⲉⲣⲙⲟⲛⲁⲭⲟⲥ	Truly great is the honour of our Roman fathers, Maximus and Dometius, the sons of the emperor who became monks.
ⲕⲉ ⲅⲁⲣ ⲁⲩⲭⲱ ⲛ̀ⲥⲱⲟⲩ ⲛ̀ⲛⲓⲭⲓⲛⲟⲩⲱⲙ ⲁ̀ ⲡⲟⲩⲗⲁⲥ ϣⲱⲟⲩⲓ̀ ϧⲉⲛ ϯⲛⲏⲥⲧⲓⲁ̀ ⲁ̀ ⲛⲁⲥⲕⲉⲥⲓⲥ ⲉ̀ⲧⲟⲩⲓ̀ⲣⲓ ⲙ̀ⲙⲱⲟⲩ ⲣⲱⲕϩ ⲛ̀ⲧϫⲟⲙ ⲙ̀ⲡ̅ⲥⲁⲧⲁⲛⲁⲥ	For they abandoned food and their tongues had dried because of fasting. As for their asceticism, it burned the power of Satan.
ⲉⲣⲉ ⲡⲟⲩⲣⲟ ϧⲉⲛ ⲡⲓⲡⲁⲗⲗⲁⲧⲓⲟⲛ ⲉϥⲟⲩⲱⲙ ⲉϥⲥⲱ ⲉϥⲟⲩⲛⲟϥ ⲙ̀ⲙⲟϥ ⲉⲣⲉ ⲛⲉϥϣⲏⲣⲓ ϩⲓ ⲡ̀ϣⲁϥⲉ ⲉⲩϣⲉⲡϧⲓⲥⲓ ⲉⲑⲃⲉ ⲡ̅ⲭ̅ⲥ̅	The emperor was in the palace eating and drinking, celebrating while his sons were in the wilderness, labouring for the sake of Christ.
ⲓ̀ⲧⲁ ⲁⲩϣⲱⲡⲓ ⲛⲉⲙ ⲡ̅ⲭ̅ⲥ̅ ϧⲉⲛ ⲧ̀ⲭⲱⲣⲁ ⲛ̀ⲧⲉ ⲛⲏⲉⲧⲟⲛϧ ⲁⲩⲉⲣϣⲁⲓ ⲛⲉⲙⲁϥ ϧⲉⲛ ⲧⲉϥⲙⲉⲧⲟⲩⲣⲟ ⲉⲑⲙⲏⲛ ⲉ̀ⲃⲟⲗ ϣⲁ ⲉⲛⲉϩ	They came to be with Christ in the region of the living, and they rejoiced with Him in His eternal kingdom.
ⲁⲛⲁⲩ ⲉ̀ⲡⲁⲓⲥⲟⲛ ⲃ̄ ⲉ̀ⲧⲁⲩϣⲓⲛⲓ ⲛ̀ⲥⲁ ⲡⲉⲛⲥⲱⲧⲏⲣ ϧⲉⲛ ⲡⲓϣ̀ⲗⲏⲗ ⲛⲉⲙ ϯⲛⲏⲥⲧⲓⲁ ⲛⲉⲙ ⲛⲓⲁⲥⲕⲉⲥⲓⲥ ⲉⲧϭⲟⲥⲓ	Behold, these two brothers who sought after our Saviour with prayer, fasting, and exalted asceticism.
ⲗⲩⲧⲟⲣⲅⲓⲁ̀ ⲛⲓⲃⲉⲛ ⲉⲑ̅ⲩ̅ ⲁⲩϣⲉⲙϣⲓ ⲙ̀ⲫϯ ⲛ̀ϧⲣⲏⲓ ⲛ̀ϧⲏⲧⲥ ⲛ̀ϫⲉ ⲛⲥⲓⲟⲩ ⲉ̀ⲧⲉⲣⲟⲩⲱⲓⲛⲓ ⲙⲁⲝⲓⲙⲟⲥ ⲛⲉⲙ ⲇⲟⲩⲙⲉⲧⲓⲟⲥ	The luminous stars, Maximus and Dometius served God in every holy liturgy.

ⲙⲁⲣⲉⲛϩⲱⲥ ⲛ̀ⲧⲉⲛϯⲱ̀ⲟⲩ ⲙ̀ⲡⲟⲩⲁ̀ⲅⲱⲛ ⲉ̀ⲧⲟⲓ ⲛ̀ϣ̀ⲫⲏⲣⲓ ⲛⲉⲙ ⲛⲟⲩⲁⲥⲕⲉⲥⲓⲥ ⲙ̀ⲙⲏⲓ ⲉ̀ⲧⲟⲩ ⲁⲓⲧⲟⲩ ⲉⲑⲃⲉ ⲡⲭ̅ⲥ̅	Let us praise and glorify their wonderous struggle and their true asceticism which they withstood for the sake of Christ.
ⲛⲓⲁⲑⲗⲓⲧⲏⲥ ⲛ̀ⲅⲉⲛⲛⲉⲟⲥ ⲟⲩⲟϩ ⲛⲓⲣⲉϥⲙⲓϣⲓ ⲛ̀ⲕⲁⲗⲱⲥ ⲛ̀ϩ̀ⲣⲏⲓ ϧⲉⲛ ⲡⲓⲥ̀ⲧⲁⲇⲓⲟⲛ ⲛ̀ⲧⲉ ϯⲙⲉⲧⲙⲟⲛⲁⲭⲟⲥ	The brave athletes and good fighters in the stadium of monasticism.
ⲱ ⲛⲓⲥⲧⲩⲗⲗⲟⲥ ⲛ̀ⲧⲉ ⲧⲧⲁϫⲣⲏⲟⲩⲧ ⲱ ⲛⲓⲥⲧⲣⲁⲧⲏ̀ⲗⲁⲧⲏⲥ ⲛ̀ⲧⲁϥⲙⲏⲓ ⲛ̀ⲧⲉ ⲡⲓⲛⲓϣϯ ⲛ̀ⲟⲩⲣⲟ ⲡⲭ̅ⲥ̅ ⲙⲁⲝⲓⲙⲟⲥ ⲛⲉⲙ ⲇⲟⲙⲉⲧⲓⲟⲥ	O firm pillars and faithful soldiers of the great king, Christ are Maximus and Dometius.
ⲱ̀ ⲛⲏ ⲉ̀ⲧⲁⲩ ⲉⲣⲕⲁⲧⲁⲫⲣⲟⲛⲓⲛ ⲙ̀ⲡⲱⲟⲩ ⲧⲏⲣϥ ⲛ̀ⲧⲉ ⲡⲓⲕⲟⲥⲙⲟⲥ ⲛⲉⲙ ϯⲙⲉⲧⲟⲩⲣⲟⲟ ⲛ̀ⲧⲉ ⲡⲟⲩⲓⲱⲧ ⲁⲩⲙⲟϣⲓ ⲛ̀ⲥⲁ ⲡⲭ̅ⲥ̅	O they who despised all the glory of the world and the kingdom of their father to follow Christ.
ⲛ̀ⲧϣⲉⲃⲓⲱ̀ ⲛ̀ⲛⲓⲑ̀ⲣⲟⲛⲟⲥ ⲛ̀ⲧⲉ ⲑⲙⲉⲧⲟⲩⲣⲟ ⲙ̀ⲡⲓⲕⲟⲥⲙⲟⲥ ⲛⲁⲓ ⲉⲑⲛⲁⲃⲱⲗⲟⲩ ⲉ̀ⲃⲟⲗ ⲛⲉⲙ ⲛⲏ ⲉⲧϩⲉⲙⲥⲓ ⲉ̀ϩ̀ⲣⲏⲓ ⲉϫⲱⲟⲩ	Instead of the thrones of the worldly kingdom which deteriorate along with those who sit on them.
ⲁϥⲉⲣϩ̀ⲙⲟⲧ ⲛⲱⲟⲩ ⲛ̀ϫⲉ ⲡⲭ̅ⲥ̅ ⲛ̀ϩⲁⲛⲑ̀ⲣⲟⲛⲟⲥ ⲉⲩⲟⲩⲁⲃ ⲛ̀ⲁⲧϣ̀ⲥⲁϫⲓ ⲉ̀ⲡⲟⲩⲧⲁⲓⲟ̀ ϧⲉⲛ ⲧⲉϥⲙⲉⲧⲟⲩⲣⲟ ⲛ̀ⲁⲧⲙⲟⲩⲛⲕ	Christ granted them holy thrones of ineffable honour in His eternal kingdom.
ⲛ̀ⲧϣⲉⲃⲓⲱ̀ ⲛ̀ϩⲁⲛⲡⲟⲣⲫⲩⲣⲁ ⲛⲉⲙ ϩⲁⲛϩⲉⲃⲥⲱ ⲛ̀ⲓⲉⲃ ⲛ̀ⲛⲟⲩⲃ ⲁϥϯϩⲓⲟ̀ⲛⲛⲟⲩ ⲛ̀ϩⲁⲛⲥ̀ⲧⲟⲗⲏ ⲛ̀ⲟⲩⲱⲓⲛⲓ ⲛ̀ⲉ̀ⲡⲟⲩⲣⲁⲛⲓⲟⲛ	Instead of purple robes and golden garments, He dressed you in luminous and heavenly vestments.
ⲛ̀ⲧϣⲉⲃⲓⲱ̀ ⲛ̀ϩⲁⲛⲭ̀ⲗⲟⲙ ⲛⲁⲓ ⲉⲑⲛⲁⲗⲱⲙ ⲛ̀ⲥⲉⲧⲁⲕⲟ ϩⲓ ⲁ̀ⲛⲁⲙⲏⲓ ⲛⲉⲙ ⲙⲁⲣⲅⲁⲓⲧⲏⲥ ⲛⲏ ⲓⲉⲑⲛⲁϣⲓⲃϯ ⲛ̀ⲭⲱⲗⲉⲙ	Instead of crowns covered with precious stones and gems which fade, ruin, and quickly alter.

ⲁϥϯⲥⲧⲉⲫⲁⲛⲟⲩ ⲙ̄ⲙⲱⲧⲉⲛ ⲛ̄ϫⲉ ⲡⲭ̄ⲥ̄ ⲡⲉⲛⲟⲩⲣⲟ ϧⲉⲛ ϩⲁⲛⲭⲗⲟⲙ ⲉⲩⲟⲓ ⲛ̄ⲁⲧⲗⲱⲙ ⲉⲩϩⲓ ⲥⲉⲧⲉⲃⲣⲏⲭ ⲛ̄ⲟⲩⲱⲓⲛⲓ ⲉ̀ⲃⲟⲗ	Christ our king crowned you with incorruptible crowns that radiate with light.
ⲛ̄ⲧϣⲉⲃⲓⲱ̀ ⲛ̄ϯⲙⲉⲧⲟⲩⲣⲟ ⲉ̀ⲧⲉ ⲟⲩⲟⲛ ⲧⲁⲥⲟⲩϫⲱⲕ ⲙ̄ⲙⲁⲩ ⲁ ⲧⲉⲧⲉⲛϣⲱⲡⲓ ⲛ̄ⲟⲩⲣⲟ ⲛⲉⲙ ⲓ̄ⲏ̄ⲥ̄ ⲡⲭ̄ⲥ̄ ϣⲁ ⲉ̀ⲛⲉϩ	Instead of the kingdom that has an end, you became kings with Jesus Christ forever.
ⲧⲱⲃϩ ⲙ̄ⲡⲟ̄ⲥ̄ ...	Pray to the Lord...

c) The Melody in the *Kīyahk* Psalmodia[108]

The *Kīyahk* Psalmodia is the liturgical book specific for the vigil praises (known as *sabʿah w-ārbaʿah*/seven and four) for the month of *Kīyahk* during the fast of the Nativity.[109] This text was first published by Aqlādyūs Labīb in 1911 and interestingly enough it is the only *madīḥ* (melody) in the *adam* tune that is in the large edition, the remaining are for the Holy Trinity or the Virgin Mary.[110] In later editions, there is the inclusion of melodies for Shenoute of Atripe, Pshoi, and Antony.[111] It was originally written in Arabic with a few words in Coptic such as the name of Christ and the name of their father. Throughout the text, the author does not hesitate to interchange the name "Abu Maqar" and "Macarius" to maintain poetic rhythm. Interestingly, Labīb mentions in the preface to this book that

---

108 Aqlādyūs Labīb, ed., *Pičōm Nte Tipsalmōdia Ethu Nte Piabot Khoiak: Mphrēg Etauthaš Nče Nenioti Ntiekklēsia Nremnkhēmi*, (Kairo: ʿain-i šams), 559-562.
109 Emile Maher Ishaq, "sabʾah wa-arbaʾah", *CE* 7.
110 Although this edition was based off the manuscripts from Dayr al-Suryān, there is room for speculation that influence from al-Baramūs had a hand.
111 Cf. *The Kiahk Psalmodia*, (NSW, Australia: St Shenouda Coptic Orthodox Monastery, 2010), 284-305.

his edition is based on that of al-Suryān,[112] but the inclusion of this unique melody (and no other melody for any saint), as well as the mention of al-Baramūs suggests that the Psalmodia that that he used from al-Suryān is most probably influenced by that of al-Baramūs.

1	I begin by the name of God, our Lord ⲓⲏⲥ ⲡⲭⲥ, and explain in reverence the meaning of Maximus and Dometius.
2	I direct my words to Mary ϯⲡⲁⲣⲑⲉⲛⲟⲥ to help me with the order ⲧⲱⲉⲣⲓ ⲛ̄ⲛⲓⲁⲓⲕⲉⲟⲥ.
3	I call out for you to strengthen me, and entreat you in Jesus' name, help me praise the fathers and brothers: Maximus and Dometius.
4	They deserted the Romans and ⲡ̄ⲟⲩⲣⲟ ⲗⲉⲟⲛⲧⲓⲟⲥ, and lived in the wilderness: Maximus and Dometius.
5	They first removed their crowns and cast them from their heads for their love for the King of Heaven: Maximus and Dometius.
6	They followed the words of the Gospel and the works of the law, and now rest in the bosom of Abraham: Maximus and Dometius.
7	Their honour was magnified when they entered into Paradise with two crowns on their heads: Maximus and Dometius.
8	They cherished life on the mountain where they befriended the beasts, leaving behind all kingdoms and wealth: Maximus and Dometius.
9	They rejected this world's glory and defeated the accursed Satan, gaining everlasting joy: Maximus and Dometius.

---

112 Labīb, *Pičōm Nte Tipsalmōdia Ethu Nte Piabot Khoiak*, 559-562.

10	Their superior, Abba Agabus, guided them before his death to go to the Mountain of Scete, the desert of Macarius.
11	David the harpist explained in his psalms that the emperor's sons would come to you, O Abba Macarius.
12	When they were in the wilderness, they looked like angels and were chosen for the papacy: Maximus and Dometius.
13	They surpassed the rituals of the monks and that of the ascetics, roaming valleys far and wide: Maximus and Dometius.
14	They journeyed without direction and were guided by the angels to the Mountain of Scete: Maximus and Dometius.
15	They healed all afflictions in the name of the holy Lord in Syria and the Mountain of Scete: Maximus and Dometius.
16	They chanted hymns before the holy Lord and grew courage: Maximus and Dometius.
17	Their crowns were shining bright when they were placed on their heads and the wilderness rejoiced: Maximus and Dometius.
18	Hail to you O fathers, O sons of Macarius, O stars of the Mountain of Scete and beacons of al-Baramūs.
19	Hail to you O Abū Maqār! Hail to you O Macarius! O father of the Mountain of Scete, together with the leading fathers.
20	My childhood and youth were spent in worries and misery, but her name is precious which is the key to the door of paradise.
21	Great indeed is your stature; the hope of all souls. Do not forget the chanter, your servant, the sinner in all his adversity.

Liturgical Hymns

22	They triumphed over all the demons by the name of the holy Lord and became a strong fort: Maximus and Dometius.
23	The pride of all monks, ⲡⲟⲩⲣⲟ ⲗⲉⲟⲛⲧⲓⲟⲥ, the sons of the ruling king: Maximus and Dometius.
24	Their father, Abba Macarius said of them that they are the pride of monastic vestments: Maximus and Dometius.
25	Their names have been inscribed alongside those of the fathers and all their forefathers: Maximus and Dometius.
26	They wore gleaming garments when they entered Paradise with bright luminous crowns: Maximus and Dometius.
27	They both became Christ's grooms and entered Paradise musing praise with the angels.
28	They attained much reverence by the name of the holy Lord and are praised with melodies and hymns: Maximus and Dometius.
29	They are a priceless gift to the holy Lord, and a cut gem to the Emperor Valentinian: Maximus and Dometius.
30	Do not forget our Patriarch to the holy Lord, and his partner our bishop, Anba (…).
31	And remember O our Lord, all the hosts of monks, and all the ranks ⲡⲓⲟⲩⲁⲓ ⲡⲓⲟⲩⲁⲓ ⲛ̀ⲛⲓⲭⲣⲏⲥⲧⲓⲁⲛⲟⲥ.
32	Hail to the three named Macarius, and all the fathers who live in the Mountain of Scete, the desert of Macarius.
33	Hail to Abba John the hegumen, and our father Abba Pshoi ⲡⲓⲣⲱⲙⲓ ⲛ̀ⲧⲉⲗⲓⲟⲥ.
34	Hail to Abba Daniel, Abba Isidoros, and the most honourable, Abba Arsenius.
35	Hail to Abba Paul, Abba Antony, and the father of the coenobites, the righteous Abba Pachomius.

36	Hail to Abba Abraham, Abba George, and to those who attained praise from the mouth of the holy Lord.
37	They were blessed with crosses by the sign of the holy cross and became knights in the desert of Macarius.
38	Hail to Abba Moses, to Abba Zacharias, and our father Abba John Kame the presbyter.
39	O Wadi Habib, the fathers likened you to Paradise, and the king's sons have inhabited you: Maximus and Dometius.
40	You are a truly great mountain, likened unto Paradise, and home to our fathers the monks: the desert of Macarius.
41	You harboured sinners and were a refuge to robbers. Abū Maqār made you similar to Paradise.
42	You are a spiritual net which saw many ethnicities, and turned back evil doers and robbers, making them leading fathers.
43	They became spiritual people, popes, bishops, and priests, and you wore the crowns, O sons of Macarius.
44	The luminous crowns you wore shone brightly over your head like the angels.
45	Blessed are you, O Abū Maqār! Blessed are you O Macarius! O you whom the faithful came to be covered from the sins of their soul.
46	O you who received the evildoers and washed off the rust of the soul for all who lived or visited the desert of Macarius.
47	Your memory is in all places and with all people, O dwelling of the monks: the desert of Macarius.
48	A lit pillar is what Macarius saw at the highest point of the mountain and built Dayr al-Baramūs.

| 49 | The righteous fathers who live there cry out saying, "Holy!" in a vigil day and night to the children of Macarius. |
| 50 | And hail to Mary, who intercedes on everyone's behalf, the friend of this great name and the key to the door of paradise. |

d) Liturgical hymns for the 17ᵗʰ *Tōbi*¹¹³

These are taken from the manuscripts at the monastery of St Antony and preserved in a handwritten book by Ṣamūʾīl al-Suryānī known as *tartīb al-bayʿah* (the order of the monasteries). This book is a collection of various liturgical hymns that are specific to different monasteries:¹¹⁴

Vespers Gospel Response	
Coptic	English trans.
ⲚⲒⲪⲰⲤⲦⲎⲢ ⲚⲦⲈ ϮⲘⲈⲐⲘⲎ ⲞⲨⲞϨ ⲚⲒⲚⲒϢϮ ⲚⲀⲢⲬⲎⲄⲞⲤ ⲚⲦⲈⲦⲈⲚ ⲤⲨⲚⲞⲆⲒⲀ ⲈⲐⲞⲨ ⲘⲀⲜⲒⲘⲞⲤ ⲚⲈⲘ ⲆⲞⲘⲈⲦⲒⲞⲤ	The luminaries of truth and the great leaders of our holy community are Maximus and Dometius
ⲬⲈⲢⲈ ⲚⲈⲚⲒⲞϮ ⲚⲆⲒⲔⲈⲞⲤ ⲘⲀⲜⲒⲘⲞⲤ ⲚⲈⲘ ⲆⲞⲘⲈⲦⲒⲞⲤ ⲚⲚⲈⲦⲀⲨϨⲒ ⲘⲠϨⲞ ⲘⲠⲀⲒⲔⲞⲤⲘⲞⲤ ⲞⲨⲞϨ ⲘⲈⲚⲢⲈ ⲠⲬⲤ ⲠⲞⲤ	Hail to our righteous fathers, Maximus and Dometius who rejected this world and loved Christ the Lord.

---

113 There are no liturgical hymns specific for the commemoration during of 14ᵗʰ of *Tōbi*.
114 Ṣamūʾīl al-Suryānī, *Tartīb al-bayʿah, 396*.

Matins Gospel Response	
ⲛⲁⲓ ⲉⲧⲁⲥⲑⲟⲩⲱⲧⲉⲛ ϧⲉⲛ ⲟⲩⲣⲁⲛ ⲛ̀ϫⲉ ϯⲧⲣⲓⲁⲥ ⲛ̀ⲣⲉϥⲧⲁⲛϧⲟ ⲉⲑⲣⲉⲛⲙⲟϣⲓ ⲛ̀ⲥⲁ ⲛⲟⲩϣⲉⲛⲧⲁⲧⲥⲓ ⲛ̀ⲧⲉⲛⲉⲣⲫⲟⲣⲓⲛ ⲙ̀ⲡⲟⲩⲥⲭⲏⲙⲁ ⲉ̄ⲑ̄ⲩ̄	These whom the life-giving Trinity have gathered in their name that we should follow in their footsteps and be clothed by their holy habit.
Gospel Response	
ⲉⲩϯ ⲉⲧⲟⲧⲉⲛ ⲛ̀ⲛⲓⲱϣ ⲉⲧⲥ̀ϧⲏⲟⲩⲧ ϧⲉⲛ ⲡⲓⲉⲩⲁⲅⲅⲉⲗⲓⲟⲛ ⲛ̀ⲧⲉ ⲑⲁⲓ ⲧⲉ ϯⲙⲉⲧⲙⲁⲓⲥⲟⲛ ⲡ̀ϫⲱⲕ ⲉⲃⲟⲗ ⲛ̀ⲛⲓⲁⲣⲉⲧⲏ ⲧⲏⲣⲟⲩ	They handed to us the promises written in the gospel, which is brotherly love, the perfection of all virtues.
Aspasmos	
ⲭⲉⲣⲉ ⲙⲁⲝⲓⲙⲟⲥ ⲛⲉⲙ ⲇⲟⲙⲉⲧⲓⲟⲥ ⲛⲉⲛⲓⲟϯ ⲛ̀ⲣⲱⲙⲉⲟⲥ ⲛⲓⲁⲅⲓⲟⲥ ⲉⲧⲥ̀ⲙⲁⲣⲱⲟⲩⲧ	Hail! Maximus and Dometius, our holy and blessed Roman fathers.
ⲛⲁⲓ ⲛⲓϣϯ ⲙ̀ⲫⲱⲥⲧⲏⲣ ⲙⲁⲝⲓⲙⲟⲥ ⲛⲉⲙ ⲇⲟⲙⲉⲧⲓⲟⲥ ⲁⲩⲭⲁⲩ ⲉⲩⲉⲣⲟⲩⲱⲓⲛⲓ ϧⲉⲛ ⲧⲉⲛⲙⲏϯ ϯⲛⲟⲩ	These great luminaries, Maximus and Dometius, became luminous now in our midst.
ϩⲓⲛⲁ...	That [we may praise You...]

Iconography of Saints Maximus and Dometius

THE TWO 13ᵀᴴ-CENTURY WALL PAINTINGS THAT SURVIVE FROM the monastery of St Antony in the Red Sea[115] and the monastery of al-Baramūs[116] are the earliest known representations of these saints in the Coptic tradition.

In their depiction, both brothers are shown wearing a striped hood, a cloak with crosses, a gridle on their waist, and carrying crosses. Maximus is known by his beard, and Dometius is known by his younger and beardless appearance (see figure 1,4, and 5). Their iconography is similar to their representation in the *Life*. During their early years before joining the Egyptian desert, they were clothed in the Syrian habit which is cited as a black garment. One saint of a Syrian background is included in the iconography program of the two monasteries mentioned above, who is St Barsoum the Syrian (see figure 3). He is seen wearing a black hood that extends into a stole. It is possible that this is the representation that is meant in the *Life*.

Furthermore, when the brothers had met Abba Macarius, they desired to wear the same habit as him. The *Life* tells us that Abba Agabus saw Abba Macarius in a vision whereby Abba Macarius said:

> *I saw a monk standing in front of me. He was a tall man, dressed in clothes that had black bands and a hood on his head with crosses on it. He had in his hand a cross.* (#15)

---

115 Elizabeth S Bolman, ed., *Monastic visions: wall paintings in the Monastery of St. Antony at the Red Sea*, (Yale University Press, 2002), 55. For comments on the inscription see pp. 228.
116 Silvia Pasi, "The wall paintings of the church of Al-Adra in the monastery of Deir el-Baramūs (Wadi-el-Natrun)", *Zograf* 34 (2010): 37-52.

Only during his time with the two brothers does Abba Macarius bless them to wear the monastic habit of Scete:

> *They put out for me a small mat on the ground in the corner of the cave, while they stayed on the other side and slept in one space. They took a belt and a cloak and put them before me on the ground and then they were silent. (#65)*

In the wall painting at St Antony's, they are clothed in the same manner as Abba Macarius, no longer wearing the black garments belonging to the Syrian habit. Christ is in the midst holding the two halos of the saints as though crowing them with glory.

An interesting observation from the *Life* is the continued presence of the Cherub. We know from the life and sayings of Abba Macarius, that the Cherub appears to him on several occasions,[117] and for this reason he is referred to as "the friend of the Cherub" by the Coptic community.

Even in today's neo-Coptic iconography, Abba Macarius is often depicted with a Cherub by his side. One of the earliest examples of this is found in the monastery of St Antony, whereby the Cherub takes the hand of Macarius and points toward the icons of Maximus and Dometius with a gesture of blessing (see figure 2). This seems to be consistent with the narrative that the Cherub led Abba Macarius to the place where he was instructed to build the monastery of al-Baramūs.

Finally, their cloaks which are covered in crosses are unlike any of the other monks. In fact, it seems to be a royal cloak that bears some resemblance to the Coptic clerical *burnus* (cape).[118]

---

117 Tim Vivian, *Saint Macarius, the spiritbearer: coptic texts relating to Saint Macarius the Great*, (New York: St Vladimir's Seminary Press, 2004), 84-84, 140, 168- 170, 182.
118 Archbishop Bassilios, "Coptic Vestments", *CE5*.

It may perhaps be an indication to their royal background as sons of Emperor Valentinian. The author of the *Life*, writes:

> *I will not cease to name them sons of the emperor until each one knows their dignity, their angelic life, and their way of life, for they loved Christ more than the entire glory of this world and have followed Him with all their heart. (#45)*

Figure 1. Maximus & Dometius. 13th-century St Antony's Monastery, Red Sea. Photo by the author.

Figure 2. Maximus, Dometius, the Cherub, and Macarius. 13th-century St Antony's Monastery, Red Sea. Photo by the author.

Figure 3. Barsoum. 13th-century St Antony's. Photo by the author.

Figure 4. Maximus and Dometius. 13th-century al-Baramūs. Photo by the author.

Figure 5. A 20th-century wall painting in the Monastery of St Pshoi. Photo by the author.

APPENDIX 1

Manuscripts Consulted

Appendix 1.1: 18th-century manuscript of the Difnār

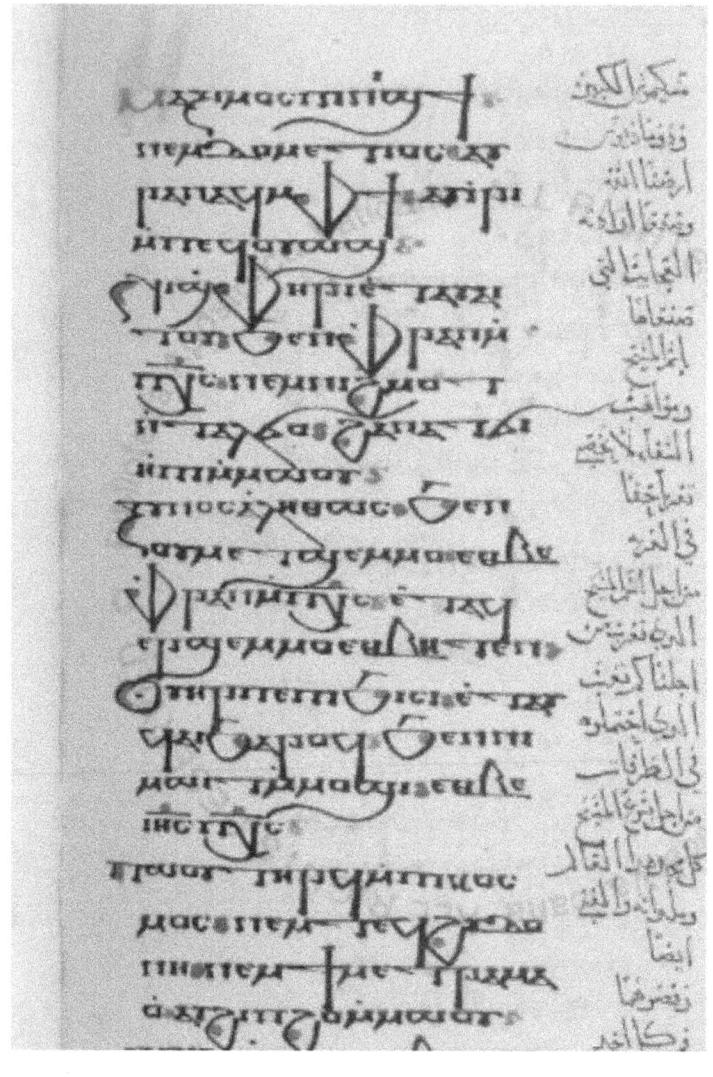

Appendix 1.2: Vat.Copt.67. 13^(th)-c. manuscript containing the Bohairic life.

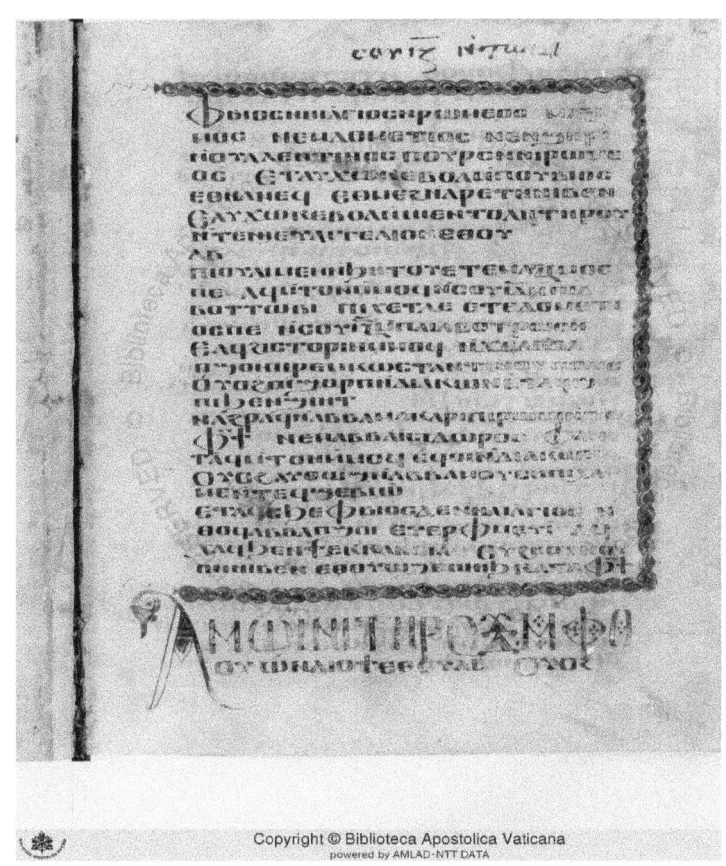

APPENDIX 2

The *Life* of Maximus and Dometius
Transcription of the Bohairic manuscript

1. Ⲫⲃⲓⲟⲥ ⲛ̀ⲛⲓⲁⲅⲓⲟⲥ ⲛ̀ⲣⲱⲙⲉⲟⲥ Ⲙⲁⲍⲓⲙⲟⲥ ⲛⲉⲙ Ⲇⲟⲙⲉⲧⲓⲟⲥ ⲛⲉⲛϣⲏⲣⲓ ⲛ̀ⲟⲩⲁⲗⲉⲛⲧⲓⲟⲥ ⲡⲟⲩⲣⲟ ⲛ̀ⲛⲓⲣⲱⲙⲉⲟⲥ ⲉⲧⲁⲩϫⲱⲕ ⲙ̀ⲡⲟⲩⲃⲓⲟⲥ ⲉⲑⲛⲁⲛⲉϥ ⲉⲑⲙⲉϩ ⲛ̀ⲁⲣⲉⲧⲏ ⲛⲓⲃⲉⲛ ⲉⲁⲩϫⲱⲕ ⲉⲃⲟⲗ ⲛ̀ⲛⲓⲉⲛⲧⲟⲗⲏ ⲧⲏⲣⲟⲩ ⲛ̀ⲧⲉ ⲡⲓⲉⲩⲁⲅⲅⲉⲗⲓⲟⲛ ⲉ̄ⲑ̄ⲩ̄ ⲡⲓⲟⲩⲁⲓ ⲙⲉⲛ ⲛ̀ϩⲏⲧⲟⲩ ⲉⲧⲉ Ⲙⲁⲍⲓⲙⲟⲥ ⲡⲉ ⲁϥⲙ̀ⲧⲟⲛ ⲙ̀ⲙⲟϥ ⲛ̀ⲥⲟⲩⲓ̅ⲇ̅ ⲙ̀ⲡⲓⲁⲃⲟⲧ Ⲧⲱⲃⲓ ⲡⲓⲭⲉⲧ ⲇⲉ ⲉⲧⲉ Ⲇⲟⲙⲉⲧⲓⲟⲥ ⲡⲉ ⲛ̀ⲥⲟⲩⲓ̅ⲍ̅ ⲙ̀ⲡⲁⲓⲁⲃⲟⲧ ⲣⲱ ⲟⲛ

2. ⲉⲁϥϩⲓⲥⲧⲟⲣⲓⲛ ⲙ̀ⲙⲟϥ ⲛ̀ϫⲉ ⲁⲃⲃⲁ Ⲡϣⲱⲓ ⲡⲓⲣⲉⲙⲕⲟⲛⲥⲧⲁⲛⲟⲩⲡⲟⲗⲓⲥ ⲟⲩⲟϩ ⲡⲓϣⲟⲣⲡ ⲛ̀ⲇⲓⲁⲕⲱⲛ ⲉⲧⲁϥϣⲱⲡⲓ ϧⲉⲛ Ϣⲓϩⲏⲧ ⲛⲁϩⲣⲁϥ ⲛ̀ⲁⲃⲃⲁ Ⲙⲁⲕⲁⲣⲓⲟⲥ ⲡⲓⲣⲱⲙⲓ ⲛ̀ⲧⲉ Ⲫϯ ⲛⲉⲙ ⲁⲃⲃⲁ Ⲓⲥⲓⲇⲱⲣⲟⲥ ⲫⲁⲓ ⲉⲧⲁϥⲙ̀ⲧⲟⲛ ⲙ̀ⲙⲟϥ ⲉϥⲟⲓ ⲛ̀ⲇⲓⲁⲕⲱⲛ ⲟⲩⲟϩ ⲁϥⲑⲱϣ ⲛ̀ⲁⲃⲃⲁ Ⲙⲱⲥⲏ ⲡⲓⲭⲁⲙⲉ ⲛ̀ⲧⲉϥϣⲉⲃⲓⲱ. ⲉⲧⲁϥϭⲉ ⲫⲃⲓⲟⲥ ⲇⲉ ⲛ̀ⲛⲁⲓⲁⲅⲓⲟⲥ ⲛ̀ⲑⲟϥ ⲁⲃⲃⲁ Ⲡϣⲱⲓ ⲉⲟⲩⲉⲣⲫⲙⲉⲩⲓ ⲁϥⲭⲁϥ ϧⲉⲛ ϯⲉⲕⲕ̀ⲗⲏⲥⲓⲁ ⲉⲟⲩϩⲛⲟⲩ ⲛ̀ⲟⲩⲟⲛ ⲛⲓⲃⲉⲛ ⲉⲑⲟⲩⲱϣ ⲉⲱⲛϧ ⲕⲁⲧⲁ Ⲫϯ.

3. Ⲁⲙⲱⲓⲛⲓ ⲧⲏⲣⲟⲩ ⲙ̀ⲫⲟⲟⲩ ⲱ ⲛⲁⲓⲟϯ ⲉ̄ⲑ̄ⲩ̄ ⲟⲩⲟϩ ⲛ̀ⲑⲉⲟⲫⲟⲣⲟⲥ ⲛ̀ⲧⲉⲧⲉⲛⲑⲱⲟⲩϯ ⲉⲣⲟⲓ ϧⲉⲛ ⲟⲩϯϩⲑⲏϥ ⲛ̀ⲧⲁϫⲱ ⲉⲣⲱⲧⲉⲛ ⲛ̀ⲛⲓⲁⲣⲉⲧⲏ

ⲛⲉⲙ ⲛⲓϣⲫⲏⲣⲓ ⲛⲉⲙ ⲛⲓϫⲟⲙ ⲛ̀ⲧⲉ ⲛⲁⲓⲁⲅⲓⲟⲥ ⲛ̀ⲣⲱⲙⲉⲟⲥ Ⲙⲁⲝⲓⲙⲟⲥ ⲛⲉⲙ Ⲇⲟⲙⲉⲧⲓⲟⲥ ⲛⲉⲛϣⲏⲣⲓ ⲛ̀Ⲟⲩⲁⲗⲉⲛⲧⲓⲛⲟⲥ ⲡⲓⲙⲁⲓⲛⲟⲩϯ ⲛ̀ⲟⲩⲣⲟ.

4. ⲁⲥϣⲱⲡⲓ ϧⲉⲛ ⲡⲥⲛⲟⲩ ⲛ̀ⲁⲃⲃⲁ Ⲙⲁⲕⲁⲣ ⲫⲏⲉ̅ⲑ̅ⲩ̅ ⲙ̀ⲡ̅ⲛ̅ⲁ̅ⲧⲟⲫⲟⲣⲟⲥ ⲡⲓⲣⲱⲙⲓ ⲛ̀ⲧⲉ Ⲫϯ ⲉⲧⲁ ⲧⲁⲣⲭⲏ ⲛ̀ⲧⲉ Ϣⲓϩⲧ ϣⲱⲡⲓ ⲉⲃⲟⲗϩⲓⲧⲟⲧϥ ⲛ̀ⲑⲟϥ ⲅⲁⲣ ⲡⲉ ⲉⲧⲁϥⲉⲣϣⲟⲣⲡ ⲛ̀ⲧⲱϫⲓ ⲙ̀ⲡⲁⲓⲁϩⲁⲗⲟⲗⲓ ⲛ̀ⲧⲉ ⲡ̅ⲟ̅ⲥ̅ ⲥⲁⲃⲁⲱⲑ ⲉⲧⲉ Ϣⲓϩⲧ ⲡⲉ ϣⲁⲧⲉϥⲭⲱ ⲛ̀ϧⲏⲧϥ ⲙ̀ⲡⲕⲁⲣⲡⲟⲥ ⲛ̀ϯⲙⲉⲧⲁⲛⲟⲓⲁ ⲙ̀ⲙⲏⲓ ϩⲓⲧⲉⲛ Ⲫϯ.

5. ⲱ ⲡⲓⲧⲱⲟⲩ ⲉⲧⲥⲙⲁⲣⲱⲟⲩⲧ ⲛ̀ⲧⲉ Ϣⲓϩⲧ ⲡⲓⲧⲱⲟⲩ ⲉⲧⲁ Ⲫϯ ϣⲱⲡⲓ ϩⲓϫⲱϥ ⲛⲉⲙ ⲛⲉϥⲁⲅⲅⲉⲗⲟⲥ ⲱ ⲡⲓⲧⲱⲟⲩ ⲛ̀ⲣⲉϥⲭⲁⲛⲟⲃⲓ ⲉⲃⲟⲗ ⲱ ⲡⲓⲧⲱⲟⲩ ⲉⲧⲁϥⲉⲣⲉ ⲛⲓⲣⲉϥⲉⲣⲛⲟⲃⲓ ⲛⲁⲩ ⲉⲪϯ ⲱ ⲛⲉⲙ ⲡⲁⲓⲧⲱⲟⲩ ⲙ̀ⲡ̅ⲛ̅ⲁ̅ⲧⲓⲕⲟⲛ ⲫⲁⲓ ⲉⲧⲁϥⲉⲣⲉ ⲡⲁⲓⲏⲓ ⲧⲏⲣϥ ⲙⲟϩ ⲛ̀ⲥⲑⲟⲓⲛⲟⲩϥⲓ ϩⲓⲧⲉⲛ ⲛⲓⲉⲩⲭⲏ ⲛ̀ⲧⲉ ⲛⲓⲁⲅⲓⲟⲥ ⲉⲧϣⲟⲡ ⲛ̀ϧⲏⲧϥ. ⲱ ⲛⲉⲙ ⲡⲁⲓⲧⲱⲟⲩ ⲉ̅ⲑ̅ⲩ̅ ⲛ̀ⲧⲉ ⲡⲓϩⲟⲥⲉⲙ ⲫⲁⲓ ⲉⲧⲁϥϣⲱⲡⲓ ⲛ̀ⲟⲩϩⲟⲥⲉⲙ ⲙ̀ⲡ̅ⲛ̅ⲁ̅ⲧⲓⲕⲟⲛ ⲉϥⲓⲱⲓ ⲉⲃⲟⲗ ⲛ̀ⲛⲓⲑⲱⲗⲉⲃ ⲛ̀ⲧⲉ ϯⲯⲩⲭⲏ. ⲁⲓⲛⲁϣⲫⲏⲣⲓ ⲉⲑⲃⲉ ⲡⲓⲧⲁⲓⲟ ⲉⲧⲁϥⲧⲁϩⲟⲕ ⲛⲁϣ ⲛ̀ⲣⲏϯ ⲱ ⲡⲓⲧⲱⲟⲩ ⲉⲧⲧⲁⲓⲏⲟⲩⲧ ⲛ̀ⲧⲉ ⲡⲓϩⲙⲟⲩ ⲫⲁⲓ ⲉⲧⲁ ⲟⲩⲙⲏϣ ⲛ̀ϩⲙⲟⲩ ⲛ̀ⲧⲉ ⲡⲓⲕⲁϩⲓ ⲛ̀ⲗⲟⲅⲓⲕⲟⲛ ⲫⲓⲣⲓ ⲉⲃⲟⲗⲛ̀ϧⲏⲧϥ ⲕⲁⲧⲁ ϯⲙⲉⲧⲙⲉⲑⲣⲉ ⲛ̀ⲧⲉ ⲡⲉⲛⲥ̅ⲱ̅ⲣ̅. ⲛⲁⲓ ⲉⲧⲁⲩϫⲟⲩⲕⲉⲣ ⲛ̀ⲛⲓⲯⲩⲭⲏ ⲉⲧⲁⲩⲱⲗϥ ϧⲉⲛ ⲛⲁⲓⲁⲛⲟⲙⲓⲁ. ⲱ ⲡⲓⲧⲱⲟⲩ ⲉ̅ⲑ̅ⲩ̅ ⲛ̀ⲧⲉ Ϣⲓϩⲧ ⲫⲙⲁⲛⲑⲱⲟⲩϯ ⲛ̀ⲧⲉ ⲛⲓⲁⲅⲅⲉⲗⲟⲥ ⲛⲉⲙ ⲛⲓⲣⲱⲙⲓ ⲉⲩⲥⲟⲡ.

6. ϫⲉ ϩⲓⲛⲁ ⲛ̀ⲧⲁϫⲟⲥ ϧⲉⲛ ⲟⲩϣⲱⲧ ⲉⲃⲟⲗ ⲡⲓⲧⲱⲟⲩ ⲫⲁⲓ ⲉⲧⲁϥⲉⲣⲉ ⲛⲓⲥⲓⲛϣⲟⲩⲓ ⲛ̀ⲣⲉϥϩⲱⲗⲉⲙ ⲛⲉⲙ ⲛⲏⲉⲧⲁⲩⲓⲣⲓ ⲛ̀ϩⲁⲛⲕⲉϩⲃⲏⲟⲩⲓ ⲉⲩⲧⲁⲥⲑⲏⲛⲟⲩⲧ ⲉⲃⲟⲗ ϣⲱⲡⲓ ⲙ̀ⲡⲣⲟⲫⲏⲧⲏⲥ ⲟⲩⲟϩ ⲛ̀ⲣⲉϥⲥⲁϫⲓ ⲛⲉⲙ Ⲫϯ ⲡⲓⲇⲏⲙⲓⲟⲩⲣⲅⲟⲥ. Ⲧⲉⲣⲙⲉⲛⲓⲁ ⲅⲁⲣ ⲛ̀Ϣⲓϩⲧ ⲡⲉ ⲫⲙⲁⲛⲑⲱⲟⲩϯ ⲛ̀ⲛⲏⲉⲧⲕⲱϯ ⲛ̀ⲥⲁ Ⲫϯ ϧⲉⲛ ⲡⲟⲩϩⲏⲧ ⲧⲏⲣϥ ⲛⲁⲓ ⲉⲧⲁ Ⲫϯ ⲡⲓⲗⲟⲅⲟⲥ ⲑⲟⲩⲱⲧ ⲙ̀ⲙⲱⲟⲩ ⲉϧⲟⲩⲛ ϧⲉⲛ ⲡⲓⲇ̅ ⲛ̀ⲗⲁⲕϩ ⲛ̀ⲧⲉ ⲡⲕⲁϩⲓ ϩⲓⲧⲉⲛ ϯⲥⲙⲏ ⲡⲓⲉⲩⲁⲅⲅⲉⲗⲓⲟⲛ ⲫⲁⲓ ⲉⲧⲭⲱ ⲙ̀ⲙⲟⲥ ϫⲉ ⲫⲏⲉⲑⲙⲉⲓ ⲙ̀ⲙⲟϥ ⲙⲁⲣⲉϥⲭⲟⲗϥ ⲉⲃⲟⲗ ⲟⲩⲟϩ ⲛ̀ⲧⲉϥⲱⲗⲓ ⲙ̀ⲡⲉϥⲥ̅ⲧ̅ⲩ̅ ⲛ̀ⲧⲉϥⲙⲟϣⲓ ⲛ̀ⲥⲱⲓ. ϧⲉⲛ ⲫⲁⲓ ⲅⲁⲣ ⲁϥⲭⲱ ⲛ̀ϧⲏⲧⲟⲩ ⲛ̀ⲛⲓⲙⲕⲁⲩϩ ⲛ̀ⲧⲉ ⲡⲉϥⲥ̅ⲧ̅ⲩ̅ ⲉ̅ⲑ̅ⲩ̅ ϩⲓⲧⲉⲛ ⲡⲉϥⲃⲱⲕ ⲁⲃⲃⲁ Ⲙⲁⲕⲁⲣⲓⲟⲥ ⲫⲁⲓ ⲉⲧⲟⲓ ⲛ̀ⲧⲩⲡⲟⲥ ⲛⲱⲟⲩ ϧⲉⲛ ϩⲱⲃ ⲛⲓⲃⲉⲛ ϫⲉ ϩⲓⲛⲁ ϧⲉⲛ ϯϫⲟⲙ ⲛ̀ⲧⲉ ⲡⲓⲥ̅ⲧ̅ ⲉ̅ⲑ̅ⲩ̅ ⲛ̀ⲧⲟⲩϭⲟϫⲓ ⲛ̀ⲥⲁ ϯϫⲟⲙ ⲧⲏⲣⲥ ⲛ̀ⲧⲉ ⲡⲓⲁⲛⲧⲓⲕⲓⲙⲉⲛⲟⲥ ⲉⲃⲟⲗϧⲉⲛ ⲡϣⲁϥⲉ ϩⲓⲛⲁ ϫⲉ ⲛ̀ⲧⲁϣⲧⲉⲙⲱⲥⲕ ϧⲉⲛ ⲡⲁⲓⲥⲁϫⲓ ⲛ̀ⲧⲉ ϯϩⲩⲡⲟⲑⲉⲥⲓⲥ ⲉⲧⲁⲛⲭⲁⲥ ⲉϧⲣⲏⲓ ⲛ̀ϣⲟⲣⲡ ϯⲛⲁⲕⲟⲧⲧ

ϩⲓϫⲉⲛ ⲡⲓⲡⲣⲟⲕⲓⲙⲉⲛⲟⲛ ⲛ̄ⲧⲁⲥⲁϫⲓ ⲕⲁⲧⲁ ⲫⲏⲉⲧⲉ ⲡⲓⲡ̅ⲛ̅ⲁ̅ ⲉ̅ⲑ̅ⲩ̅ ⲛⲁⲉⲣⲭⲩⲣⲟⲕⲓⲛ ⲙ̀ⲙⲟϥ ⲛⲏⲓ.

7. ⲉⲡⲓⲇⲏ ⲁⲥϣⲁⲛϣⲱⲡⲓ ⲛ̄ⲧⲁⲥⲱⲧⲉⲙ ⲉⲁⲃⲃⲁ Ⲙⲁⲕⲁⲣ ⲡⲓⲣⲱⲙⲓ ⲛ̄ⲧⲉ Ⲫ̄ϯ ⲉϥⲥⲁϫⲓ ⲛⲉⲙ ⲛⲓϧⲉⲗⲗⲟⲓ ⲛⲉ ϣⲁϥϫⲟⲥ ⲛⲱⲟⲩ ϫⲉ ⲁⲙⲱⲓⲛⲓ ⲛ̄ⲧⲉⲧⲉⲛⲛⲁⲩ ⲉⲡⲓⲡ̅ ⲛ̄ⲧⲉ ⲛⲓⲕⲟⲩϫⲓ ⲛ̀ϣⲉⲙⲙⲱⲟⲩ ⲡϩⲱⲃ ϩⲓ ⲁⲛⲁⲅⲕⲏ ⲉⲣⲟⲓ ϧⲉⲛ ⲟⲩϩⲟϩ ⲛ̄ⲧⲉ Ⲫ̄ϯ ⲛ̄ⲧⲁⲟⲩⲱⲛϩ ⲉⲃⲟⲗ ⲛ̀ⲑⲙⲉⲧϫⲱⲣⲓ ⲛ̄ⲛⲁⲓⲁⲅⲓⲟⲥ ⲛⲉⲙ ⲧⲟⲩⲡⲟⲗⲓⲧⲓⲁ ⲉⲑⲛⲁⲛⲉⲥ.

8. ⲁⲥϣⲱⲡⲓ ⲇⲉ ⲉϥⲟⲓ ⲛ̀ⲟⲩⲣⲟ ⲛ̀ϫⲉ ⲟⲩⲗⲉⲛⲧⲓⲛⲟⲥ ⲡ̀ϣⲏⲣⲓ ⲙ̄ⲡⲓϣⲁⲙϣⲉⲛⲟⲩϯ ⲛ̀ⲟⲩⲣⲟ ⲓⲟⲩⲃⲓⲁⲛⲟⲥ ⲫⲁⲓ ⲉ̀ⲧⲁϥϣⲟⲣϣⲉⲣ ⲛ̀ⲛⲓⲉⲣⲫⲏⲟⲩⲓ ⲧⲏⲣⲟⲩ ⲛ̄ⲧⲉ ⲛⲓϣⲁⲙϣⲉ ⲓⲇⲱⲗⲟⲛ ⲉⲧⲥⲟϥ ⲁϥⲫⲱⲣⲕ ⲙ̄ⲡⲥⲱϫⲡ ⲛ̄ⲛⲟⲩⲥⲉⲛϯ. ⲛⲉ ⲟⲩⲟⲛ ⲟⲩⲛⲓϣϯ ⲛ̀ϩⲓⲣⲏⲛⲏ ϣⲟⲡ ⲡⲉ ϧⲉⲛ ⲛⲓⲉⲕⲕⲗⲏⲥⲓⲁ ⲛ̄ⲧⲉ Ⲫ̄ϯ ⲉⲧϣⲟⲡ ϧⲉⲛ ϯⲟⲓⲕⲟⲩⲙⲉⲛⲏ ϩⲱⲥⲧⲉ ⲛ̄ⲧⲟⲩⲙⲟⲩϯ ⲉⲣⲟϥ ⲛ̀ⲑⲟϥ Ⲟⲩⲁⲗⲉⲛⲧⲓⲟⲥ Ⲕⲱⲥⲧⲁⲛⲧⲓⲛ ⲙ̀ⲃⲉⲣⲓ.

9. ⲗⲟⲓⲡⲟⲛ ⲁϥⲉⲛ ⲛⲉϥϣⲏⲣⲓ ⲉⲡϣⲱⲓ ⲛ̀ⲕⲁⲗⲱⲥ Ⲙⲁⲝⲓⲙⲟⲥ ⲛⲉⲙ Ⲇⲟⲙⲉⲧⲓⲟⲥ ⲧⲟⲩⲕⲟⲩϫⲓ ⲛ̀ⲥⲱⲛⲓ ϧⲉⲛ ⲙⲉⲧϣⲁⲙϣⲉⲛⲟⲩϯ ⲛⲓⲃⲉⲛ ⲛⲉⲙ ϯⲥⲃⲱ ⲉⲑⲛⲁⲛⲉⲥ ϧⲉⲛ ϩⲁⲛⲯⲁⲗⲙⲟⲥ ⲛⲉⲙ ϩⲁⲛⲛⲏⲥⲧⲓⲁ ⲛⲉⲙ ϩⲁⲛϣⲗⲏⲗ ⲛ̀ϫⲱⲣϩ ⲛⲉⲙ ⲙⲉⲣⲓ ⲛⲉⲙ ϩⲁⲛⲙⲉⲗⲉⲧⲏ ⲉⲩⲙⲏⲛ ⲉⲃⲟⲗ ϩⲱⲥⲧⲉ ⲛ̄ⲧⲉ ⲡⲓⲡⲁⲗⲁⲧⲓⲟⲛ ⲉⲣ ⲙ̀ⲫⲣⲏϯ ⲛ̀ⲟⲩⲙⲟⲛⲁⲥⲧⲏⲣⲓⲟⲛ ⲙ̀ⲙⲟⲛⲁⲭⲟⲥ ϧⲉⲛ ⲛⲉϥⲉϩⲟⲟⲩ ⲟⲩⲟϩ ⲛⲁϥϩⲣⲟ ⲙ̀ⲙⲱⲟⲩ ⲡⲉ ⲉⲉⲣⲁⲥⲕⲓⲛ ⲧⲏⲣⲟⲩ ⲓⲥϫⲉⲛ ⲡⲟⲩⲕⲟⲩϫⲓ ϣⲁ ⲡⲟⲩⲛⲓϣϯ ⲙ̀ⲫⲣⲏϯ ⲛ̀ϩⲁⲛⲥⲱⲧⲡ ⲙ̀ⲙⲟⲛⲁⲭⲟⲥ ⲥⲭⲉⲗⲟⲥ ⲛ̄ⲧⲟⲩⲙⲟⲩϯ ⲛ̀ⲛⲁⲓⲁⲅⲓⲟⲥ ϩⲓⲧⲉⲛ ⲟⲩⲟⲛ ⲛⲓⲃⲉⲛ ⲓⲥϫⲉ ⲉⲩⲟⲓ ⲛ̀ⲕⲟⲩϫⲓ ϫⲉ ⲛⲓϧⲉⲗⲗⲟⲓ ⲉⲑⲃⲉ ⲛⲟⲩϩⲃⲏⲟⲩⲓ ⲉⲑⲛⲁⲛⲉⲩ ⲛⲉⲙ ⲡⲟⲩⲥⲙⲟⲧ ⲛ̀ϣⲁⲙϣⲉⲛⲟⲩϯ.

10. ⲗⲟⲓⲡⲟⲛ ϧⲉⲛ ⲡ̀ϫⲓⲛⲑⲣⲉ ⲛⲁⲓⲙⲁⲕⲁⲣⲓⲟⲥ Ⲙⲁⲝⲓⲙⲟⲥ ⲛⲉⲙ Ⲇⲟⲙⲉⲧⲓⲟⲥ ⲁⲓⲁⲓ ⲟⲩⲟϩ ⲛ̄ⲧⲟⲩϭⲓ ⲡⲣⲟⲕⲟⲡⲧⲏ ϧⲉⲛ ⲛⲓϩⲃⲏⲟⲩⲓ ⲉⲑⲛⲁⲛⲉⲩ ⲕⲁⲧⲁ Ⲫ̄ϯ ⲁⲩⲕⲱϯ ⲛ̀ⲥⲁ ⲫⲃⲓⲟⲥ ⲛ̀ⲛⲓⲁⲅⲅⲉⲗⲟⲥ ⲉⲧⲉ ϯⲙⲟⲛⲁⲭⲟⲥ ⲧⲉ ⲟⲩⲟϩ ⲛⲁⲩⲥⲟϭⲛⲓ ⲡⲉ ⲛⲉⲙ ⲛⲟⲩⲉⲣⲏⲟⲩ ⲉⲩϫⲱ ⲙ̀ⲙⲟⲥ ϫⲉ ⲁⲛⲛⲁϣⲫⲱⲧ ⲛ̀ⲁϣ ⲛ̀ⲣⲏϯ ⲛ̀ⲧⲉⲛⲉⲣⲙⲟⲛⲁⲭⲟⲥ ⲟⲩⲟϩ ⲡⲉϫⲉ ⲡⲓⲕⲟⲩϫⲓ ⲙ̀ⲡⲓⲛⲓϣϯ ϫⲉ ⲙⲁⲣⲉⲛϫⲉⲙⲗⲱⲓϫⲓ ⲙ̀ⲡⲉⲛⲓⲱⲧ ⲟⲩⲟϩ ⲛ̄ⲧⲉⲭⲟⲥ ⲛⲁϥ ϫⲉ ⲁⲛⲛⲁϩⲱⲗ ⲉⲛⲓⲕⲓⲉⲩ ⲛ̄ⲧⲉⲛϣⲗⲏⲗ ϧⲉⲛ ⲡ̀ⲧⲟⲡⲟⲥ ⲟⲩⲟϩ ⲁϥϣⲁⲛⲭⲁⲛ ⲉⲃⲟⲗ ⲡⲓⲙⲁ ϫⲉ ⲉⲧⲉⲛⲟⲩⲁϣϥ ⲧⲉⲛⲛⲁϩⲱⲗ ⲉⲣⲟϥ.

11. ⲉⲧⲁⲩⲥⲟϭⲛⲓ ⲇⲉ ⲉⲡⲟⲩⲱⲧ ⲁϥⲁⲓⲧⲟⲩ ⲛ̀ⲣⲉⲙϩⲉ ⲛⲉ ⲟⲩⲟⲛ ⲟⲩⲡⲣⲉⲥⲃⲩⲧⲉⲣⲟⲥ ⲇⲉ ⲉϥϣⲟⲡ ϧⲉⲛ ⲡⲧⲟⲡⲟⲥ ⲙ̀ⲡⲓⲧ̅ⲏ̅ ⲛ̀ⲉⲡⲓⲥⲕⲟⲡⲟⲥ ⲉⲡⲉϥⲣⲁⲛ ⲡⲉ ⲓⲱ̅ⲁ̅ ⲉⲟⲩⲙⲟⲛⲁⲭⲟⲥ ⲡⲉ ⲟⲩⲟϩ ⲫⲁⲓ ⲛⲁⲣⲉ ⲛⲓⲟⲩⲣⲱⲟⲩ ⲥⲟϭⲛⲓ ⲉⲣⲟϥ ⲡⲉ ⲛ̀ⲟⲩⲙⲏϣ ⲛ̀ⲥⲟⲡ ⲛⲉⲙ ⲛⲓⲉⲡⲓⲥⲕⲟⲡⲟⲥ ⲛ̀ⲧⲉ ⲡⲓⲙⲁ ⲉⲧⲉⲙⲙⲁⲩ. ⲉⲧⲁⲩϫⲓⲙⲓ ⲟⲩⲛ ⲛ̀ⲟⲩⲉϩⲟⲟⲩ ⲉϥϩⲏϣ ⲛ̀ϫⲉ ⲛⲓⲙⲁⲕⲁⲣⲓⲟⲥ ⲁⲩϯ ϩⲓⲱⲧⲟⲩ ⲛ̀ϩⲁⲛϩⲃⲱⲥ ⲉⲛⲁⲛⲉⲩ ⲟⲩⲟϩ ⲁⲩⲁⲗⲏⲓ ⲉⲛⲟⲩϩⲑⲱⲣ ⲁⲩⲓ ⲉⲃⲟⲗ ϫⲉ ⲁⲩϣⲉⲛⲱⲟⲩ ⲉⲛⲓⲕⲉⲁ ⲉϣⲗⲏⲗ ϧⲉⲛ ⲡⲧⲟⲡⲟⲥ ⲛ̀ⲛⲉⲛⲓⲟϯ ⲉ̅ⲑ̅ⲩ̅ ⲛ̀ⲉⲡⲓⲥⲕⲟⲡⲟⲥ.

12. ⲉⲧⲁⲩϣⲉ ⲇⲉ ⲛⲱⲟⲩ ⲉⲛⲓⲕⲉⲁ ⲉϣⲗⲏⲗ ϧⲉⲛ ⲡⲧⲟⲡⲟⲥ ⲁⲩϫⲓⲙⲓ ⲙ̀ⲡⲓⲡⲣⲉⲥⲃⲩⲧⲉⲣⲟⲥ ⲉ̅ⲑ̅ⲩ̅ ⲓⲱ̅ⲁ̅ ⲫⲏⲉⲧⲁⲛⲉⲣϣⲟⲣⲡ ⲛ̀ϥⲓⲣⲓ ⲉⲣⲟϥ ⲟⲩⲟϩ ⲁϥϣⲟⲡⲟⲩ ⲉⲣⲟϥ ϧⲉⲛ ⲟⲩⲙⲉⲧⲉⲣⲙⲣⲁϣ ⲛⲉⲙ ⲟⲩⲧⲓⲙⲏ ⲟⲩⲟϩ ⲁⲩⲧⲁⲙⲟϥ ⲉⲡⲓⲣⲏϯ ⲉⲧⲟⲩⲟⲩⲱϣ ⲉⲉⲣⲙⲟⲛⲁⲭⲟⲥ. ⲛ̀ⲑⲟϥ ⲇⲉ ϩⲓⲧⲉⲛ ⲡⲓϩⲙⲟⲧ ⲛ̀ⲧⲉ Ⲫϯ ⲛⲁϥⲉⲣⲇⲟⲕⲓⲙⲁⲍⲓⲛ ⲙ̀ⲡⲟⲩⲙⲉⲩⲓ ⲡⲉ ϩⲓⲛⲁ ⲛ̀ⲧⲉϥⲉⲙⲓ ⲁⲕⲣⲓⲃⲱⲥ ⲉⲛⲟⲩⲙⲉⲩⲓ ⲙ̀ⲡⲁⲧⲉϥ ϫⲉ ϩⲗⲓ ⲛ̀ⲥⲁϫⲓ ⲛⲱⲟⲩ ϩⲟⲧⲉ ⲇⲉ ⲉⲧⲁϥⲛⲁⲩ ⲉⲧⲟⲩⲡⲣⲟϩⲉⲣⲥⲓⲥ ⲉⲥⲥⲟⲩⲧⲱⲛ ⲉϧⲟⲩⲛ ⲉⲪϯ ⲁϥⲣⲁϣⲓ ⲉⲙⲁϣⲱ ⲟⲩⲟϩ ⲁϥϯⲛⲟⲙϯ ⲛⲱⲟⲩ. ⲛ̀ⲑⲱⲟⲩ ⲇⲉ ⲛⲁⲩϯϩⲟ ⲉⲣⲟϥ ⲡⲉ ϩⲓⲛⲁ ⲛ̀ⲧⲟⲩϣⲱⲡⲓ ϧⲁⲧⲟⲧϥ ⲛ̀ⲑⲟϥ ⲇⲉ ⲙ̀ⲡⲉϥⲉⲣⲁⲛⲉⲭⲉⲥⲑⲉ ⲛⲱⲟⲩ ⲉϥϫⲱ ⲙ̀ⲙⲟⲥ ϫⲉ ϯⲉⲣϩⲟϯ ϧⲁⲧϩⲏ ⲙ̀ⲡⲉⲧⲉⲛⲓⲱⲧ ⲡⲟⲩⲣⲟ ϯⲛⲁϣⲉⲣⲡⲁⲓϩⲱⲃ ⲫⲁⲓ ⲁⲛ ⲁⲗⲗⲁ ⲓⲥϫⲉ ⲧⲉⲧⲉⲛⲟⲩⲱϣ ⲉⲉⲣⲙⲟⲛⲁⲭⲟⲥ ⲧⲱⲟⲩⲛ ⲛ̀ⲧⲉⲧⲉⲛϣⲉⲛⲱⲧⲉⲛ ⲉϯⲥⲩⲣⲓⲁ ⲁⲓⲥⲱⲧⲉⲙ ⲉⲑⲃⲉ ⲟⲩⲁⲛⲁⲭⲱⲣⲏⲧⲏⲥ ⲛ̀ⲧⲉ ⲡⲓⲙⲁ ⲉⲧⲉⲙⲙⲁⲩ ⲉϥϣⲟⲡ ϧⲉⲛ ⲟⲩⲡⲉⲧⲣⲁ ϩⲓϫⲉⲛ ⲫⲓⲟⲙ ⲟⲩⲟϩ ⲫⲁⲓ ⲁ ⲡⲉϥⲥⲱⲓⲧ ⲙⲁϩ ϯⲥⲩⲣⲓⲁ ⲧⲏⲣⲥ ⲛⲉⲙ Ⲡⲁⲗⲉⲥⲧⲓⲛⲏ ⲉⲡⲉϥⲣⲁⲛ ⲡⲉ Ⲁⲅⲁⲡⲟⲥ ⲉⲟⲩⲣⲉⲙⲧⲁⲣⲥⲟⲥ ⲡⲉ ⲛ̀ⲧⲉ ϯⲔⲩⲗⲓⲕⲓⲁ. ⲫⲁⲓ ⲛⲁϥⲟⲓ ⲙ̀Ⲡⲁⲩⲗⲟⲥ ϧⲉⲛ ⲡⲉϥⲛⲁϩϯ ⲛⲉⲙ ⲛⲉϥϩⲃⲏⲟⲩⲓ ⲓⲥϫⲉ ⲟⲩⲛ ⲡⲓϩⲱⲃ ⲣⲁⲛⲱⲧⲉⲛ ⲙⲁϣⲉⲛⲱⲧⲉⲛ ⲉⲡⲉϥⲙⲁ ⲉⲧⲁⲩⲥⲱⲧⲉⲙ ⲇⲉ ⲁⲩⲣⲁϣⲓ ⲉⲙⲁϣⲱ ⲟⲩⲟ ϧⲉⲛ ⲫⲁⲓ ⲁϥϣⲗⲏⲗ ⲉϫⲱⲟⲩ ⲁϥⲧⲫⲱⲟⲩ ⲉⲃⲟⲗ ϧⲉⲛ ⲟⲩϩⲓⲣⲏⲛⲏ.

13. ⲛ̀ⲑⲱⲟⲩ ⲇⲉ ⲁⲩϣⲉⲛⲱⲟⲩ ⲉⲃⲟⲗϩⲓⲧⲟⲧϥ ϧⲉⲛ ⲟⲩⲛⲓϣϯ ⲛ̀ⲣⲁϣⲓ ⲟⲩⲟϩ ⲁⲩϩⲓⲧⲟⲧⲟⲩ ⲉϣⲉ ⲉⲧⲟⲩⲡⲟⲗⲓⲥ ⲉⲛⲁⲩ ⲉⲛⲟⲩⲓⲟϯ ⲁⲗⲗⲁ ⲁⲩϩⲱⲗ ⲉϯⲥⲩⲣⲓⲁ ϧⲉⲛ ⲟⲩⲥⲱⲟⲩⲧⲉⲛ ⲉⲧⲁⲩϣⲓⲛⲓ ⲇⲉ ⲛ̀ⲥⲁ ⲡⲉⲥⲥ̅ⲩ̅ Ⲁⲅⲁⲡⲟⲥ ⲁⲩⲧⲁⲙⲱⲟⲩ ⲉⲡⲉϥⲙⲁ ⲟⲩⲟϩ ⲉⲧⲁⲩⲉⲣⲁⲡⲁⲛⲧⲁⲛ ⲉⲣⲟϥ ⲁϥϣⲟⲡⲟⲩ ⲉⲣⲟϥ ϧⲉⲛ ⲟⲩⲛⲓϣϯ ⲛ̀ⲣⲁϣⲓ ⲛ̀ⲑⲱⲟⲩ ⲇⲉ ⲁⲩⲧⲁⲙⲟϥ ⲉϩⲱⲃ ⲛⲓⲃⲉⲛ.

14. ⲡⲓϧⲉⲗⲗⲟ ⲟⲩⲛ ⲛ̀ⲑⲉⲟⲫⲟⲣⲟⲥ ⲉⲧⲉⲙⲙⲁⲩ ⲉⲧⲁϥⲛⲁⲩ ⲉⲧⲟⲩⲁⲅⲁⲡⲏ ⲉϧⲟⲩⲛ ⲉⲪϯ ⲥⲁⲧⲟⲧϥ ⲁϥϯ ⲉⲭⲱⲟⲩ ⲙ̀ⲡⲓⲥⲭⲏⲙⲁ ⲉ̅ⲑ̅ⲩ̅ ⲛ̀ⲧⲉ ⲛⲓⲙⲟⲛⲁⲭⲟⲥ ⲛ̀ⲧⲉ ϯⲥⲩⲣⲓⲁ ⲛⲓⲙⲟⲛⲁⲭⲟⲥ ⲅⲁⲣ ⲛ̀ⲧⲉ ⲡⲓⲙⲁ ⲉⲧⲉⲙⲙⲁⲩ ⲥⲉⲉⲣⲫⲟⲣⲓⲛ ⲁⲛ ⲙ̀ⲙⲁⲣϭⲛⲁϩ ⲟⲩⲇⲉ ϩⲱⲕ ⲁⲗⲗⲁ ⲟⲩϩⲉⲃⲥⲱ ⲛ̀ⲭⲁⲙⲉ. ⲡⲉⲧⲟⲩⲉⲣⲫⲟⲣⲓⲛ ⲙ̀ⲙⲟⲥ ⲫⲁⲓ ⲅⲁⲣ ⲡⲉ ⲡⲥⲭⲏⲙⲁ ⲛ̀ⲛⲁ ϯⲥⲩⲣⲓⲁ ⲡⲉ.

15. ⲗⲟⲓⲡⲟⲛ ϯⲧⲁⲙⲟ ⲙ̀ⲙⲱⲧⲉⲛ ⲕⲁⲧⲁ ⲫⲣⲏϯ ⲉⲧⲁⲩϫⲟⲥ ⲛⲏⲓ ⲛ̀ⲑⲱⲟⲩ ⲛⲁⲓⲁⲅⲓⲟⲥ ϫⲉ ϩⲟⲧⲉ ⲉⲧⲁϥⲛⲟⲓ ⲉⲉⲙⲧⲟⲛ ⲙ̀ⲙⲟϥ ⲛ̀ϫⲉ ⲡⲓϧⲉⲗⲗⲟ ⲉ̅ⲑ̅ⲩ̅ ⲁⲅⲁⲡⲟⲥ ⲁⲛϣⲉⲛϥ ϫⲉ ⲁϫⲉ ⲟⲩⲥⲁϫⲓ ⲛⲁⲛ ϫⲉ ⲡⲉⲛⲓⲱⲧ ⲉ̅ⲑ̅ⲩ̅ ⲛ̀ⲧⲉⲛⲱⲛϧ ⲉⲣⲟϥ ⲙⲉⲛⲉⲛⲥⲱⲕ. ⲛ̀ⲑⲟϥ ⲇⲉ ⲡⲉϫⲁϥ ⲛⲁⲛ ϫⲉ ⲁⲓⲛⲁⲩ ⲉⲣⲟⲓ ϧⲉⲛ ⲡⲁⲓⲉϫⲱⲣϩ ⲉⲓⲟϩⲓ ⲉⲣⲁⲧ ϩⲓϫⲉⲛ ⲧⲁⲓⲡⲉⲧⲣⲁ ⲉⲧⲥⲁⲣⲏⲥ ⲙ̀ⲙⲟⲛ ⲉⲓⲛⲁⲩ ⲉⲟⲩⲙⲟⲛⲁⲭⲟⲥ ⲉϥⲟϩⲓ ⲉⲣⲁⲧϥ ⲙ̀ⲡⲁⲙⲑⲟ ⲉⲃⲏⲗ ⲉⲟⲩⲣⲱⲙⲓ ⲡⲉ ⲉϥϣⲏⲟⲩ ⲉⲣⲉ ⲟⲩⲟⲛ ϩⲁⲛϩⲃⲱⲥ ⲧⲟⲓ ⲉϫⲱϥ ⲉϥⲟⲓ ⲛ̀ϩⲓⲣϩⲓⲣ ⲛ̀ⲭⲁⲙⲉ ⲛⲉⲙ ⲟⲟⲩⲕⲗⲁϥⲧ ϩⲓϫⲉⲛ ⲧⲉϥⲁⲫⲉ ⲉⲣⲉ ⲟⲩⲟⲛ ϩⲁⲛⲥ̅ⲧ̅ ⲧⲟⲓ ⲉⲣⲟⲥ ⲉⲣⲉ ⲟⲩⲟⲛ ⲟⲩϣⲃⲱⲧ ⲙ̀ⲃⲁⲓ ϧⲉⲛ ⲧⲉϥϫⲓϫ ⲛⲉⲙ ⲟⲩⲥ̅ⲧ̅. ϧⲉⲛ ⲡϫⲓⲛⲑⲣⲓⲛⲁⲩ ⲉⲣⲟϥ ⲁⲓⲉⲣϩⲟϯ ⲛ̀ⲑⲟϥ ⲇⲉ ⲁϥϧⲱⲛⲧ ⲉⲣⲟⲓ ⲁϥⲉⲣⲥⲡⲁⲍⲉⲥⲑⲉ ⲙ̀ⲙⲟⲓ ⲟⲩⲟϩ ⲡⲉϫⲁϥ ⲛⲏⲓ ϫⲉ ⲕⲥⲱⲟⲩⲛ ϫⲉ ⲁⲛⲟⲕ ⲛⲓⲙ ⲡⲉϫⲏⲓ ⲛⲁϥ ϫⲉ ⲙ̀ⲙⲟⲛ ⲡⲁⲓⲱⲧ ⲉ̅ⲑ̅ⲩ̅ ⲡⲉϫⲁϥ ⲛⲏⲓ ϫⲉ ⲁⲛⲟⲕ ⲙⲁⲕⲁⲣ ⲡⲓⲣⲉⲙⲛ̀ⲭⲏⲙⲓ ⲉⲧⲁⲓⲓ ⲉⲑⲁϩⲉⲙ ⲛⲉⲕϣⲏⲣⲓ ⲛ̀ⲧⲁⲟⲗⲟⲩ ϩⲁⲣⲟⲓ ⲉϩⲣⲏⲓ ⲉϫⲏⲙⲓ. ⲡⲉϫⲏⲓ ⲛⲁϥ ϫⲉ ⲭⲛⲁⲟⲗⲧ ⲛⲉⲙⲱⲟⲩ ⲁⲛ ⲁⲛⲟⲕ ⲡⲁⲓⲱⲧ. ⲡⲉϫⲁϥ ⲛⲏⲓ ϫⲉ ⲙ̀ⲙⲟⲛ ⲁⲗⲗⲁ ϯⲧⲁⲙⲟ ⲙ̀ⲙⲟⲕ ϫⲉ ⲙⲉⲛⲉⲛⲥⲁ ⲕⲉⲅ̅ ⲛⲉϩⲟⲟⲩ ⲭⲛⲁⲙⲧⲟⲛ ⲙ̀ⲙⲟⲕ ⲟⲩⲟϩ ⲛ̀ⲧⲉⲕϣⲉⲛⲁⲕ ϩⲁ ⲡ̅ⲟ̅ⲥ̅ ⲟⲩⲟϩ ⲡⲟⲩⲣⲟ ϥⲛⲁⲟⲩⲱⲣⲡ ⲛ̀ⲥⲁ ⲛⲉϥϣⲏⲣⲓ ⲉⲛⲧⲉϥⲟⲗⲟⲩ ⲉⲕⲱⲥⲧⲁⲛⲧⲓⲛⲟⲩⲡⲟⲗⲓⲥ. ⲗⲟⲓⲡⲟⲛ ⲁⲛⲁⲩ ϩⲟⲛϩⲉⲛ ⲉⲧⲟⲧⲟⲩ ϩⲓⲛⲁ ⲛ̀ⲧⲟⲩⲓ ⲉϩⲣⲏⲓ ⲉϫⲏⲙⲓ ⲛ̀ⲧⲟⲩϣⲱⲡⲓ ϧⲁⲧⲟⲧ ϫⲉ Ⲫϯ ⲡⲉ ⲉⲧⲁϥⲑⲁϩⲙⲟⲩ ⲛⲏⲓ ⲉϩⲁⲛϣⲏⲣⲓ. ⲓⲥ ϩⲏⲡⲡⲉ ⲟⲩⲛ ⲁⲓϫⲟⲥ ⲛⲁⲕ.

16. ⲟⲩⲟϩ ⲛⲁⲓ ⲉⲧⲁϥϫⲟⲧⲟⲩ ⲛⲏⲓ ⲁϥⲉⲣⲁⲑⲟⲩⲱⲛϩ ⲉⲃⲟⲗ ϩⲁⲣⲟⲓ. ϯⲛⲟⲩ ⲛⲁϣⲏⲣⲓ ϯⲧⲁⲙⲟ ⲙ̀ⲙⲱⲧⲉⲛ ϫⲉ ⲓⲥ ⲟⲩⲙⲏϣ ⲛ̀ⲉϩⲟⲟⲩ ϯⲥⲱⲧⲉⲙ ⲉⲡϣⲉⲛⲛⲟⲟⲩϥⲓ ⲙ̀ⲡⲓⲣⲱⲙⲓ ⲉⲧⲉⲙⲙⲁⲩ ⲁⲃⲃⲁ ⲙⲁⲕⲁⲣ. ⲟⲩⲟϩ ϧⲉⲛ ⲫⲁⲓ ϯϫⲱ ⲙ̀ⲙⲟⲥ ⲛⲱⲧⲉⲛ ϫⲉ ⲉϣⲱⲡ ⲛ̀ⲧⲉ ⲡⲟⲩⲣⲟ ⲉⲙⲓ ⲉⲣⲱⲧⲉⲛ ϥⲛⲁⲭⲁ ⲑⲏⲛⲟⲩ ⲙ̀ⲡⲁⲓⲙⲁ ⲁⲛ ⲗⲟⲓⲡⲟⲛ ⲙⲉⲛⲉⲛⲥⲁ ⲡϫⲱⲕ ⲉⲃⲟⲗ ⲙ̀ⲡⲁⲓⲃⲓⲟⲥ ⲙⲁϣⲉⲛⲱⲧⲉⲛ ⲉϩⲣⲏⲓ ⲉϫⲏⲙⲓ ϣⲱⲡⲓ ⲛⲱⲧⲉⲛ ϧⲁⲧⲉⲛ ⲫⲏⲉ̅ⲑ̅ⲩ̅ ⲁⲃⲃⲁ ⲙⲁⲕⲁⲣ ϣⲁⲧⲉ ⲡ̅ⲟ̅ⲥ̅ ϫⲉⲙ ⲡⲉⲧⲉⲛϣⲓⲛⲓ.

17. ⲛⲁⲓ ⲇⲉ ⲉⲧⲁϥϫⲟⲧⲟⲩ ⲛⲱⲟⲩ ⲛ̀ϫⲉ ⲡⲓϧⲉⲗⲗⲟ ⲁ̀ⲅⲁⲡⲟⲥ ⲁϥⲙⲟⲧⲛ ⲙ̀ⲙⲟϥ ϧⲉⲛ ⲟⲩϩⲓⲣⲏⲛⲏ ⲛⲉ ⲁⲩⲉⲣ Ϛ̅ ⲅⲁⲣ ⲛ̀ⲣⲟⲙⲡⲓ ⲡⲉ ⲉⲩϣⲟⲡ ⲛⲉⲙⲁϥ ⲟⲩⲟϩ ⲁⲡⲉϥⲡ̅ⲛ̅ⲁ̅ ⲕⲱⲃ ⲉϩⲣⲏⲓ ⲉϫⲱⲟⲩ ⲙ̀ⲫⲣⲏϯ ⲉⲧⲁ ⲡⲓⲡ̅ⲛ̅ⲁ̅ ⲛ̀ⲧⲉ Ⲏⲗⲓⲁⲥ ⲕⲱⲃ ⲉϫⲉⲛ Ⲉⲗⲓⲥⲉⲟⲥ ⲙ̀ⲡⲓⲥⲏⲟⲩ.

18. ⲁⲅⲓⲥ ⲇⲉ ⲟⲩⲛ ⲛ̀ⲧⲉⲛⲧⲁⲙⲱⲧⲉⲛ ⲉⲛⲓⲙⲏⲓⲛⲓ ⲛⲉⲙ ⲛⲓϣⲫⲏⲣⲓ ⲛⲉⲙ ⲛⲓϩⲙⲟⲧ ⲡ̀ⲧⲁⲗϭⲟ ⲉⲧⲁ Ⲫϯ ⲉⲣⲉⲛⲉⲣⲅⲓⲛ ⲙ̀ⲙⲱⲟⲩ ⲉⲃⲟⲗϩⲓⲧⲉⲛ ⲛⲉⲛϫⲓϫ ⲛ̀ⲛⲁⲓⲁⲅⲓⲟⲥ ϩⲱⲥⲧⲉ ⲛ̀ⲧⲉ ⲡⲟⲩⲥⲱⲓⲧ ⲥⲱⲣ ⲉⲃⲟⲗ ϧⲉⲛ ϯⲠⲁⲗⲉⲥⲧⲓⲛⲏ ⲧⲏⲣⲥ ⲛⲉⲙ ⲧⲭⲱⲣⲁ ⲛ̀ⲧⲉ Ⲡⲓⲥⲓⲇⲓⲁ ⲉⲑⲃⲉ ⲛⲓⲧⲁⲗϭⲟ ⲉⲧⲟⲩⲓⲣⲓ ⲙ̀ⲙⲱⲟⲩ ϧⲉⲛ ⲛⲏⲉⲧϣⲱⲛⲓ ϧⲉⲛ ⲫⲣⲁⲛ ⲙ̀ⲡⲉⲛⲟ̅ⲥ̅ Ⲓⲏ̅ⲥ̅ Ⲡⲭ̅ⲥ̅ ⲟⲩⲙⲏϣ ⲅⲁⲣ ϧⲉⲛ ⲛⲏⲉⲧⲉ ⲛⲓⲡ̅ⲛ̅ⲁ̅ ⲛ̀ⲕⲁⲑⲁⲣⲧⲟⲛ ⲛⲉⲙⲱⲟⲩ ⲁⲩϣⲁⲛⲥⲱⲧⲉⲙ ⲉⲡⲟⲩⲣⲁⲛ ⲙ̀ⲙⲁⲩⲁⲧϥ ϣⲁⲩⲓ ⲉⲃⲟⲗ ϩⲁⲣⲱⲟⲩ ⲟⲩⲟϩ ⲛ̀ⲧⲟⲩⲟⲩϫⲁⲓ ⲥⲁⲧⲟⲧⲟⲩ ϩⲓⲧⲉⲛ ⲡⲓϩⲙⲟⲧ ⲛ̀ⲧⲉ Ⲫϯ ⲡⲉⲛⲥ̅ⲱ̅ⲣ̅.

19. ⲥⲱⲧⲉⲙ ⲉⲧⲁⲓⲛⲓϣϯ ⲛ̀ϣⲫⲏⲣⲓ ⲉⲧⲁⲥϣⲱⲡⲓ ⲉⲃⲟⲗϩⲓⲧⲟⲧⲟⲩ. ⲁⲩⲉⲛ ⲟⲩⲣⲱⲙⲓ ϣⲁⲣⲱⲟⲩ ⲉⲃⲟⲗϧⲉⲛ ⲁⲥⲕⲁⲗⲱⲛ ⲉⲣⲉ ⲟⲩⲟⲛ ⲟⲩⲡ̅ⲛ̅ⲁ̅ ⲛ̀ⲣⲉϥϣⲓⲛⲓ ⲛⲉⲙⲁϥ. ⲉⲧⲓ ⲟⲩⲛ ⲉϥⲟⲩⲏⲟⲩ ⲙ̀ⲡⲓⲙⲁⲛϣⲱⲡⲓ ⲛ̀ⲧⲉ ⲛⲁⲓⲁⲅⲓⲟⲥ ⲁϥⲱϣ ⲉⲃⲟⲗ ϧⲉⲛ ⲟⲩⲛⲓϣϯ ⲛ̀ϧⲣⲱⲟⲩ ⲉϥϫⲱ ⲙ̀ⲙⲟⲥ ϫⲉ ⲱⲃⲓⲁ ⲛ̀ⲧⲟⲧⲗ Ⲙⲁⲕⲁⲣ ⲡⲓⲣⲉⲙⲛ̀ⲭⲏⲙⲓ ⲡⲓⲁⲛⲁⲭⲱⲣⲓⲧⲏⲥ ⲁⲛⲭⲁ ⲛⲓϣⲁϥⲉⲩ ⲛ̀ⲧⲉ ⲭⲏⲙⲓ ⲛⲁⲕ ⲁⲕⲓ ⲉⲡⲁⲓⲙⲁ ⲟⲛ ⲟⲩⲟϩ ⲓⲥ ϩⲏⲡⲡⲉ ⲛⲉⲕϣⲗⲏⲗ ⲥⲉϩⲓⲥⲓ ⲛⲁⲛ ⲙ̀ⲡⲁⲓⲕⲉⲙⲁ ⲉⲕϯⲛⲧⲟⲧⲕ ⲛⲉⲙ ⲛⲁⲓⲣⲱⲙⲉⲟⲥ. ⲫⲁⲓ ⲇⲉ ⲉⲧⲁϥϫⲟϥ ⲁϥⲓ ⲉⲃⲟⲗϧⲉⲛ ⲡⲓⲣⲱⲙⲓ ⲛ̀ϫⲉ ⲡⲓⲡ̅ⲛ̅ⲁ̅ ⲛ̀ⲁⲕⲁⲑⲁⲣⲧⲟⲛ ⲟⲩⲟϩ ⲟⲩⲟⲛ ⲛⲓⲃⲉⲛ ⲉⲧⲁⲩⲥⲱⲧⲉⲙ ⲁⲩϯⲱⲟⲩ ⲙ̀Ⲫϯ.

19. Ⲛⲉ ⲟⲩⲟⲛ ⲟⲩⲕⲟϩ ⲛ̀ⲧⲱⲟⲩ ϧⲉⲛ ⲡⲓⲙⲁⲛⲙⲟϣⲓ ⲉⲑⲛⲁ ⲉϧⲟⲩⲛ ⲉⲓⲕⲟⲛⲓⲟⲛ ⲉⲣⲉ ⲟⲩⲛⲓϣϯ ⲛ̀ⲇⲣⲁⲕⲱⲛ ϣⲟⲡ ⲛ̀ϩⲏⲧⲥ ⲟⲩⲟϩ ⲫⲁⲓ ⲛⲉ ϣⲁϥⲧⲁⲕⲉ ⲟⲩⲙⲏϣ ⲛ̀ⲧⲉ ⲛⲓⲣⲱⲙⲓ ⲉⲑⲙⲟϣⲓ ϧⲉⲛ ⲡⲓⲙⲁⲙⲙⲟϣⲓ ⲉⲧⲉⲙⲙⲁⲩ. ϩⲟⲧⲉ ⲉⲧⲁ ⲛⲁ Ⲓⲕⲟⲛⲓⲟⲛ ⲛⲁⲩ ⲉⲡⲓⲧⲁⲕⲟ ⲉⲧϣⲟⲡ ⲁⲩϩⲱⲗ ϣⲁ ⲛⲓⲁⲅⲓⲟⲥ ⲉⲩⲧⲁⲙⲟ ⲙ̀ⲙⲱⲟⲩ ⲉⲡⲧⲁⲕⲟ ⲛ̀ⲧⲉ ⲡⲓⲑⲏⲣⲓⲟⲛ ⲉⲧϩⲱⲟⲩ ⲉⲧⲉⲙⲙⲁⲩ. ⲧⲟⲧⲉ ⲁⲡⲓⲙⲁⲕⲁⲣⲓⲟⲥ Ⲙⲁⲝⲓⲙⲟⲥ ⲥϧⲉ ⲟⲩⲕⲟⲩϫⲓ ⲛ̀ⲥϧⲁⲓ ⲉϥϫⲱ ⲙ̀ⲙⲟⲥ ϫⲉ ϧⲉⲛ ⲫⲣⲁⲛ ⲙ̀ⲡⲟ̅ⲥ̅ ⲥⲁⲃⲁⲱⲑ Ⲫϯ ⲛ̀ⲁⲃⲃⲁ Ⲙⲁⲕⲁⲣ ⲛⲉⲙ ⲁⲃⲃⲁ Ⲁⲅⲁⲡⲟⲥ ⲡⲉⲛⲓⲱⲧ ⲛ̀ⲣⲱⲙⲓ ⲉⲧⲉⲣⲫⲟⲣⲓⲛ ⲙ̀Ⲡⲭ̅ⲥ̅ ⲡⲓⲗⲟⲅⲟⲥ ⲛ̀ⲧⲉ ⲫⲓⲱⲧ ϫⲉ ⲉϣⲱⲡ ⲛ̀ⲧⲟⲩⲉⲛ ⲡⲁⲓⲕⲟⲩϫⲓ ⲛ̀ⲥϧⲁⲓ ⲉⲣⲟⲕ ⲙ̀ⲡⲉⲕⲙⲟϩ ⲛ̀ⲑⲟⲕ ϧⲁ ⲡⲓⲇⲣⲁⲕⲱⲛ ⲉⲕⲉ̀ⲓ ⲉⲃⲟⲗ ⲉⲣⲉ ⲣⲱⲕ ϣⲟⲧⲉⲙ ⲛ̀ⲧⲉⲕⲉⲛⲕⲟⲧ ϧⲉⲛ ⲑⲙⲏϯ ⲙ̀ⲡⲓⲙⲁⲙⲙⲟϣⲓ ⲛ̀ⲧⲉⲕϣⲧⲉⲙⲕⲓⲙ ⲉⲣⲟⲕ ⲉⲃⲟⲗϧⲉⲛ ⲡⲓⲙⲁ

ⲉⲧⲉⲙⲙⲁⲩ ϣⲁⲧⲉ ⲛⲓϩⲁⲗⲁϯ ⲛ̀ⲧⲉ ⲧⲫⲉ ⲟⲩⲱⲙ ⲛ̀ⲛⲉⲕⲁϥⲟⲩⲓ. ⲉⲧⲁⲩϭⲓ ⲇⲉ ⲙ̀ⲡⲓⲥϧⲁⲓ ⲁⲩⲧⲏⲓϥ ⲛ̀ⲟⲩⲣⲱⲙⲓ ⲉⲁϥⲧⲁⲗⲟϥ ⲉⲟⲩϩⲑⲟ ⲁϥϩⲱⲗ ⲁϥⲭⲱ ⲙ̀ⲡⲓⲥϧⲁⲓ ϩⲓⲣⲱϥ ⲙ̀ⲡⲓⲃⲏⲃ ⲛ̀ⲧⲉ ⲡⲓⲑⲏⲣⲓⲟⲛ ⲟⲩⲟϩ ⲁϥⲫⲱⲧ ⲥⲁⲧⲟⲧϥ.

20. Ⲱ ⲛⲉⲙ ϯϣⲫⲏⲣⲓ ⲉⲧⲁⲥϣⲱⲡⲓ ⲙ̀ⲡⲓⲛⲁⲩ ⲉⲧⲉⲙⲙⲁⲩ ⲡⲓⲇⲣⲁⲕⲱⲛ ⲅⲁⲣ ⲉⲧϩⲱⲟⲩ ϧⲉⲛ ϯⲟⲩⲛⲟⲩ ⲉⲧⲉⲙⲙⲁⲩ ⲥⲁⲧⲟⲧϥ ⲁϥⲓ ⲉⲃⲟⲗϧⲉⲛ ⲡⲉϥⲃⲏⲃ ⲟⲩⲟϩ ⲛⲁϥⲉⲛⲕⲟⲧ ⲉϥϩⲓⲱⲟⲩⲧ ⲥⲁⲡⲉⲥⲏⲧ ⲛ̀ⲧϥⲉ ϧⲉⲛ ⲑⲙⲏϯⲙ̀ⲡⲓⲙⲁⲙⲙⲟϣⲓ ⲉⲩⲉⲣⲑⲉⲱⲣⲓⲛ ⲙ̀ⲙⲟϥ ⲛ̀ϫⲉ ⲟⲩⲟⲛ ⲛⲓⲃⲉⲛ ⲛⲏⲉⲑⲟⲩⲛⲟⲩ ⲙ̀ⲙⲟϥ ⲛ̀ⲟⲩⲉϩⲟⲟⲩ ⲙ̀ⲙⲟϣⲓ ⲛ̀ⲧⲟⲓ ϣⲁⲧⲟⲩⲛⲁⲩ ⲉⲣⲟϥ ⲛ̀ϥϣⲕⲓⲙ ⲉⲣⲟϥ ⲁⲛ ϩⲟⲗⲱⲥ ⲉⲃⲟⲗϧⲉⲛ ⲡⲉϥⲙⲁ ⲉⲩϩⲓⲱⲛⲓ ⲉⲣⲟϥ ⲟⲩⲟϩ ⲛⲁⲩϯⲱⲟⲩ ⲙ̀Ⲫϯ ⲫⲏⲉⲧⲓⲣⲓ ⲛ̀ⲛⲓϣⲫⲏⲣⲓ ϧⲉⲛ ⲛⲏⲉⲑⲟⲩ ⲛ̀ⲧⲁϥ.

21. Ⲟⲩⲣⲱⲙⲓ ⲇⲉ ϩⲱϥ ⲁϥⲓ ⲉⲃⲟⲗϧⲉⲛ Ⲗⲩⲥⲧⲣⁱⁿ ⲉⲛⲁⲩ ⲉⲧϣⲫⲏⲣⲓ ⲉⲧⲁⲥϣⲱⲡⲓ ⲛⲁⲣⲉ ⲡⲉϥⲥⲱⲙⲁ ⲧⲏⲣϥ ⲕⲏⲕ ⲛ̀ⲥⲉϩⲧ ⲡⲉ ⲟⲩⲟϩ ⲉⲧⲁϥⲓ ϣⲁ ⲛⲏⲉⲑⲟⲩ ϧⲉⲛ ⲡⲉϥϫⲓⲛⲛⲁⲩ ⲉⲣⲱⲟⲩ ⲙ̀ⲙⲁⲩⲁⲧϥ ⲉⲃⲟⲗϩⲓⲧⲉⲛ ⲡⲉϥⲛⲓϣϯ ⲛ̀ⲛⲁϩϯ ⲁϥⲧⲟⲩⲃⲟ ⲥⲁⲧⲟⲧϥ ⲉⲃⲟⲗϩⲁ ⲡⲓⲥⲉϩⲧ ⲟⲩⲟϩ ⲛⲁⲣⲉ ⲟⲩⲟⲛ ⲛⲓⲃⲉⲛ ϯⲱⲟⲩ ⲙ̀ⲡⲉⲛⲟ̅ⲥ̅ Ⲓⲏ̅ⲥ̅ Ⲡ̅ⲭ̅ⲥ̅ ⲉⲑⲃⲉ ⲛⲓⲧⲁⲗϭⲟ ⲉⲧⲉϥⲓⲣⲓ ⲙ̀ⲙⲱⲟⲩ ϧⲉⲛ ⲛⲉⲛϫⲓϫ ⲛ̀ⲛⲁⲓⲙⲁⲕⲁⲣⲓⲟⲥ.

22. Ⲁⲩⲉⲛ ⲟⲩⲁⲓ ϣⲁⲣⲱⲟⲩ ⲉⲃⲟⲗϧⲉⲛ Ⲙⲁⲕⲇⲁⲗⲁⲛ ⲛ̀ⲧⲉ ϯⲠⲓⲥⲓⲇⲓⲁ ⲉⲣⲉ ⲡⲉϥϩⲟ ⲥⲱⲧⲉⲣ ϩⲓⲫⲁϩⲟⲩ ⲙ̀ⲙⲟϥ ϩⲓⲧⲉⲛ ⲧⲉⲛⲉⲣⲅⲓⲁ ⲛⲟⲩⲇⲉⲙⲱⲛ ⲓⲥ Ⲅ̅ϯ ⲛ̀ⲣⲟⲙⲡⲓ ⲟⲩⲟϩ ⲉⲧⲁⲩⲛⲁⲩ ⲉⲣⲟϥ ⲛ̀ϫⲉ ⲛⲏⲉⲑⲟⲩ ⲁⲩⲉⲣⲙⲕⲁϩ ⲛ̀ϩⲏⲧ ⲉⲙⲁϣⲱ ⲉⲑⲃⲉ ⲡⲓⲣⲏϯ ⲉⲛⲁϥⲟⲓ ⲙ̀ⲙⲟϥ ⲟⲩⲟϩ ⲉⲧⲁⲩϭⲓ ⲛ̀ⲟⲩⲕⲟⲩϫⲓ ⲙ̀ⲙⲱⲟⲩ ⲁⲩⲉⲣⲥⲫⲣⲁⲅⲓⲍⲓⲛ ⲙ̀ⲙⲟϥ ϧⲉⲛ ⲫⲣⲁⲛ ⲙ̀ⲡⲉⲛⲟ̅ⲥ̅ Ⲓⲏ̅ⲥ̅ Ⲡ̅ⲭ̅ⲥ̅ ⲁⲓϫⲟϣϥ ⲉϫⲱϥ ⲟⲩⲟϩ ϧⲉⲛ ϯⲟⲩⲛⲟⲩ ⲁⲡⲉϥϩⲟ ⲥⲱⲟⲩⲧⲉⲛ. Ⲱ ⲛⲉⲙ ⲛⲁⲓϩⲙⲟⲧ ⲉⲧⲟⲓ ⲛ̀ⲛⲓϣϯ ⲉⲧⲁ ⲡϣⲏⲣⲓ ⲙ̀Ⲫϯ ⲁⲓⲧⲟⲩ ⲛⲉⲙ ⲛⲓϣⲏⲣⲓ ⲛ̀ⲟⲩⲣⲟ ⲕⲉ ⲅⲁⲣ ϧⲉⲛ ⲟⲩⲙⲉⲑⲙⲏⲓ ⲛⲏⲉⲧⲉⲣⲁⲅⲁⲡⲁⲛ ⲙ̀Ⲫϯ ϣⲁϥⲉⲣϩⲱⲃ ⲛⲉⲙⲱⲟⲩ ϧⲉⲛ ϩⲱⲃ ⲛⲓⲃⲉⲛ ⲉⲑⲛⲁⲛⲉⲩ.

23. ϯϯϩⲟ ⲇⲉ ⲉⲣⲱⲧⲉⲛ ⲙ̀ⲡⲉⲛⲑⲣⲉϩⲗⲓ ⲉⲣⲁⲑⲛⲁϩϯ ⲉⲛⲏⲉⲧϫⲱ ⲙ̀ⲙⲱⲟⲩ ⲕⲉ ⲅⲁⲣ ⲁⲛⲟⲕ ϩⲱ ϧⲁ ⲡⲓⲉⲗⲁⲭⲓⲥⲧⲟⲥ Ⲡⲓϣⲟⲓ ⲉⲧⲓ ⲉⲓϩⲉⲛ Ⲕⲱⲥⲧⲁⲛⲧⲓⲛⲟⲩⲡⲟⲗⲓⲥ ϧⲁⲧϩⲏ ⲙ̀ⲡⲁϯⲉⲙⲓ ⲣⲱ ⲉⲡⲧⲏⲣϥ ϫⲉ ⲁⲣⲉ Ϣⲓϩⲏⲧ ⲛ̀ⲑⲱⲛ ⲁⲓⲥⲱⲧⲉⲙ ⲉⲃⲟⲗϩⲓⲧⲉⲛ ⲛⲓⲡⲣⲁⲅⲙⲁⲧⲉⲩⲧⲏⲥ ⲉⲑⲃⲉ ⲛⲓⲧⲁⲗϭⲟ ⲉⲧⲉⲣⲉ ⲛⲁⲓⲁⲅⲓⲟⲥ ⲓⲣⲓ ⲙ̀ⲙⲱⲟⲩ ϧⲉⲛ ⲫⲣⲁⲛ ⲙ̀ⲡⲉⲛⲟ̅ⲥ̅ Ⲓⲏ̅ⲥ̅ Ⲡ̅ⲭ̅ⲥ̅ ⲡⲓⲗⲟⲅⲟⲥ ⲟⲩⲟϩ ⲁⲓϩⲱⲗ ⲉϯⲤⲩⲣⲓⲁ ⲉⲧⲓ ⲉⲓⲟⲓ ⲛ̀ⲕⲟⲥⲙⲓⲕⲟⲥ ϣⲁϯⲛⲁⲩ ϧⲉⲛ ⲛⲁⲃⲁⲗ ⲉⲛⲏⲉⲧⲁⲓⲥⲟⲑⲙⲟⲩ ⲛ̀ⲧⲉ ⲡⲁϩⲏⲧ ⲑⲱⲧ ⲉⲁⲓϫⲟⲥ ϧⲉⲛ

ⲛⲁⲙⲉⲩⲓ ϫⲉ ⲛⲁⲛⲉ ⲡⲓϫⲓⲛⲛⲁⲩ ⲛ̀ⲧⲉ ⲛⲓⲃⲁⲗ ⲉϩⲟⲧⲉ ⲡⲓϫⲓⲛⲥⲱⲧⲉⲙ ϧⲉⲛ
ⲛⲓⲙⲁϣϫ. ⲓⲥϫⲉⲛ ⲡⲓⲉϩⲟⲟⲩ ⲅⲁⲣ ⲉⲧⲉⲙⲙⲁⲩ ⲉⲧⲁⲓⲛⲁⲩ ⲉⲛⲟⲩϩⲃⲏⲟⲩⲓ
ⲉⲑⲛⲁⲛⲉⲩ ⲁⲡⲁϩⲏⲧ ⲑⲱⲧ ⲉⲉⲣⲙⲟⲛⲁⲭⲟⲥ ⲁⲗⲗⲁ ⲙ̀ⲡⲓϣϫⲉⲙϫⲟⲙ ϣⲁ
ⲡⲓⲛⲁⲩ ⲉⲧⲁ Ⲫϯ ⲉⲣⲃⲟⲏⲑⲓⲛ ⲉⲣⲟⲓ ⲁϥⲉⲛⲧ ⲉⲃⲟⲗϧⲉⲛ ⲛⲓϭⲓⲣϣⲟⲩϣ ⲛ̀ⲧⲉ
ⲡⲓⲕⲟⲥⲙⲟⲥ ⲁⲓⲓ ⲉϢⲓϩⲏⲧ. ⲗⲟⲓⲡⲟⲛ ϫⲉ ⲛⲏⲉⲧⲁⲓ ⲥⲟⲑⲙⲟⲩ ϧⲉⲛ ϯⲥⲩⲣⲓⲁ
ⲛⲉⲙ ⲛⲏⲉⲧⲁⲓ ⲥⲟⲙⲟⲩ ϩⲓ ⲡⲁϫⲱⲙ. ϯⲛⲟⲩ ϫⲉ ⲙⲏⲡⲱⲥ ⲛ̀ⲧⲁⲥⲱⲕ ϧⲉⲛ
ⲡⲁⲓⲥⲁϫⲓ ⲙ̀ⲡⲁⲓⲣⲏϯ ⲉⲓⲧⲁϫⲣⲟ ⲛ̀ϯⲙⲉⲧⲙⲉⲑⲣⲉ ⲛ̀ⲧⲁⲉⲣⲡⲱⲃϣ ⲛ̀ⲛⲓϩⲙⲟⲧ
ⲉⲑⲛⲁⲛⲉⲩ. ⲗⲟⲓⲡⲟⲛ ⲧⲉⲛⲛⲁⲕⲟⲧⲧⲉⲛ ⲡⲁⲗⲓⲛ ⲉϫⲉⲛ ⲛⲓϩⲙⲟⲧ ⲛ̀ⲧⲁⲗϭⲟ
ⲉⲧⲉ Ⲡ̅ⲭ̅ⲥ̅ ⲡⲉⲛⲛⲟⲩϯ ⲁⲓⲧⲟⲩ ⲉⲃⲟⲗϩⲓⲧⲉⲛ ⲛⲓⲁϣⲏⲣⲓ ⲛ̀ⲟⲩⲣⲟ ⲛⲁⲓ ⲉⲧⲁⲩϯ
ⲙ̀Ⲡ̅ⲭ̅ⲥ̅ ϩⲓⲱⲧⲟⲩ ⲙ̀ⲫⲣⲏϯ ⲙ̀Ⲡⲁⲩⲗⲟⲥ ⲛⲉⲙ Ⲧⲓⲙⲟⲑⲉⲟⲥ ⲉⲑⲃⲉ ⲫⲁⲓ ⲁ
ϯϫⲟⲙ ⲛ̀ⲧⲉ ⲛⲏⲉⲧⲉⲙⲙⲁⲩ ⲉⲣϩⲱⲃ ϧⲉⲛ ⲛⲁⲓⲕⲉⲭⲱⲟⲩⲛⲓ ⲛ̀ⲧⲁⲓⲙⲁⲓⲏ.

24. Ⲛⲉ ⲟⲩⲟⲛ ⲟⲩⲡⲣⲉⲥⲃⲩⲧⲉⲣⲟⲥ ⲇⲉ ⲟⲛ ϧⲉⲛ Ⲅⲁⲃⲃⲁⲗⲱⲛ ϯⲃⲁⲕⲓ
ⲛ̀ⲧⲉ ⲛⲓⲅⲁⲃⲃⲁⲗⲉⲟⲥ ⲉⲡⲉϥⲣⲁⲛ ⲡⲉ Ⲍⲁⲭⲁⲣⲓⲁⲥ ⲫⲁⲓ ⲇⲉ ⲁⲟⲩⲠ̅Ⲛ̅Ⲁ̅
ⲛ̀ⲁⲣⲭⲟⲛⲧⲓⲕⲟⲛ ϫⲱⲓⲗⲓ ⲉⲣⲟϥ ⲉϥⲓⲣⲓ ⲛ̀ϩⲁⲛⲙⲏⲓⲛⲓ ⲛⲉⲙ ϩⲁⲛϣⲫⲏⲣⲓ
ϩⲓⲧⲉⲛ ⲛⲓⲇⲉⲙⲱⲛ ϩⲱⲥⲧⲉ ⲛ̀ⲧⲉϥⲥⲱⲣⲉⲙ ⲛ̀ⲛⲓⲅⲁⲃⲁⲗⲗⲉⲟⲥ ⲧⲏⲣⲟⲩ
ⲟⲩⲟϩ ⲉⲧⲁ ⲡⲓⲉⲡⲓⲥⲕⲟⲡⲟⲥ ⲛ̀ⲧⲉ ⲅⲁⲃⲁⲗⲗⲱⲛ ⲛⲁⲩ ⲉⲡⲧⲁⲕⲟ ⲉⲧⲁϥϣⲱⲡⲓ
ϧⲉⲛ ⲡⲓⲱϣ ⲁϥϭⲓ ⲛⲉⲙⲁϥ ⲛ̀ϩⲁⲛⲕⲉⲡⲣⲉⲥⲃⲩⲧⲉⲣⲟⲥ ⲟⲩⲟϩ ⲁϥⲓ ϣⲁ
ⲛⲏⲉ̅ⲑ̅ⲩ̅ ⲁϥⲧⲁⲙⲱⲟⲩ ⲉϩⲱⲃ ⲛⲓⲃⲉⲛ ⲉⲧⲁϥϣⲱⲡⲓ. ⲉⲧⲁⲩⲥⲱⲧⲉⲙ ⲇⲉ
ⲉⲛⲁⲓⲛ̀ⲧⲟⲧϥ ⲙ̀ⲡⲓⲉⲡⲓⲥⲕⲟⲡⲟⲥ ⲁⲩⲉⲣⲙⲕⲁϩ ⲛ̀ϩⲏⲧ ⲉⲙⲁϣⲱ ⲟⲩⲟϩ
ⲡⲉϫⲱⲟⲩ ⲛⲁϥ ϫⲉ ⲡⲱⲥ ⲙ̀ⲡⲉⲕⲉⲛϥ ⲛⲉⲙⲁⲕ ⲛ̀ⲑⲟϥ ⲡⲉϫⲁϥ ⲛⲱⲟⲩ ϫⲉ
ⲙ̀ⲡⲉϥⲥⲱⲧⲉⲙ ⲛ̀ⲥⲱⲓ ⲛⲁⲓⲟϯ ⲉ̅ⲑ̅ⲩ̅. ⲁϥⲉⲣⲟⲩⲱ ⲛ̀ϫⲉ ⲡⲡⲓⲉⲡⲓⲥⲕⲟⲡⲟⲥ
ⲡⲉϫⲁϥ ⲛⲱⲟⲩ ϫⲉ ϯϯϩⲟⲉⲣⲱⲧⲉⲛ ⲛⲁⲓⲟϯ ⲉ̅ⲑ̅ⲩ̅ ⲛ̀ⲧⲉⲧⲉⲛⲟⲩⲱⲣⲡ
ⲛ̀ⲥⲱϥ ⲛ̀ⲑⲱⲧⲉⲛ ⲡⲁⲛⲧⲱⲥ ⲛ̀ⲧⲉϥⲓ.

25. ⲡⲓⲁⲅⲓⲟⲥ ⲇⲉ Ⲙⲁⲝⲓⲙⲟⲥ ⲉⲧⲁϥϭⲓ ⲛ̀ⲟⲩϫⲱⲙ ⲁϥⲥϧⲁⲓ ⲙ̀ⲡⲁⲓⲣⲏϯ
ⲉϥϫⲱ ⲙ̀ⲙⲟⲥ ϫⲉ ⲁⲛⲟⲕ ⲡⲉ ⲡⲓϫⲱⲃ Ⲙⲁⲝⲓⲙⲟⲥ ⲡⲓⲃⲱⲕ ⲛ̀ⲧⲉ Ⲡ̅ⲭ̅ⲥ̅
ⲉⲓⲥϧⲁⲓ ϧⲉⲛ ⲧⲁϫⲓϫ ⲙ̀ⲙⲟⲛ ⲙ̀ⲙⲟⲓ ϫⲉ ϧⲉⲛ ϯϫⲟⲙ ⲛ̀ⲧⲉ Ⲡ̅ⲟ̅ⲥ̅ ⲥⲁⲃⲁⲱⲑ
Ⲫϯ ⲛ̀ⲧⲉ ⲛⲓⲁⲡⲟⲥⲧⲟⲗⲟⲥ ⲛⲉⲙ ⲛⲓⲡⲣⲟⲫⲏⲧⲏⲥ ⲛⲉⲙ ⲁⲃⲃⲁ Ⲙⲁⲕⲁⲣ
ⲡⲓⲣⲉⲙⲛ̀ⲭⲏⲙⲓ ⲫⲁⲓ ⲉⲧⲁ ⲁ̀ⲅⲁⲡⲟⲥ ⲡⲉⲛⲓⲱⲧ ⲛⲁⲩ ⲉⲣⲟϥ ϧⲉⲛ ⲡⲓϩⲟⲣⲁⲙⲁ
ⲉⲓⲥϧⲁⲓ ⲛ̀Ⲍⲁⲭⲁⲣⲓⲁⲥ ϫⲉ ⲓⲥϫⲉ ϯⲥⲃⲱ ⲛ̀ⲧⲉ ⲛⲓⲁⲡⲟⲥⲧⲟⲗⲥ ⲡⲉ
ⲉⲧⲉⲕϯⲥⲃⲱ ⲛ̀ϩⲏⲧⲥ ⲓⲉ ⲟϩⲓ ⲙ̀ⲡⲉⲣⲏϯ. ⲓⲥϫⲉ ⲑⲁ ⲛⲓⲇⲉⲙⲱⲛ ⲧⲉ ⲟⲩⲟϩ
ⲕⲟⲓ ⲛ̀ⲁⲧⲥⲱⲧⲉⲙ ⲛ̀ⲥⲁ ⲡⲉⲕⲉⲡⲓⲥⲕⲟⲡⲟⲥ ⲉϥϯⲥⲃⲱ ⲛⲁⲕ ⲉⲡⲉⲕⲟⲩϫⲁⲓ ⲓⲉ
ⲧⲉⲛⲟⲩϩⲥⲁϩⲛⲓ ⲙ̀ⲡⲓⲇⲉⲙⲱⲛ ⲉⲧⲉⲙⲙⲁⲩ ϧⲉⲛ ⲫⲣⲁⲛ ⲛ̀Ⲓ̅ⲏ̅ⲥ̅ ⲡⲓⲗⲟⲅⲟⲥ
ⲙ̀ⲙⲏⲓ ⲛ̀ⲧⲉ Ⲫϯ ⲉⲣⲉ ⲡⲓⲇⲉⲙⲱⲛ ⲉⲧⲉⲙⲙⲁⲩ ⲓ ⲉϫⲱⲕ ⲛ̀ⲧⲉϥϩⲓⲟ̀ ⲙ̀ⲙⲟⲕ

ⲟⲩⲟϩ ⲛ̀ⲥⲉⲉⲙⲓ ⲧⲏⲣⲟⲩ ⲉⲧⲥⲟⲣⲙⲉⲥ ⲉⲧⲉⲕⲭⲏ ⲛ̀ϧⲏⲧⲥ. ⲧⲟⲧⲉ ⲁϥⲥϧⲉ ⲫⲣⲁⲛ ⲛ̀ⲁⲃⲃⲁ Ⲙⲁⲕⲁⲣ ⲥⲁⲃⲟⲗ ⲛ̀ϯⲉⲡⲓⲥⲧⲟⲗⲏ ⲁϥⲧⲏⲓⲥ ⲙ̀ⲡⲓⲉⲡⲓⲥⲕⲟⲡⲟⲥ ⲟⲩⲟϩ ⲁϥⲧϥⲟϥ. Ⲱ ϯϣⲫⲏⲣⲓ ⲉⲧⲁⲥϣⲱⲡⲓ ⲙ̀ⲡⲓⲛⲁⲩ ⲉⲧⲁ ⲡⲓⲉⲡⲓⲥⲕⲟⲡⲟⲥ ϯⲛⲁϥ ⲛ̀ϯⲉⲡⲓⲥⲧⲟⲗⲏ ⲉϥϫⲱ ⲙ̀ⲙⲟⲥ ϫⲉ ⲛⲓⲁⲛⲁⲭⲱⲣⲓⲧⲏⲥ ϣⲓⲛⲓ ⲉⲣⲟⲕ.

26. ⲡⲓⲱⲟⲩ ⲛⲁⲕ Ⲡ̅ⲭ̅ⲥ̅ ⲡⲓⲗⲟⲅⲟⲥ ⲛ̀ⲧⲉ Ⲫϯ ⲛⲉⲙ ⲛⲓϫⲟⲙ ⲉⲧⲉⲕⲟⲩⲱⲛϩ ⲙ̀ⲙⲱⲟⲩ ⲉⲃⲟⲗϧⲉⲛ ⲛⲏⲉⲧⲟⲓ ⲛⲁⲕ ⲙ̀ⲃⲱⲕ ⲟⲩⲟϩ ⲉⲧϣⲉⲙϣⲓ ⲙ̀ⲡⲉⲕⲣⲁⲛ ⲉ̅ⲑ̅ⲩ̅ ⲟⲩⲇⲉ ⲅⲁⲣ ⲙ̀ⲡⲉ ⲡⲓⲇⲉⲙⲱⲛ ⲉⲧⲉⲙⲙⲁⲩ ⲛ̀ⲣⲉϥⲧⲁⲕⲉ ⲯⲩⲭⲏ ⲭⲁⲣⲱϥ ϣⲁⲧⲉϥϣⲁϣ ⲛ̀ϯⲉⲡⲓⲥⲧⲟⲗⲏ ⲁⲗⲗⲁ ϧⲉⲛ ϯⲟⲩⲛⲟⲩ ⲁϥϣⲱϫⲓ ⲉϫⲱϥ ⲁϥⲣⲁϧⲧϥ ϩⲓϫⲉⲛ ⲡⲕⲁϩⲓ ϧⲉⲛ ⲑⲙⲏϯ ⲛ̀ⲛⲏⲉⲧⲟϩⲓ ⲉⲣⲁⲧⲟⲩ ⲟⲩⲟϩ ⲁϥϩⲓⲧ ⲙ̀ⲙⲟϥ ⲉϥⲉϣ ϩⲣⲱⲟⲩ ⲉⲃⲟⲗ ⲟⲩⲟϩ ⲁϥⲟⲩⲁϩϥ ⲙ̀ⲫⲣⲏϯ ⲛ̀ⲟⲩⲟⲩϩⲟⲣ ϩⲱⲥⲧⲉ ⲛ̀ⲧⲉ ϯⲃⲁⲕⲓ Ⲅⲁⲃⲁⲗⲗⲱⲛ ⲑⲱⲟⲩϯ ⲉϩⲣⲏⲓ ⲉϫⲱϥ ⲛ̀ⲥⲉⲛⲁⲩ ⲉⲣⲟϥ ⲛ̀ⲥⲉⲉⲣϣⲫⲏⲣⲓ ⲙ̀ⲡⲉⲧϣⲟⲩϣⲟⲩ ⲙ̀ⲙⲟϥ ϧⲁϫⲉⲛ ⲟⲩⲕⲟⲩϫⲓ ϫⲉ ⲉⲧⲁϥϣⲱⲡⲓ ⲙ̀ⲙⲟϥ. ⲁϥϩⲓ ⲇⲉ ϧⲉⲛ ⲧⲁⲓⲃⲁⲥⲁⲛⲟⲥ ⲙ̀ⲡⲁⲓⲣⲏϯ ⲙ̅ⲏ̅ ⲛ̀ⲉϩⲟⲟⲩ ⲧⲟⲧⲉ ⲁⲩⲉⲛϥ ϣⲁ ⲛⲓⲁⲅⲓⲟⲥ ⲉϥⲥⲟⲛϩ ⲙ̀ⲡⲉⲇⲏⲥ: ⲛ̀ⲑⲱⲟⲩ ⲇⲉ ⲉⲧⲁⲩⲛⲁⲩ ⲉⲡⲉⲧϩⲉⲙⲕⲟ ⲁⲩⲉⲣⲙⲕⲁϩ ⲛ̀ϩⲏⲧ ⲉⲙⲁϣⲱ ⲟⲩⲟϩ ⲉⲧⲁⲩϭⲓ ⲛ̀ⲟⲩⲕⲟⲩϫⲓ ⲙ̀ⲙⲱⲟⲩ ⲁⲩⲉⲣⲫⲣⲁⲅⲓⲍⲓⲛ ⲙ̀ⲙⲟϥ ⲁⲩⲭⲟϣϥ ⲉϫⲱϥ ϧⲉⲛ ⲫⲣⲁⲛ ⲙ̀Ⲡ̅ⲭ̅ⲥ̅ ⲟⲩⲟϩ ⲥⲁⲧⲟⲧϥ ⲁϥⲟⲩϫⲁⲓ ⲉⲃⲟⲗϩⲁ ⲇⲉⲙⲱⲛ ⲁϥϣⲱⲡⲓ ϧⲁⲧⲉⲛ ⲛⲓⲁⲅⲓⲟⲥ ⲛ̅ⲅ̅ ⲛ̀ⲉϩⲟⲟⲩ ϣⲁⲧⲟⲩⲥⲁⲃⲟϥ ⲉϥⲙⲱⲓⲧ ⲛ̀ⲧⲉ ⲡⲓⲟⲩϫⲁⲓ ⲛ̀ⲥⲉⲧⲫⲟϥ ϧⲉⲛ ⲟⲩϩⲓⲣⲏⲛⲏ ⲉϥϯⲱⲟⲩ ⲙ̀Ⲫϯ.

27. ϧⲉⲛ ⲛⲁⲓⲧⲁⲗϭⲟ ⲇⲉ ⲧⲏⲣⲟⲩ ⲉⲧϣⲟⲡ ⲉⲃⲟⲗϩⲓⲧⲉⲛ ⲛⲁⲓⲙⲁⲕⲁⲣⲓⲟⲥ ⲙ̀ⲡⲟⲩϭⲓⲥⲓ ⲛ̀ϩⲏⲧ ⲉⲡⲧⲏⲣϥ ⲟⲩⲇⲉ ⲛⲁⲩϣⲟⲩϣⲟⲩ ⲙ̀ⲙⲱⲟⲩ ⲁⲛ ⲡⲉ ⲟⲩⲇⲉ ⲙ̀ⲡⲟⲩϫⲉ ⲟⲩⲥⲁϫⲓ ⲛ̀ⲟⲩⲣⲱⲙⲓ ϧⲉⲛ ⲟⲩⲉⲣϣⲓϣⲓ ⲁⲗⲗⲁ ⲛⲁⲩⲑⲉⲃⲓⲟ ⲙ̀ⲙⲱⲟⲩ ⲡⲉ ⲥⲁⲡⲉⲥⲏⲧ ⲛ̀ⲥⲟⲛ ⲛⲓⲃⲉⲛ ϩⲱⲥ ⲉⲩϣⲟϣϥ ⲟⲩⲟϩ ⲉⲩⲓⲣⲓ ⲙ̀ⲙⲱⲟⲩ ⲛ̀ⲁⲧⲉⲙⲡϣⲁ ⲉⲩϫⲱ ⲙ̀ⲙⲟⲥ ⲛ̀ⲛⲁⲩ ⲛⲓⲃⲉⲛ ϫⲉ ⲡⲓϩⲙⲟⲧ ⲫⲁ Ⲫϯ ⲡⲉ ⲙ̀ⲙⲁⲩⲁⲧϥ ⲁⲛⲟⲛ ⲇⲉ ⲁⲛⲟⲓ ⲛ̀ϩⲁⲛⲭⲱⲃ ⲟⲩⲟϩ ⲛ̀ⲣⲉϥⲉⲣⲛⲟⲃⲓ.

28. Ⲛⲉ ⲟⲩⲟⲛ ⲟⲩⲡⲣⲉⲥⲃⲩⲧⲉⲣⲟⲥ ⲇⲉ ϧⲉⲛ Ⲥⲉⲗⲉⲩⲕⲓⲁ ⲛ̀ⲧⲉ ϯϨⲓⲥⲁⲩⲣⲓⲁ ⲉϣⲱⲡ ⲛ̀ⲧⲉϥⲕⲏⲛ ⲉϥⲉⲣϩⲱⲃ ϧⲉⲛ ⲛⲓϩⲃⲏⲟⲩⲓ ⲛ̀ⲁⲛⲟⲙⲟⲛ ϣⲁϥϩⲱⲗ ⲛ̀ⲧⲉϥⲟϩⲓ ⲉⲣⲁⲧϥ ⲉⲡⲓⲙⲁⲛⲉⲣϣⲟⲩϣⲱⲟⲩϣⲓ ⲛ̀ⲧⲉ Ⲫϯ. ⲛⲁϥⲧⲁⲕⲛⲟⲩⲧ ⲅⲁⲣ ⲡⲉ ⲛⲉⲙ ⲟⲩⲥϩⲓⲙⲓ ⲛ̀ⲥⲁⲙⲁⲣⲓⲧⲏⲥ ϩⲱⲥ ⲇⲉ ⲉϥⲙⲏⲛ ⲉⲃⲟⲗϧⲉⲛ ⲛⲁⲓⲙⲉⲧⲁⲥⲉⲃⲏⲥ ⲙ̀ⲡⲁⲓⲣⲏϯ ⲁⲫϯ ⲟⲩⲱϣ ⲉϩⲓϣⲓϣ ⲛ̀ⲛⲏⲉⲧⲉ ⲡⲓⲡⲣⲉⲥⲃⲩⲧⲉⲣⲟⲥ ⲉⲧⲉⲙⲙⲁⲩ ⲓⲣⲓ ⲙ̀ⲙⲱⲟⲩ ϧⲉⲛ ϯϨⲓⲥⲁⲩⲣⲓⲁ ⲧⲏⲣⲥ ϫⲉ ϩⲓⲛⲁ ⲛ̀ⲧⲉ ⲡⲕⲉⲥⲉⲡⲓ ⲛⲁⲩ ⲛ̀ⲧⲟⲩⲉⲣϩⲟϯ. ⲗⲟⲓⲡⲟⲛ ϧⲉⲛ

ⲡⲓⲉϩⲟⲟⲩ ⲛ̀ⲧⲉ ⲡⲉϥⲉⲣⲫⲙⲉⲩⲓ ⲙ̀ⲡⲓⲁⲅⲓⲟⲥ Ⲓⲅⲛⲁⲧⲓⲟⲥ ⲁϥϣⲉⲛⲁϥ ⲟⲛ
ⲉϯⲉⲕⲕⲗⲏⲥⲓⲁ ϫⲉ ϩⲓⲛⲁ ⲛ̀ⲧⲉϥϣⲉⲙϣⲓ ϩⲟⲧⲉ ⲟⲩⲛ ⲉⲧⲁϥⲕⲏⲛ ⲉϥϫⲱ
ⲛ̀ϯⲉⲩⲭⲏ ⲛ̀ⲧⲉ ⲡⲓⲉⲩⲁⲅⲅⲉⲗⲓⲟⲛ ⲙⲉⲛⲉⲛⲥⲁ ⲛⲓⲧⲱⲃϩ ⲁϥϯ ⲙ̀ⲡⲉϥⲟⲩⲟⲓ
ⲉⲡⲓⲙⲁⲛⲉⲣϣⲟⲩϣⲱⲟⲩϣⲓ ϫⲉ ⲁϥⲛⲁϣⲉⲙϣⲓ ϧⲉⲛ ⲟⲩⲙⲉⲧⲁⲧϩⲟϯ.
ⲥⲁⲧⲟⲧϥ ⲁⲟⲩⲁⲅⲅⲉⲗⲟⲥ ⲛ̀ⲧⲉ ⲡ̅ⲟ̅ⲥ̅ ϣⲁⲣⲓ ⲉⲣⲟϥ ϧⲉⲛ ⲟⲩⲛⲓϣϯ ⲛ̀ⲉⲣϩⲟⲧ
ⲉϥⲛⲁϣⲧ ⲉⲙⲁϣⲱ ϩⲱⲥⲧⲉ ⲡⲓϣⲁⲣ ⲛ̀ⲧⲉ ⲡⲉϥⲥⲱⲙⲁ ⲛⲟⲩϥⲧ ⲙ̀ⲫⲣⲏϯ
ⲛ̀ⲟⲩⲁⲥⲕⲟⲥ ⲟⲩⲟϩ ⲥⲁⲧⲟⲧϥ ⲁϥϩⲉⲓ ⲉϫⲉⲛ ⲡⲓⲕⲁϩⲓ ⲁϥⲉⲣⲫⲣⲏϯ
ⲛ̀ⲟⲩⲣⲉϥⲙⲱⲟⲩⲧ ⲟⲩⲟϩ ⲁⲩϥⲁⲓ ⲙ̀ⲙⲟϥ ⲁⲩϭⲓⲧϥ ⲉⲡⲉϥⲏⲓ ϧⲉⲛ ⲟⲩⲛⲓϣϯ
ⲙ̀ⲙⲉⲉⲃⲓⲏⲛ.

29. ⲫⲁⲓ ⲙⲉⲛⲉⲛⲥⲁ ⲓ̅ ⲛ̀ⲉϩⲟⲟⲩ ⲁⲡⲉϥⲥⲱⲙⲁ ⲧⲏⲣϥ ⲉϥⲉⲣϩⲟⲧ
ϩⲱⲥⲧⲉ ⲛ̀ⲥⲉⲥⲉⲕ ϥⲉⲛⲧ ⲉⲃⲟⲗϩⲁⲣⲟϥ ⲟⲩⲟϩ ⲛ̀ⲧⲉ ⲛⲉϥⲕⲁⲥ ⲃⲱϣ ⲉⲃⲟⲗ
ⲟⲩⲟϩ ⲛⲁϥϯϩⲣⲱⲟⲩ ⲉⲃⲟⲗϧⲉⲛ ⲟⲩⲥⲙⲏ ⲉⲥⲉⲛϣⲁϣⲓ ⲙ̀ⲡⲓⲉϩⲟⲟⲩ
ⲛⲉⲙ ⲡⲓⲉϫⲱⲣϩ ⲉⲑⲃⲉ ϯⲟⲩⲁⲙⲉϥ ⲉⲑⲟⲩⲱⲙ ⲛ̀ⲥⲱϥ. ⲛⲁϥⲣⲓⲙⲓ ⲇⲉ
ⲉϥⲉⲣⲟⲙⲟⲗⲟⲅⲓⲛ ⲙ̀ⲡⲉⲙⲑⲟ ⲉⲃⲟⲗ ⲛ̀ⲟⲩⲟⲛ ⲛⲓⲃⲉⲛ ⲛ̀ⲛⲓⲙⲉⲧⲁⲥⲉⲃⲏⲥ
ⲧⲏⲣⲟⲩ ⲉⲧⲁϥⲁⲓⲧⲟⲩ. ⲫⲁⲓ ⲁⲩⲧⲁⲗⲟϥ ⲉϫⲉⲛ ⲟⲩϭⲗⲟϫ ⲁϥϥⲁⲓ ⲙ̀ⲙⲟϥ
ϩⲓⲧⲉⲛ ϩⲁⲛⲣⲱⲙⲓ ⲁⲩϭⲓⲧϥ ⲉⲣⲁⲧⲟⲩ ⲛ̀ⲛⲏⲉⲑ̅ⲩ̅ ⲛⲉⲃⲓⲁⲓⲕ ⲛ̀ⲧⲉ Ⲫϯ
ⲉⲧϭⲟⲥⲓ.

30. ⲉⲧⲁⲩⲭⲁϥ ⲇⲉ ⲉϧⲣⲏⲓ ⲙ̀ⲡⲟⲩⲙⲑⲟ ⲁⲩⲉⲣⲙⲕⲁϩⲛ̀ϩⲏⲧ ϧⲉⲛ
ⲡϫⲓⲛⲑⲣⲟⲩⲛⲁⲩ ⲉⲡⲉϥϩⲉⲙⲕⲟ ⲟⲩⲟϩ ⲛⲁⲩϫⲱ ⲙ̀ⲙⲟⲥ ⲛⲁϥ ⲡⲉ ϫⲉ ⲟⲩ
ⲡⲉ ⲉⲧⲁⲕⲁⲓϥ ϣⲁⲧⲉ ⲫⲁⲓ ϣⲱⲡⲓ ⲙ̀ⲙⲟⲕ. ⲛ̀ⲑⲟϥ ⲇⲉ ⲡⲉϫⲁϥ ⲛⲱⲟⲩ
ϫⲉ ⲭⲱ ⲛⲏⲓ ⲉⲃⲟⲗ ⲛⲁⲓⲟϭ ⲉⲑ̅ⲩ̅ ⲁⲡ̅ⲭ̅ⲥ̅ ⲕⲏⲛ ⲉⲉⲣϣⲟⲣⲡ ⲛ̀ⲧⲁⲙⲱⲧⲉⲛ
ⲉⲛⲁⲡⲣⲁⲝⲓⲥ ⲉⲧϩⲱⲟⲩ ⲡⲉϫⲱⲟⲩ ⲛⲁϥ ϫⲉ ϩⲁⲣⲁ ⲁⲕⲥⲱⲟⲩⲛ ⲙ̀ⲡ̅ⲭ̅ⲥ̅
ⲛ̀ⲕⲁⲗⲱⲥ ⲟⲩⲟϩ ⲁⲕⲉⲙⲓ ⲇⲉ ϥϣⲟⲡ ⲉϥⲛⲁⲩ ⲉⲛⲉⲕϩⲃⲏⲟⲩⲓ ⲉⲧⲉⲕⲓⲣⲓ
ⲙ̀ⲙⲱⲟⲩ. ⲡⲉϫⲁϥ ϫⲉ ⲁϩⲁ ⲛⲁⲟ̅ⲥ̅ ⲛ̀ⲓⲟϯ ⲁϥϯⲥⲃⲱ ⲛⲏⲓ ⲛ̀ⲕⲁⲗⲱⲥ.

31. ⲧⲟⲧⲉ ⲛⲓⲙⲁⲕⲁⲣⲓⲟⲥ ⲛ̀ⲁⲑⲗⲏⲧⲏⲥ ⲛ̀ⲧⲉ ⲡ̅ⲭ̅ⲥ̅ Ⲓ̅ⲏ̅ⲥ̅ ⲉⲩⲥⲱⲟⲩⲛ ⲙ̀Ⲫϯ
ϫⲉ ϥⲟⲩⲱϣ ⲁⲛ ⲛ̀ⲧⲉ ϩⲗⲓ ⲧⲁⲕⲟ ⲉϥϧⲁⲃⲉⲙ ϧⲉⲛ ⲛⲉϥⲛⲟⲃⲓ ⲁⲗⲗⲁ
ⲙⲁⲗⲗⲟⲛ ϥⲟⲩⲱϣ ⲉⲑⲣⲟⲩⲕⲟⲧⲟⲩ ϩⲁⲣⲟϥ ⲧⲏⲣⲟⲩ ϧⲉⲛ ⲟⲩⲙⲉⲧⲁⲛⲟⲓⲁ
ⲙ̀ⲙⲏⲓ ⲁⲩϭⲓ ⲛ̀ⲟⲩⲕⲟⲟⲩϫⲓ ⲙ̀ⲙⲱⲟⲩ ⲁⲩⲉⲣⲥⲫⲣⲁⲅⲓⲍⲛ ⲙ̀ⲙⲟϥ ϧⲉⲛ ⲫⲙⲏⲓⲛⲓ
ⲙ̀ⲡⲓⲥ̅ⲧ̅ ⲁⲓⲭⲟϣϥ ⲉϫⲱϥ ⲉⲩϫⲱ ⲙ̀ⲙⲟⲥ ϫⲉ ⲡ̅ⲟ̅ⲥ̅ Ⲓ̅ⲏ̅ⲥ̅ ⲡ̅ⲭ̅ⲥ̅ ⲡⲓϣⲓⲛⲓ
ⲛ̀ⲁⲗⲏⲑⲓⲛⲟⲥ ⲛ̀ⲧⲉ ⲛⲉⲛⲯⲩⲭⲏ ⲛⲉⲙ ⲛⲉⲛⲥⲱⲙⲁ ⲫⲛⲉⲑⲟⲩⲱϣ ⲁⲛ ⲛ̀ⲧⲉ ϩⲗⲓ
ⲧⲁⲕⲟ ϧⲉⲛ ⲛⲏⲉⲧⲁⲩⲥⲱⲣⲉⲙ ⲁⲗⲗⲁ ⲉⲑⲣⲟⲩⲧⲁⲥⲑⲱⲟⲩ ⲧⲏⲣⲟⲩ ⲉϧⲟⲩⲛ
ⲉⲧⲉⲕϣⲁⲓⲣⲓ ⲛ̀ⲗⲟⲅⲓⲕⲏ ϩⲓⲧⲉⲛ ϯⲙⲉⲧⲁⲛⲟⲓⲁ ⲟⲩⲟϩ ⲛ̀ⲧⲉⲥⲟⲩϫⲁⲓ ⲛ̀ϫⲉ

ⲧⲟⲩⲯⲩⲭⲏ ⲛ̅ⲑⲟⲕ ⲉⲕⲉⲉⲣⲫⲁⲏ̅ⲣⲓ ⲉⲧⲏⲣⲟⲩ ϩⲓⲧⲉⲛ ⲛⲓⲉⲩⲭⲏ ⲛ̅ⲧⲉ ⲁⲅⲁⲡⲟⲥ ⲟⲑⲉⲛⲓⲱⲧ ⲛⲉⲙ ⲡⲉⲕⲃⲱⲕ Ⲙⲁⲕⲁⲣ ⲧⲟⲧⲉ ⲉⲧⲁⲁⲩⲭⲱϣ ⲙ̅ⲡⲡⲓⲙⲱⲟⲩ ⲉϫⲱϥ ⲟⲩⲟϩ ⲁϥⲟⲩϫⲁⲓ ⲛ̅ϫⲉ ⲡⲉϥⲥⲱⲙⲁ ⲉⲁⲩϣⲱⲟⲩⲓ ⲛ̅ϫⲉ ⲛⲉϥⲉⲣⲃⲟⲧ ⲁϥⲧⲁⲗϭⲟ. ⲛⲓⲁⲅⲓⲟⲥ ⲇⲉ ⲁⲩⲧϥⲟϥ ϧⲉⲛ ⲟⲩϩⲓⲣⲏⲛⲏ ⲉⲩϫⲱ ⲙ̅ⲙⲟⲥ ⲛⲁϥ ϫⲉ ⲓⲥ ϩⲏⲡⲡⲉ ⲁⲕⲟⲩϫⲁⲓ ⲙ̅ⲡⲉⲣⲉⲣⲛⲟⲃⲓ ⲛ̅ⲕⲉⲥⲟⲡ ϫⲉ ⲙⲏⲡⲱⲥ ⲛ̅ⲧⲉ ⲡϫⲱⲛⲧ ⲙ̅Ⲫϯ ⲧⲁϩⲟⲕ ⲟⲛ ⲛ̅ⲧⲉⲕⲙⲟⲩ ⲛ̅ⲕⲁⲕⲱⲥ. ⲗⲟⲓⲡⲟⲛ ⲁϥϣⲉⲛⲁϥ ⲉⲛⲏⲉⲧⲉⲛⲟⲩϥ ⲉϥⲟⲩⲟϫ ⲟⲩⲟϩ ⲁϥϭⲱⲟⲩ ⲙ̅Ⲫϯ ⲛ̅ⲥⲏⲟⲩ ⲛⲓⲃⲉⲛ ⲉⲑⲃⲉ ⲡⲓⲟⲩϫⲁⲓ ⲉⲧⲁϥⲧⲁϩⲟϥ ϩⲓⲧⲉⲛ ⲛⲓϣⲗⲏⲗ ⲛ̅ⲧⲉ ⲛⲓⲁⲅⲓⲟⲥ.

32. ⲁⲙⲉⲗⲓ ⲛⲉ ⲟⲩⲟⲛ ⲫⲓⲗⲟⲥⲟⲫⲟⲥ ⲃ̅ ϧⲉⲛ ⲁⲑⲏⲛⲁⲥ ⲛⲉ ϩⲁⲛϩⲉⲗⲗⲏⲛⲟⲥ ⲅⲁⲣ ⲛⲉ ⲉⲧⲁⲩⲥⲱⲧⲉⲙ ⲉⲑⲃⲉ ⲛⲓⲧⲁⲗϭⲟ ⲉⲧϣⲟⲡ ⲉⲃⲟⲗϩⲓⲧⲉⲛ ⲛⲓⲁⲅⲓⲟⲥ ϧⲉⲛ ϯϫⲟⲙ ⲛ̅ⲧⲉ Ⲡ̅ⲭ̅ⲥ̅ Ⲓ̅ⲏ̅ⲥ̅ ⲛⲁⲩϯϣⲑⲟⲩⲓⲧ ϧⲁⲣⲱⲟⲩ ⲡⲉ ⲉⲩϫⲱ ⲙ̅ⲙⲟⲥ ⲉⲣⲱⲟⲩ ϫⲉ ⲥⲉϩⲓⲟⲩⲓ ⲛ̅ⲛⲓⲇⲉⲙⲱⲛ ⲉⲃⲟⲗϧⲉⲛ ⲛⲓⲣⲱⲙⲓ ⲁⲩϣⲁⲛϣⲗⲏⲗ ⲉϫⲱⲟⲩ ϧⲉⲛ ⲫⲣⲁⲛ ⲙ̅Ⲡ̅ⲭ̅ⲥ̅. ⲙⲏ ⲛⲁⲓ ⲛⲉ ⲛⲓⲛⲟⲩϯ ⲛ̅ⲧⲉ ⲛⲓⲁⲑⲏⲛⲟⲥ. ⲁⲩⲧⲱⲟⲩⲛⲟⲩ ⲇⲉ ⲛ̅ϫⲉ ⲛⲓϣⲁⲙϣⲉ ⲓⲇⲱⲗⲟⲛ ⲉⲧⲉⲙⲙⲁⲩ ϧⲉⲛ ⲟⲩⲡⲛⲁⲟⲣⲅⲓⲁ ⲛ̅ⲭⲣⲟϥ ⲉⲩⲟⲩⲱϣ ⲉⲉⲣⲡⲓⲣⲁⲍⲓⲛ ⲛ̅ⲛⲏⲉ̅ⲑ̅ⲩ̅ ⲁⲩⲱⲗⲕ ⲛ̅ⲛⲟⲩϫⲓϫ ⲉⲣⲱⲟⲩ ⲟⲩⲟϩ ⲁⲩⲙⲟⲣⲟⲩ ⲛ̅ⲥⲁⲛⲧⲱⲓⲥ ⲙ̅ⲫⲣⲏϯ ⲛ̅ϩⲁⲛⲭⲁϭⲉⲩ ⲛ̅ϫⲉ ⲗⲁⲫⲟⲥ ⲟⲩⲟϩ ⲁⲩⲙⲁϣⲑⲁⲙ ⲛ̅ⲛⲟⲩⲃⲁⲗ ⲙ̅ⲫⲣⲏϯ ⲛ̅ϩⲁⲛⲃⲉⲗⲗⲉⲩ ⲉⲩϫⲱ ⲙ̅ⲙⲟⲥ ⲙ̅ⲡⲁⲓⲣⲏϯ ϫⲉ ⲓⲥϫⲉ ϩⲁⲛⲡⲣⲟⲫⲏⲧⲏⲥ ⲛⲉ ⲟⲩⲟϩ ⲥⲉϩⲓⲟⲩⲓ ⲛ̅ⲛⲓⲇⲉⲙⲱⲛ ⲉⲃⲟⲗ ⲥⲉⲛⲁⲉⲙⲓ ⲉⲡⲉⲛϩⲱⲃ. ⲁⲩϭⲓ ⲇⲉ ⲛ̅ⲕⲉⲟⲩⲁⲓ ⲛⲉⲙⲱⲟⲩ ϩⲱⲥ ⲉϥϭⲓⲙⲱⲓⲧ ϧⲁϫⲱⲟⲩ ϩⲓ ⲫⲙⲱⲓⲧ ⲁⲩⲕⲱⲗϩ ⲉⲡⲡⲓⲣⲟ.

33. ⲡⲓⲁⲅⲓⲟⲥ ⲇⲉ Ⲇⲟⲙⲉⲧⲓⲟⲥ ⲁϥⲉⲣⲟⲩⲱ ⲛⲱⲟⲩ ⲉϥϫⲱ ⲙ̅ⲙⲟⲥ ϫⲉ ⲉⲣⲉⲧⲉⲛⲟⲩⲉϣ ⲟⲩ ⲙ̅ⲡⲁⲓⲙⲁ ⲟⲩⲟϩ ⲡⲉϫⲱⲟⲩ ⲛⲁϥ ϫⲉ ⲉⲧⲁⲛⲓϣⲁⲣⲱⲧⲉⲛ ⲛⲓⲁⲅⲓⲟⲥ ⲛ̅ⲧⲉ Ⲫϯ ⲉϯϩⲟ ⲉⲣⲱⲧⲉⲛ ϩⲓⲛⲁ ⲛ̅ⲧⲉ ⲡⲉⲧⲉⲛⲛⲁⲓⲧⲁϩⲟⲛ ⲛ̅ⲧⲉⲧⲉⲛϣⲗⲏⲗ ⲉϫⲱⲛ ⲛ̅ⲧⲉ ⲡⲓⲟⲩϫⲁⲓ ⲧⲁϩⲟⲛ ϫⲉ ⲟⲩⲏⲓ ⲁⲛⲟⲛ ϩⲁⲛⲭⲁϭⲟ ⲛ̅ⲕⲉⲗⲁⲫⲟⲥ ⲟⲩⲟϩ ⲙ̅ⲃⲉⲗⲗⲉⲩ ⲓⲥ ϩⲏⲡⲡⲉ ⲭⲛⲁⲩ ⲉⲡⲁⲓⲣⲱⲙⲓ ϫⲉ ⲛ̅ⲑⲟϥ ⲁϥϭⲓⲙⲱⲓⲧ ⲛⲁⲛ ⲁϥⲉⲛⲧⲉⲛ ⲉⲡⲁⲓⲙⲁ. ⲡⲉϫⲉ ⲡⲓⲁⲅⲓⲟⲥ Ⲇⲟⲙⲉⲧⲓⲟⲥ ⲛⲱⲟⲩ ϧⲉⲛ ⲟⲩⲙⲉⲧⲁⲧⲡⲗⲟⲩⲥ ϫⲉ Ⲡ̅ⲟ̅ⲥ̅ Ⲓ̅ⲏ̅ⲥ̅ Ⲡ̅ⲭ̅ⲥ̅ ⲉϥⲉⲧⲁⲗϭⲉ ⲑⲏⲛⲟⲩ ⲟⲩⲟϩ ⲉⲥⲉϣⲱⲡⲓ ⲛⲱⲧⲉⲛ ⲙ̅ⲫⲣⲏϯ ⲉⲧⲁⲣⲉⲧⲉⲛⲉⲣⲉⲧⲓⲛ. Ⲛ̅ϯⲟⲩⲛⲟⲩ ⲇⲉ ⲁⲩⲉⲣⲕⲉⲗⲁⲫⲟⲥ ⲟⲩⲟϩ ⲁⲩⲉⲣⲃⲉⲗⲗⲉⲩ ⲛⲟⲩϫⲓϫ ⲱⲗⲕ ⲉⲣⲱⲟⲩ ⲉⲁⲩϣⲱⲡ ⲛ̅ⲭⲁϭⲟⲥⲁⲧⲟⲧⲟⲩ ⲇⲉ ⲁⲩⲱϣ ⲉⲃⲟⲗϧⲉⲛ ⲟⲩⲛⲓϣϯ ⲛ̅ⲥⲙⲏ ⲉⲩϫⲱ ⲙ̅ⲙⲟⲥ ⲫⲣⲱⲙⲓ ⲙ̅Ⲫϯ ⲛⲁⲓ ⲛⲁⲛ ϫⲉ ⲉⲧⲁⲛⲓ ⲉⲡⲁⲓⲙⲁⲉⲉⲣⲡⲓⲣⲁⲍⲓⲛ ⲙ̅ⲙⲱⲧⲉⲛ.

34. ⲟⲩⲟϩ ⲥⲁⲧⲟⲧⲟⲩ ⲁⲩϭⲓⲧⲟⲩ ϩⲓϫⲉⲛ ϩⲁⲧⲉⲛ ⲛⲉⲛϭⲁⲗⲁⲩϫ ⲛ̀ⲛⲏⲉ̅ⲑ̅ⲩ̅ ϧⲉⲛ ⲟⲩⲛⲓϣϯ ⲛ̀ⲛⲁϩϯ ⲉⲩϫⲱ ⲙ̀ⲙⲟⲥ ϫⲉ ⲧⲉⲛϯϩⲟ ⲉⲣⲱⲧⲉⲛ ⲛⲁⲓ ⲛⲁⲛ ⲁⲣⲓⲃⲟⲏⲑⲓⲛ ⲉⲣⲟⲛ ⲟⲩⲟϩ ⲧⲉⲛⲛⲁϣⲱⲡⲓ ⲛ̀ⲭⲣⲓⲥⲧⲓⲁⲛⲟⲥ ⲓⲥϫⲉⲛ ⲫⲟⲟⲩ ⲉⲃⲟⲗ ⲛ̀ⲧⲉⲛⲉⲣⲃⲱⲕ ⲙ̀ⲡ̅ⲭ̅ⲥ̅. ⲟⲩⲟϩ ⲡⲉϫⲉ ⲡⲓⲉ̅ⲑ̅ⲩ̅ Ⲙⲁⲝⲓⲙⲟⲥ ⲛⲱⲟⲩ ϫⲉ ⲁⲛ ⲧⲉⲧⲉⲛⲛⲁϩϯ ⲧⲁⲫⲙⲏ ϫⲉ Ⲓ̅ⲏ̅ⲥ̅ ⲡⲉ ⲡϣⲏⲣⲓ ⲙ̀Ⲫ̅ϯ. ⲛ̀ⲑⲱⲟⲩ ⲇⲉ ⲡⲉϫⲱⲟⲩ ϫⲉ ⲥⲉ ⲧⲉⲛⲛⲁϩϯ ϧⲉⲛ ⲡⲉⲛϩⲏⲧ ⲧⲏⲣϥ ⲛⲉⲛϭⲓⲥⲉⲩ ⲉ̅ⲑ̅ⲩ̅ ϫⲉ Ⲓ̅ⲏ̅ⲥ̅ ⲡⲉ ⲡϣⲏⲣⲓ ⲙ̀Ⲫ̅ϯ ⲟⲩⲟϩ ⲙ̀ⲙⲟⲛ ⲕⲉⲟⲩⲁⲓ ⲉⲃⲏⲗ ⲉⲣⲟϥ. ⲉⲧⲁⲩⲥⲱⲧⲉⲙ ⲇⲉ ⲉⲛⲁⲓⲥⲁϫⲓ ⲛ̀ϫⲉ ⲛⲓⲉⲃⲓⲁⲓⲕ ⲛ̀ⲧⲉ Ⲡ̅ⲭ̅ⲥ̅ ⲛ̀ⲧⲟⲧⲟⲩ ⲛ̀ⲛⲏⲉⲧⲉ ⲙ̀ⲙⲁⲩ ⲁⲩϣⲗⲏⲗ ⲉϫⲉⲛ ⲟⲩⲕⲟⲩϫⲓ ⲛ̀ⲛⲉϩ ⲁⲩⲑⲏⲓϥ ⲛⲱⲟⲩ ⲉⲩϫⲱ ⲙ̀ⲙⲟⲥ ϫⲉ ⲙⲁϣⲉⲛⲱⲧⲉⲛ ⲉⲡⲧⲟⲡⲟⲥ ⲙ̀ⲡⲓⲁⲅⲓⲟⲥ Ⲗⲉⲟⲛⲧⲓⲟⲥ ⲟⲩⲟϩ ϫⲱⲕⲉⲙ ϧⲉⲛ ⲧⲉϥⲛⲓϣϯ ⲛ̀ϣⲱϯ ⲟⲩⲟϩ ⲛ̀ⲧⲉⲧⲉⲛⲑⲁϩⲥ ⲑⲏⲛⲟⲩ ϧⲉⲛ ⲡⲁⲓⲕⲟⲩϫⲓ ⲛ̀ⲛⲉϩ ⲟⲩⲟϩ ⲛ̀ⲧⲉⲧⲉⲛⲛⲁϩϯ ϫⲉ ⲡⲓⲟⲩϫⲁⲓ ⲛⲁⲧⲁϩⲉ ⲑⲏⲛⲟⲩ.

35. ⲟⲩⲟϩ ⲁⲩⲓⲣⲓ ⲕⲁⲧⲁ ⲫⲣⲏϯ ⲉⲧⲁ ⲛⲓⲁⲅⲓⲟⲥ ϫⲟⲥ ⲛⲱⲟⲩ ⲟⲩⲟϩ ⲁⲩⲟⲩϫⲁⲓ ϧⲉⲛ ϯϫⲟⲙ ⲛ̀ⲧⲉ Ⲡ̅ⲭ̅ⲥ̅. ⲥⲁⲧⲟⲧⲟⲩ ⲇⲉ ⲁⲩϭⲓⲱⲙⲥ ⲉⲫⲣⲁⲛ ⲙ̀ⲫⲓⲱⲧ ⲛⲉⲙ ⲡϣⲏⲣⲓ ⲛⲉⲙ ⲡⲓⲡ̅ⲛ̅ⲁ̅ ⲉ̅ⲑ̅ⲩ̅ ⲟⲩⲟϩ ⲁⲩϣⲱⲡⲓ ⲛ̀ⲭⲣⲓⲥⲧⲓⲁⲛⲟⲥ. ϧⲉⲛ ⲡⲓⲙⲁ ⲉⲧⲉⲙⲙⲁⲩ ⲟⲩⲟϩ ⲁⲩϭⲓⲱϣ ⲛ̀ⲧϣⲫⲏⲣⲓ ⲉⲧⲁⲥϣⲱⲡⲓ ⲙ̀ⲙⲱⲟⲩ ϧⲉⲛ Ⲁⲑⲏⲛⲁⲥ ⲑⲃⲁⲕⲓ ⲛ̀ⲛⲓⲁⲑⲛⲛⲉⲟⲥ ⲓⲥϫⲉⲛ ⲡⲓⲉϩⲟⲟⲩ ⲇⲉ ⲉⲧⲉⲙⲙⲁⲩ ⲁⲟⲩⲙⲏϣ ϣⲱⲡⲓ ⲛ̀ⲭⲣⲓⲥⲧⲓⲁⲛⲟⲥ ⲉⲃⲟⲗ ⲛ̀ϧⲏⲧⲟⲩ ⲉⲩⲧⲱⲟⲩ ⲙ̀Ⲫ̅ϯ ⲡⲓⲗⲟⲅⲟⲥ ⲉⲧⲁϥϭⲓⲥⲁⲣⲝ. ⲉϣⲱⲡ ⲅⲁⲣ ⲁⲛϣⲁⲛⲟⲩⲱϣ ⲉϫⲱ ⲙ̀ⲡⲁϣⲁⲓ ⲛ̀ⲛⲓϩⲙⲟⲧ ⲛ̀ⲧⲁⲗϭⲟ ⲉⲧⲁ Ⲫϯ ⲉⲣⲉⲛⲉⲣⲅⲓⲛ ⲙ̀ⲙⲱⲟⲩ ϧⲉⲛ ⲛⲉⲛϫⲓϫ ⲛ̀ⲛⲓⲁⲅⲓⲟⲥ ⲡⲓⲥⲏⲟⲩ ⲛⲁⲙⲟⲩⲛⲕ ⲉⲣⲟⲓ ⲉⲓⲥⲁϫⲓ.

36. Ⲟⲩ ⲡⲣⲁⲅⲙⲁⲧⲉⲩⲥ ⲅⲁⲣ ⲛ̀ⲧⲉ ϯⲃⲁⲕⲓ Ⲁⲛⲧⲟⲭⲓⲁ ⲉϥϩⲏⲗ ϣⲁ ⲛⲁⲓⲙⲁⲕⲁⲣⲓⲟⲥ ⲕⲁⲧⲁ ⲕⲟⲩϫⲓ ⲉϥϭⲓⲥⲙⲟⲩ ⲉⲃⲟⲗϩⲓⲧⲟⲧⲟⲩ ⲉϥⲱⲗⲓ ⲙ̀ⲡⲟⲩϩⲱⲃ ⲛ̀ϫⲓϫ ⲛ̀ⲧⲟⲧⲟⲩ: ⲛⲁⲩⲉⲣϩⲱⲃ ⲅⲁⲣ ⲡⲉ ⲉⲛⲓⲥⲭⲟⲗⲁⲕⲓ ⲧⲉ ⲉⲃⲟⲗ ⲟⲩⲛ ϩⲓⲧⲉⲛ ⲡⲉϥⲛⲁϩϯ ⲉϧⲟⲩⲛ ⲉⲛⲁⲓⲁⲅⲓⲟⲥ ⲉϥⲥϩⲉ ⲡⲟⲩⲣⲁⲛ ⲉⲛⲓⲥⲭⲟⲗⲁⲕⲓ ⲁϥⲁⲓⲧⲟⲩ ⲛ̀Ⲥ̅ⲧ̅ⲥ̅ ϧⲉⲛ ⲑⲙⲏⲧ ⲙ̀ⲡⲓⲗⲟⲅⲟ ⲛ̀ⲧⲉ ⲡⲉϥϫⲟⲓ ϧⲉⲛ ⲡⲓϣϭⲏⲣ ⲛ̀ⲉⲛ ⲫⲓⲟⲙ. ⲁⲥϣⲱⲡⲓ ⲇⲉ ⲉⲣⲉ ⲡⲓϫⲟⲓ ⲭⲏ ϧⲉⲛ Ⲕⲱⲥⲧⲁⲛⲧⲓⲛⲟⲡⲟⲗⲓⲥ ⲛⲉⲙ ⲡⲉϥⲡⲣⲁⲅⲙⲁⲧⲓⲁ ⲉⲡϫⲓⲛⲧⲏⲥ ⲉⲃⲟⲗ ⲙ̀ⲙⲁⲩ ⲉⲡⲓⲇⲏ ⲅⲁⲣ ⲉⲣⲉ ⲡⲓⲗⲩⲙⲏⲛ ⲛ̀ⲧⲉ ϯⲃⲁⲕⲓ ⲉϥⲭⲏ ϧⲉⲛ ⲧⲉⲥⲙⲏϯ ⲥⲁϧⲟⲩⲛ ⲛ̀ⲛⲓⲥⲟⲃⲧ.

37. ⲧⲟⲧⲉ ⲟⲩⲛ ⲉⲧⲁϥⲉⲙⲓ ⲛ̀ϫⲉ ⲡⲟⲩⲣⲟ ϫⲉ ⲥⲉⲛⲁϣϯ ⲛ̀ϫⲉ ⲛⲓϩⲱⲓⲙⲓ ⲁϥⲟⲩⲁϩⲥⲁϩⲛⲓ ⲉⲑⲣⲟⲩⲭⲱ ⲛ̀ⲛⲓⲉϫⲏⲟⲩ ⲥϧⲟⲩⲛ ⲉⲑⲃⲉ ⲡⲉⲛϣⲟⲧ

APPENDIX 2

ⲛ̄ⲛⲓϣⲱⲙⲓ ⲛ̀ⲧⲉ ⲫⲓⲟⲙ ϩⲁⲛϩⲁⲗⲩⲥⲓⲥ ⲅⲁⲣ ⲙ̀ⲃⲉⲛⲓⲡⲓ ⲉⲧϭⲟⲗⲕ ⲉⲡⲓⲙⲁⲛⲓ ⲉϧⲟⲩⲛ ⲗⲟⲓⲡⲟⲛ ⲁⲩⲥⲉⲕ ⲛⲓϩⲁⲗⲩⲥⲓⲥ ⲁⲩⲭⲁ ⲛⲓⲉϫⲏⲟⲩ ⲉϧⲟⲩⲛ ⲉⲑⲣⲟⲩⲙⲟⲛⲓ ϧⲉⲛ ⲡⲓⲗⲩⲙⲏⲛ. ⲉⲧⲓ ⲟⲩⲛ ⲉϥⲟϩⲓ ⲉⲣⲁⲧϥ ⲛ̀ϫⲉ ⲡⲓⲙⲁⲅⲓⲥⲧⲣⲓⲁⲛⲟⲥ ⲛ̀ⲧⲉ ⲡⲟⲩⲣⲟ ⲛⲉⲙ ⲛⲓⲙⲁⲧⲟⲓ ⲛⲁϥϭⲓϩⲣⲁϥ ⲡⲉ ⲛⲉⲙ ⲛⲓⲉϫⲏⲟⲩ ⲉⲑⲙⲟⲛⲓ ⲉϧⲟⲩⲛ ⲉⲧⲁϥϯϩⲑⲏϥ ⲟⲩⲛ ⲁϥⲛⲁⲩ ⲉⲡⲓⲗⲁⲟⲩⲟ ⲛ̀ⲧⲉ ⲡⲓϫⲟⲓ ⲉⲧⲁⲛⲉⲣϣⲟⲣⲡ ⲙ̀ϥⲓⲣⲓ ⲉⲣⲟϥ ⲉϥⲫⲟⲣϣ ⲉⲃⲟⲗ ϩⲓϫⲉⲛ ⲡⲕⲁϩⲓ ⲉⲣⲉ ⲛⲓⲛⲉϥ ⲑⲱⲣⲡ ⲉⲣⲟϥ ⲕⲁⲧⲁ ⲧⲟⲩⲥⲩⲛⲏⲑⲓⲁ ⲁϥⲛⲁⲩ ⲉϥⲣⲁⲛ ⲙ̀ⲡⲓⲁⲅⲓⲟⲥ Ⲙⲁⲝⲓⲙⲟⲥ ⲛⲉⲙ Ⲇⲟⲙⲉⲧⲓⲟⲥ ⲉⲩⲥϧⲏⲟⲩⲧ ⲉⲛⲓⲥⲭⲟⲗⲁⲕⲓ ⲉⲧⲧⲟⲓ ⲉⲡⲓⲗⲁⲟⲩⲟ. ⲉⲧⲁϥⲱϣ ⲇⲉ ⲛ̄ⲛⲓⲣⲁⲛ ⲉϥⲉⲣⲕⲉⲗⲉⲩⲓⲛ ⲉⲑⲣⲟⲩⲙⲟⲩϯ ⲛⲁϥ ⲉⲛⲓⲛⲉϥ ⲟⲩⲟϩ ⲡⲉϫⲁϥ ⲛⲱⲟⲩ ϫⲉ ⲟⲩ ⲛⲉ ⲛⲁⲓⲣⲁⲛ ⲉⲧⲥϧⲏⲟⲩⲧ ϩⲓϫⲉⲛ ⲡⲉⲧⲉⲛⲗⲁⲟⲩⲟ. ⲡⲉϫⲱⲟⲩ ⲛⲁϥ ϫⲉ ϩⲁⲛⲣⲱⲙⲓ ⲛⲉ ⲉⲩⲟⲩⲁⲃ ⲉⲧϣⲟⲡ ϧⲉⲛ ⲧⲉⲛⲭⲱⲣⲁ. ⲡⲉϫⲉ ⲡⲓⲙⲁⲅⲓⲥⲧⲣⲓⲁⲛⲟⲥ ⲛⲱⲟⲩ ϥⲱⲟⲩ ⲡⲉ ⲡⲁⲓϫⲟⲓ ⲡⲉϫⲱⲟⲩ ⲛⲁϥ ϫⲉ ⲙ̀ⲙⲟⲛ ⲁⲗⲗⲁ ⲉⲧⲁⲛϭⲉ ⲛⲟⲩⲣⲁⲛ ⲉⲉⲛ ⲗⲁⲟⲩⲟ ⲉⲑⲃⲉ ⲛⲟⲩϣⲗⲏⲗ ⲉⲑⲩ ϩⲓⲛⲁ ⲛ̀ⲧⲉⲛϫⲓⲙⲓ ⲛ̀ⲟⲩⲃⲟⲏⲑⲓⲁ ⲛⲉⲙ ⲡⲉⲛϫⲟⲓ ϧⲉⲉⲛ ⲡⲉⲛϫⲓⲛⲉⲣϩⲱⲧ. ⲡⲉϫⲁϥ ⲛⲱⲟⲩ ϫⲉ ⲧⲉⲧⲉⲛⲥⲱⲟⲩⲛ ⲙ̀ⲡⲟⲩⲙⲁ ⲛ̀ⲕⲁⲗⲱⲥ ϫⲉ ⲉⲩϣⲟⲡ ⲑⲱⲛ. ⲡⲉϫⲱⲟⲩ ⲛⲁϥ ϫⲉ ⲥⲉ ⲡⲉⲛⲟ̅ⲥ̅ ⲉⲩϣⲟⲡ ϧⲉⲛ ϯⲤⲩⲣⲓⲁ.

38. Ⲧⲟⲧⲉ ⲁⲡⲓⲙⲁⲅⲓⲥⲧⲣⲓⲁⲛⲟⲥ ⲁϥⲟⲩⲁϩⲥⲁϩⲛⲓ ⲉⲥⲱⲛϩ ⲛ̀ⲛⲓⲛⲉϥ ⲛ̀ⲥⲉⲃⲓⲧⲟⲩ ϣⲁ ⲡⲟⲩⲣⲟ ⲛ̀ⲑⲟϥ ⲇⲉ ⲡⲓⲙⲁⲅⲓⲥⲧⲣⲓⲁⲛⲟⲥ ⲁϥⲉⲣϣⲟⲣⲡ ⲉⲣⲱⲟⲩ ⲁϥⲧⲁⲙⲉ ⲡⲟⲩⲣⲟ ⲟⲩⲟϩ ⲁϥⲭⲟⲥ ⲉⲑⲣⲟⲩⲉⲛⲟⲩ ⲙ̀ⲡⲉϥⲙⲑⲟ ⲫⲣⲁⲛ ⲇⲉ ⲙ̀ⲡⲟⲩⲣⲟ ⲉⲧⲉⲙⲙⲁⲩ ⲡⲉ Ⲑⲉⲟⲇⲱⲥⲓⲟⲥ ⲉⲡⲓⲗⲏ ⲅⲁⲣ Ⲑⲉⲟⲇⲱⲥⲓⲟⲥ ⲛⲉ ⲟⲩⲅⲉⲛⲟⲥ ⲛ̀ⲣⲉⲙⲛ̀ⲭⲏⲙⲓ ⲡⲉ ⲫⲁⲓ ⲇⲉ ⲛⲁϥⲟⲓ ⲛ̀ⲥⲧⲣⲁⲧⲏⲗⲁⲧⲏⲥ ⲛ̀ϣⲟⲣⲡ ⲡⲉ ⲉⲛⲓϣⲑⲱⲣ ⲛ̀ⲧⲉ Ⲟⲩⲁⲗⲉⲛⲧⲓⲛⲟⲥ ⲡⲟⲩⲣⲟ ⲁⲓⲥⲁϫⲓ ⲉϥⲓⲱⲧ ⲛ̀ⲛⲁⲓⲁⲅⲓⲟⲥ. ⲉⲧⲁϥⲛⲁⲩ ⲅⲁⲣ ⲉⲐⲉⲟⲇⲱⲥⲓⲟⲥ ϫⲉ ⲟⲩⲣⲱⲙⲓ ⲛ̀ϫⲱⲣⲓ ⲡⲉ ⲁϥⲑⲁϣϥ ⲛ̀ⲁⲣⲭⲱⲛ ⲉϫⲉⲛ ⲛⲓⲙⲁⲛϭⲱⲣⲉⲙ ⲧⲏⲣⲟⲩ ⲛ̀ⲧⲉ ⲛⲓϩⲑⲱⲣ ⲉⲧϧⲉⲛ ⲡⲓⲙⲁϩⲓ ⲛ̀ⲧⲉ ⲧⲉϥⲙⲉⲧⲟⲩⲣⲟ.

39. ⲗⲟⲓⲡⲟⲛ ⲁⲛⲁⲓⲁⲅⲓⲟⲥ ⲛⲉ ⲁⲩⲉⲣⲡⲟⲧⲁⲍⲉⲥⲑⲉ ⲙ̀ⲡⲁⲓⲕⲟⲥⲙⲟⲥ ⲉⲧⲓ ⲉϥⲟⲛϧ ⲛ̀ϫⲉ Ⲟⲩⲁⲗⲉⲛⲧⲓⲛⲟⲥ ⲡⲟⲩⲓⲱⲧ ⲛ̀ⲟⲩⲣⲟⲙⲡⲓ ⲛ̀ⲉϩⲟⲟⲩ ⲉⲧⲁϥⲙⲧⲟⲛ ⲇⲉ ⲙ̀ⲙⲟϥ ⲛ̀ϫⲉ Ⲟⲩⲁⲗⲉⲛⲧⲓⲛⲟⲥ ⲡⲟⲩⲣⲟ ⲕⲁⲧⲁ ⲛⲓϩⲁⲡ ⲙ̀ⲙⲏⲓ ⲛ̀ⲁⲧϣϧⲉⲧϧⲱⲧⲟⲩ ⲛ̀ⲧⲉ Ⲫϯ ⲛⲉⲙ ⲡϯⲙⲁϯ ⲛ̀ⲟⲩⲛⲕⲗⲏⲧⲟⲥ ⲧⲏⲣⲥ ⲁⲩⲱϣ ⲛ̀Ⲑⲉⲟⲇⲱⲥⲓⲟⲥ ⲡⲓⲥⲧⲣⲁⲧⲓⲗⲁⲧⲏⲥ ⲛ̀ⲟⲩⲣⲟ ⲛ̀ⲧϣⲉⲃⲓⲱ ⲛ̀Ⲟⲩⲁⲗⲉⲛⲧⲓⲛⲟⲥ ϥⲓⲱⲧ ⲛ̀ⲛⲓⲙⲕⲁⲣⲁⲓⲟⲥ Ⲙⲁⲝⲓⲙⲟⲥ ⲛⲉⲙ Ⲇⲟⲙⲉⲧⲓⲟⲥ ⲕⲁⲧⲁ ⲫⲣⲏϯ ⲙⲁⲕⲁⲣⲓⲟⲥ Ⲙⲁⲝⲓⲙⲟⲥ ⲉⲧⲥϧⲏⲟⲩⲧ ϧⲉⲛ ⲛⲓⲓⲥⲧⲟⲣⲓⲁ ⲛ̀ⲧⲉ ϯⲉⲕⲕⲗⲏⲥⲓⲁ. ⲉⲧⲁϥⲛⲁⲩ ⲇⲉ ⲉⲛⲓⲛⲉϥ ⲉⲩⲥⲟⲛϩ ⲛ̀ϫⲉ ⲡⲟⲩⲣⲟ

ⲛ̀ⲉⲩⲥⲉⲃⲏⲥ Ⲑⲉⲟⲇⲱⲥⲓⲟⲥ ⲁϥⲑⲣⲟⲩⲃⲟⲗⲟⲩ ⲉⲃⲟⲗ ⲉϥϫⲱ ⲙ̀ⲙⲟⲥ ϫⲉ
ⲛⲁϣⲫⲏⲣⲓ ⲙ̀ⲙⲉⲗⲟⲥ ⲛⲉⲙ ⲙ̀ⲡⲉⲣⲭⲁⲩ ⲉⲩⲥⲟⲛϩ ϫⲉ ϩⲓⲛⲁ ⲙⲏⲡⲟⲧⲉ ⲛ̀ⲧⲉ
Ⲡ̄ⲭ̄ⲥ̄ ϫⲱⲛⲧ ⲉⲣⲟⲓ. ⲟⲩⲟϩ ⲡⲉϫⲉ ⲡⲓϣⲁⲙϣⲉⲛⲟⲩϯ ⲡⲟⲩⲣⲟ ⲛⲱⲟⲩ
ϧⲉⲛ ⲟⲩⲙⲉⲧⲣⲉⲙⲣⲁⲩϣ ϫⲉ ⲛⲓⲙ ⲛⲉ ⲛⲓⲣⲱⲙⲓ ⲛ̀ⲧⲉ Ⲫ̄ϯ ⲛ̀ⲧⲉⲛⲥⲱⲟⲩⲛ
ⲙ̀ⲙⲱⲟⲩ ⲡⲉϫⲱⲟⲩ ϫⲉ ⲡⲉⲛⲟ̄ⲥ̄ Ⲙⲁⲝⲓⲙⲟⲥ ⲡⲉ ⲡⲓⲟⲩⲁⲓ ⲟⲩⲟϩ Ⲇⲟⲙⲉⲧⲓⲟⲥ
ⲡⲉ ⲡⲓⲕⲉⲟⲩⲁⲓ. ⲡⲁⲗⲓⲛ ⲇⲉ ⲟⲛ ⲡⲉϫⲁϥ ⲛⲱⲟⲩ ϫⲉ ϩⲁ ⲛ̀ⲁϣ ⲛ̀ⲣⲏϯ ⲛⲉ
ϧⲉⲛ ⲡⲟⲩⲥⲙⲟⲧ. ⲁⲩⲉⲣⲟⲩⲱ ⲡⲉϫⲱⲟⲩ ⲛⲁϥ ϫⲉ ⲡⲓⲟⲩⲁⲓ ⲙⲉⲛ ⲟⲩⲣⲱⲙⲓ
ⲉϥⲟⲩⲏⲛ ⲡⲉ ⲉⲁϥⲉⲣⲙⲟⲣⲧ ⲡⲓⲭⲉⲧ ⲇⲉ ⲟⲩⲣⲱⲙⲓ ⲉϥϣⲏⲟⲩ ⲛ̀ⲟⲩⲕⲟⲩϫⲓ
ⲉⲁϥϩⲓⲁⲣⲭⲏ ⲙ̀ⲙⲟⲣⲧ. ⲧⲟⲧⲉ ⲁϥⲉⲣⲕⲉⲗⲉⲩⲓⲛ ⲛ̀ϫⲉ ⲡⲟⲩⲣⲟ ⲉⲑⲣⲟⲩϯ ⲛ̄ϯ
ⲛ̀ⲗⲟⲩⲕⲟⲩϫⲓ ⲙ̀ⲫⲟⲩⲁⲓ ⲛ̀ⲛⲓⲛⲉϥ ⲛ̀ⲥⲉⲭⲁⲩ ⲉⲃⲟⲗϧⲉⲛ ⲟⲩϩⲓⲣⲏⲛⲏ.

40. Ⲙⲉⲛⲉⲛⲥⲁ ⲛⲁⲓ ⲁⲡⲟⲩⲣⲟ ⲙⲟⲩϯ ⲉⲟⲩⲥⲓⲟⲩⲣ ⲛ̀ⲧⲉ ⲡⲓⲡⲁⲗⲁⲧⲓⲟⲛ
ⲉⲡⲉϥⲣⲁⲛ ⲡⲉ Ⲙⲁⲣⲕⲉⲗⲗⲟⲥ ⲉⲟⲩⲣⲱⲙⲓ ⲡⲉ ⲉϥϫⲟⲣ ϧⲉⲛ ⲛⲉϥϩⲃⲛⲟⲩⲓ
ⲙ̀ⲫⲣⲏϯ ⲛ̀ⲟⲩⲙⲟⲩⲓ ⲁϥϯ ⲛⲁϥ ⲛ̀ⲟⲩϩⲑⲟ ⲉϥϫⲟⲣ ϧⲉⲛ ⲧⲉϥϫⲟⲙ
ⲟⲩⲟϩ ⲁϥⲟⲩⲟⲣⲡϥ ⲉϯⲤⲩⲣⲓⲁ ϩⲓⲛⲁ ⲛ̀ⲧⲉϥⲉⲙⲓ ⲉⲡⲧⲁϫⲣⲟ ⲙ̀ⲡⲓϩⲱⲃ
ⲙ̀ⲡⲁⲧⲉϥⲧⲁⲙⲉ ϯⲟⲩⲣⲱ. ⲟⲩⲟϩ ⲙⲉⲛⲉⲛⲥⲁ ϩⲁⲛⲕⲟⲩϫⲓ ⲇⲉ ⲛ̀ⲉϩⲟⲟⲩ
ⲁϥⲕⲟⲧϥ ⲛ̀ϫⲉ ⲡⲓⲥⲓⲟⲩⲣ ϣⲁ ⲡⲟⲩⲣⲟ ⲉϥϫⲱ ⲙ̀ⲙⲟⲥ ϫⲉ ⲥⲉϣⲓⲛⲓ
ⲉⲣⲟⲕ ⲉⲙⲁϣⲱ ⲛ̀ϫⲉ ⲛⲉⲕϣⲏⲣⲓ ⲛⲉⲛⲥⲛⲏⲟⲩ ⲛ̀ϯⲟⲩⲣⲱ. ⲡⲟⲩⲣⲟ
ⲇⲉ Ⲑⲉⲟⲇⲱⲥⲓⲟⲥ ⲁϥⲣⲁϣⲓ ⲉⲙⲁϣⲱ ⲟⲩⲟϩ ⲁϥⲧⲁⲙⲉ ϯⲟⲩⲣⲱ ⲛⲉⲙ
ⲛⲏⲉⲧⲉⲛⲟⲩϥ ⲧⲏⲣⲟⲩ ⲟⲩⲟϩ ⲁϥϣⲱⲡⲓ ⲛ̀ϫⲉ ⲟⲩⲛⲓϣϯ ⲛ̀ⲣⲁϣⲓ ϧⲉⲛ
ⲡⲓⲡⲁⲗⲁⲧⲓⲟⲛ ⲧⲏⲣϥ ⲙ̀ⲡⲓⲉϩⲟⲟⲩ ⲉⲧⲉⲙⲙⲁⲩ.

41. ⲓⲧⲁ ⲙⲉⲛⲉⲛⲥⲁ ϩⲁⲛⲕⲟⲩϫⲓ ⲛ̀ⲉϩⲟⲟⲩ ⲁⲡⲟⲩⲣⲟ ⲟⲩⲱⲣⲡ ⲛ̀ⲧⲟⲩⲙⲁⲩ
ⲛⲉⲙ ⲧⲟⲩⲥⲱⲛⲓ ⲉϯⲤⲩⲣⲓⲁ ϫⲉ ⲛ̀ⲧⲟⲩⲛⲁⲩ ⲉⲣⲱⲟⲩ ⲟⲩⲟϩ ⲛ̀ⲧⲉ
ⲡⲟⲩϩⲏⲧ ⲑⲱⲧ. ⲟⲩⲟⲡ ⲁⲡⲓⲁⲅⲓⲟⲥ ϯⲛⲟⲙϯ ⲛ̀ⲧⲟⲩⲙⲁⲩ ⲛⲉⲙ ⲧⲟⲩⲥⲱⲛⲓ
ⲟⲩⲟϩ ⲛ̀ⲧⲉⲛⲫⲱⲟⲩ ϧⲉⲛ ⲟⲩϩⲓⲣⲏⲛⲏ. ⲓⲥϫⲉⲛ ⲡⲓⲉϩⲟⲟⲩ ⲉⲧⲉⲙⲙⲁⲩ
ⲁⲛⲓⲣⲉⲙⲕⲱⲥⲧⲁⲛⲧⲓⲛⲟⲩⲡⲟⲗⲓⲥ ⲉⲣⲡⲓⲙⲱⲓⲧ ϣⲁ ⲛⲓⲁⲅⲓⲟⲥ ⲙ̀ⲙⲁⲙⲟϣⲓ
ⲙ̀ⲡⲓⲉϩⲟⲟⲩ ⲛⲉⲙ ⲡⲓⲉϫⲱⲣϩ ⲉⲩⲓⲛⲓ ϣⲁⲣⲱⲟⲩ ⲛ̀ⲟⲩⲟⲛ ⲛⲓⲃⲉⲛ ⲉⲧϣⲱⲛⲓ
ⲛ̀ⲟⲩⲙⲏϣ ⲛ̀ⲣⲏϯ ⲛⲉⲙ ⲛⲏⲉⲧⲉ ⲛⲓⲡ̄ⲛ̄ⲁ̄ ⲛ̀ⲁⲕⲁⲑⲁⲣⲧⲟⲛ ⲛⲉⲙⲱⲟⲩ ⲟⲩⲟϩ
ⲁⲩϣⲁⲛϩⲟϩ ϣⲁ ⲛⲁⲓⲙⲁⲕⲁⲣⲓⲟⲥ ⲛ̀ⲧⲟⲩⲧⲱⲃϩ ⲉϫⲱⲟⲩ ϣⲁⲩⲧⲁⲗϭⲟ
ϩⲓⲧⲉⲛ ⲡⲓϩⲙⲟⲧ ⲛ̀ⲧⲉ Ⲫ̄ϯ ⲡⲉⲛⲥⲱ̄ⲣ̄.

42. Ⲙⲉⲛⲉⲛⲥⲁ ⲛⲁⲓ ⲁⲡⲟⲩⲣⲟ Ⲑⲉⲟⲇⲱⲥⲓⲟⲥ ϩⲱⲗ ϣⲁⲣⲱⲟⲩ ϣⲁⲧⲉϥϭⲓ
ⲙ̀ⲡⲟⲩⲥⲙⲟⲩ ⲛⲉⲙ ⲡⲟⲩⲥⲟϭⲛⲓ ⲟⲩⲟϩ ⲛ̀ⲧⲟⲩⲧⲥⲁⲃⲟϥ ⲉϩⲁⲛϩⲃⲛⲟⲩⲓ
ⲉⲛⲁⲛⲉⲩ ⲟⲩⲟϩ ⲉⲩⲉⲣⲛⲟϥⲣⲓ ⲛ̀ⲧⲉϥⲙⲉⲧⲟⲩⲣⲟ ⲛⲉⲙ ϯⲉⲕⲕⲗⲏⲥⲓⲁ

ⲛ̀ⲧⲉ Ⲫϯ ϧⲉⲛ ⲛⲁⲓ ⲇⲉ ⲁⲩⲧⲁϫⲣⲟⲥ ⲛ̀ⲕⲁⲗⲱⲥ ϧⲉⲛ ⲧⲁϫⲣⲟ ⲛⲓⲃⲉⲛ ⲉⲁⲣⲉϩ ⲫⲛⲁϩϯ ⲛ̀ⲛⲓⲕⲉⲁ ⲟⲩⲟϩ ⲉⲑⲣⲉϥⲭⲁ ⲛⲓϣⲏⲣⲓ ⲛ̀ⲧⲉ ϯⲉⲕⲕⲗⲏⲥⲓⲁ ⲉⲩⲧⲁⲓⲏⲟⲩⲧ ⲛ̀ⲧⲟⲧϥ ϧⲉⲛ ⲧⲓⲙⲏ ⲛⲓⲃⲉⲛ.

43. ⲗⲟⲓⲡⲟⲛ ⲉⲧⲁⲩⲟⲩⲱⲛϩ ⲉⲃⲟⲗ ⲛ̀ϫⲉ ⲛⲁⲓⲙⲁⲕⲁⲣⲓⲟⲥ ⲉⲩϯⲥⲱⲓⲧ ϧⲉⲛ ϯⲥⲩⲣⲓⲁ ⲧⲏⲣⲥ ⲛⲁϥϩⲏⲗ ϣⲁⲣⲱⲟⲩ ⲛ̀ϫⲉ ⲡⲓⲉⲩⲥⲉⲃⲏⲥ ⲛ̀ⲟⲩⲣⲟ Ⲑⲉⲟⲇⲱⲥⲓⲟⲥ ⲉϥⲥⲟϭⲛⲓ ⲉⲣⲱⲟⲩ ⲟⲩⲟϩ ⲉϥⲉⲣⲁⲡⲟⲗⲉⲩⲓⲛ ⲛ̀ⲧⲟⲩⲥⲃⲱ ⲛⲉⲙ ⲡⲟⲩⲥⲙⲟⲩ ϩⲱⲥ ⲉϥⲥⲱⲟⲩⲛ ϫⲉ ⲑⲱⲟⲩ ⲧⲉ ϯⲙⲉⲧⲟⲩⲣⲟ ϫⲉ ⲅⲁⲣ ⲁⲗⲏⲑⲱⲥ ⲁⲡⲉϥⲭⲓⲛϩⲓⲕⲟⲧ ϣⲱⲡⲓ ⲛⲁϥ ⲛ̀ϩⲏⲟⲩ ⲛⲉⲙ ⲟⲩⲥⲃⲱ ⲉⲥⲟⲓ ⲛ̀ⲛⲓϣϯ ⲟⲩⲟϩ ϩⲓⲛⲁ ⲛ̀ⲧⲁϫⲟⲥ ϧⲉⲛ ⲟⲩϣⲱⲧ ⲉⲃⲟⲗ ⲉⲧⲁϥϣⲁϣⲛⲓ ⲉⲧⲁⲓⲛⲓϣϯ ⲙ̀ⲙⲉⲧⲙⲁⲓⲛⲟⲩϯ ⲛⲉⲙ ⲧⲁⲓⲧⲓⲙⲏ ⲙ̀ⲡⲁⲓⲣⲏϯ ⲉϧⲟⲩⲛ ⲉⲛⲓⲉⲕⲕⲗⲏⲥⲓⲁ ⲛ̀ⲧⲉ Ⲫϯ ϩⲓⲧⲉⲛ ⲛⲓⲥⲃⲱⲟⲩⲓ ⲛ̀ⲱⲛϧ ⲛ̀ⲧⲉ ⲛⲁⲓⲙⲁⲕⲁⲣⲓⲟⲥ ⲟⲩⲙⲟⲛⲟⲛ ⲛ̀ⲑⲟϥ ⲙ̀ⲙⲁⲩⲁⲧϥ ⲁⲗⲗⲁ ⲛⲉⲙ ⲛⲉϥⲕⲉϣⲏⲣⲓ ⲟⲛ Ⲁⲣⲕⲁⲇⲓⲟⲥ ⲛⲉⲙ Ⲟⲛⲟⲣⲓⲟⲥ ⲉⲧⲁϥⲉⲛⲟⲩ ⲉⲡϣⲱⲓ ϩⲱⲟⲩ ϧⲉⲛ ⲧⲁⲓⲙⲉⲧⲉⲩⲥⲉⲃⲏⲥ ⲙ̀ⲡⲁⲓⲣⲏϯⲉⲃⲟⲗ ϩⲓⲧⲟⲧⲥ ⲛ̀ⲧⲥⲃⲱ ⲛⲉⲙ ⲡⲓⲥⲙⲟⲧ ⲉⲑⲛⲁⲛⲉϥ ⲛ̀ⲧⲉ ⲛⲁⲓⲙⲁⲕⲁⲣⲓⲟⲥ ⲡⲁⲓⲣⲏϯ ⲟⲛ ϯⲕⲉⲟⲩϫⲓ Ⲑⲉⲟⲇⲱⲥⲓⲟⲥ.

44. ⲙⲉⲛⲉⲛⲥⲁ ⲛⲁⲓ ⲇⲉ ⲁϥⲙⲧⲟⲛ ⲙ̀ⲙⲟϥ ⲛ̀ϫⲉ ⲡⲓⲁⲣⲭⲓⲉⲡⲓⲥⲕⲟⲡⲟⲥ ⲛ̀ⲧⲉ Ⲕⲱⲥⲧⲁⲛⲧⲓⲛⲟⲩⲡⲟⲗⲓⲥ ⲟⲩⲟϩ ⲡⲁⲛⲧⲱⲥ ⲉⲃⲟⲗϩⲓⲧⲉⲛ ⲧⲁⲓⲗⲱⲓϫⲓ ⲑⲁⲓ. Ⲉⲧⲁ Ⲫϯ ⲉⲛ ⲛⲁⲓⲁⲅⲓⲟⲥ ⲉⲱϩⲓϩⲏⲧ ⲙ̀ⲫⲣⲏϯ ⲛ̀Ⲓⲁⲕⲱⲃ ⲡⲓⲡⲁⲧⲣⲓⲁⲭⲏⲥ ⲉⲧⲁϥⲓ ⲉϧⲣⲏⲓ ⲉⲭⲏⲙⲓ ⲙ̀ⲡⲓⲥⲛⲟⲩ ⲛ̀ⲩⲗⲱⲓϫⲓ ⲙ̀ⲡⲓϩⲱⲛ ϣⲁⲧⲉϥⲉⲣⲅⲟⲗⲁⲟⲥ ⲉϥⲟϣ ⲛ̀ⲧⲉϥⲙⲁϩ ⲡⲣⲟ ⲙ̀ⲡⲕⲁϩⲓ ⲡⲁⲓⲣⲏϯ ϩⲱⲟⲩ ⲛⲁⲓⲁⲅⲓⲟⲥ Ⲙⲁⲝⲓⲙⲟⲥ ⲛⲉⲙ Ⲇⲟⲙⲉⲧⲓⲟⲥ ⲛⲁⲓϣⲏⲣⲓ ⲛ̀ⲟⲩⲣⲟ ⲛ̀ϯⲛⲁⲕⲏⲛ ⲁⲛ ⲉⲓⲙⲟⲩϯ ⲉⲣⲱⲟⲩ ϫⲉ ϣⲏⲣⲓ ⲛ̀ⲟⲩⲣⲟ ϣⲁⲧⲉ ⲟⲩⲟⲛ ⲛⲓⲃⲉⲛ ⲉⲙⲓ ⲉⲡⲟⲩⲁⲝⲓⲱⲙⲁ ⲛⲉⲙ ⲡⲟⲩⲃⲓⲟⲥ ⲛ̀ⲁⲅⲅⲉⲗⲓⲕⲟⲛ ⲛⲉⲙ ⲛⲟⲩⲡⲟⲗⲏⲧⲓⲁ ⲉⲡⲓⲇⲏ ⲁⲩⲙⲉⲛⲣⲉ Ⲡⲭ̅ⲥ̅ ⲉϩⲟⲧⲉ ⲡⲱⲟⲩ ⲧⲏⲣϥ ⲙ̀ⲡⲁⲓⲕⲟⲥⲙⲟⲥ ⲁⲩⲟⲩⲁϩⲟⲩ ⲛ̀ⲥⲱϥ ϧⲉⲛ ⲡⲟⲩϩⲏⲧ ⲧⲏⲣϥ.

45. ⲉⲑⲃⲉ ⲫⲁⲓ ⲛ̀ⲑⲟϥ ϩⲱϥ Ⲡⲭ̅ⲥ̅ Ⲓⲏ̅ⲥ̅ ⲁϥϯⲱⲟⲩ ⲛⲱⲟⲩ ⲁⲗⲏⲑⲱⲥ ϩⲱⲥⲧⲉ ⲉⲑⲣⲉϥⲉⲣⲟⲓⲕⲟⲛⲟⲙⲓⲛ ⲙ̀ⲙⲱⲟⲩ ⲉⲑⲣⲟⲩⲓ ⲉⲱϩⲓϩⲏⲧ ⲡⲓⲧⲱⲟⲩ ⲉⲑ̅ⲩ̅ ⲛ̀ⲧⲟⲩϫⲱⲕ ⲉⲃⲟⲗⲛ̀ϧⲏⲧϥ ⲟⲩⲟϩ ⲛ̀ⲥⲉⲕⲱⲧ ⲙ̀ⲙⲁⲩ ⲛ̀ⲟⲩⲉⲕⲕⲗⲏⲥⲓⲁ ϧⲉⲛ ⲡⲟⲩⲣⲁⲛ ⲁⲩⲧⲁϫⲣⲟ ⲛ̀ⲧⲉⲥⲥⲉⲛϯⲉϩⲣⲏⲓ ⲉϫⲉⲛ ϯⲡⲉⲧⲣⲁ ⲛ̀ⲁⲧⲕⲓⲙ Ⲡⲭ̅ⲥ̅ ⲉⲁⲥϣⲱⲡⲓ ⲛ̀ⲟⲩⲗⲩⲙⲏⲛ ⲛ̀ⲟⲩϫⲁⲓ ⲛ̀ⲟⲩⲟⲛ ⲛⲓⲃⲉⲛ ⲉⲑⲛⲁⲕⲟⲧⲟⲩ ϩⲁ Ⲫϯ ⲉⲑⲃⲉ ⲡⲭⲱ ⲉⲃⲟⲗ ⲛ̀ⲧⲉ ⲛⲟⲩⲛⲟⲃⲓ ⲁⲗⲏⲑⲱⲥ ⲅⲁⲣ ⲁϥⲟⲩⲛⲟϥ ⲛ̀ϫⲉ ⲡⲓⲡⲁⲣⲁⲇⲓⲥⲟⲥ ⲛ̀ⲧⲉ Ⲫϯ ⲡⲓⲥⲱϯ ⲉⲧⲁϥϣⲱⲡⲓ ⲛ̀ϯⲯⲩⲭⲏ ⲛ̀ⲛⲓⲣⲉϥⲉⲣⲛⲟⲃⲓ ϧⲉⲛ ⲡⲓⲙⲁ ⲉⲧⲉⲙⲙⲁⲩ ⲟⲩⲟϩ ⲟⲛ ϥⲛⲁⲕⲏⲛ ⲁⲛ ⲉϥϣⲟⲡ ⲛ̀ⲗⲩⲙⲏⲛ

ⲛ̀ⲧⲉ ⲡⲓⲟⲩⲭⲁⲓ ϣⲁ ⲉⲛⲉϩ ⲛ̀ⲧⲉ ⲛⲓⲉⲛⲉϩ. ⲁⲗⲗⲁ ⲙⲁⲣⲉⲛⲧⲁⲥⲑⲟ ⲉϫⲉⲛ ⲧⲙⲟⲣⲫⲏ ⲛ̀ⲧⲭⲓⲛⲓ ⲉϣⲓϩⲏⲧ ⲛ̀ⲛⲓⲙⲁⲕⲁⲣⲓⲟⲥ.

46. ϩⲟⲧⲉ ⲟⲩⲛ ⲗⲟⲓⲡⲟⲛ ⲉⲧⲁⲩⲕⲱϯ ⲛ̀ⲥⲁ ⲟⲩⲁ ⲉⲑⲣⲟⲩⲫⲱϣⲛⲉϥ ⲛ̀ⲁⲣⲭⲓⲉⲡⲓⲥⲕⲟⲡⲟⲥ ⲉⲑⲃⲁⲕⲓ ⲛ̀ⲧⲙⲉⲧⲟⲩⲣⲟ ⲁϥⲓ ϣⲁ Ⲑⲉⲟⲇⲱⲥⲓⲟⲥ ⲛ̀ϫⲉ ⲡⲓⲇⲏⲙⲟⲥ ⲧⲏⲣϥ ⲛⲉⲙ ⲟⲩⲟⲛ ⲛⲓⲃⲉⲛ ⲉⲩⲥⲟⲡ ⲉⲩⲉⲣⲉⲧⲓⲛ ⲙ̀ⲙⲟϥ ⲉⲑⲣⲟⲩϩⲉⲙⲥⲟ ⲙ̀Ⲙⲁⲝⲓⲙⲟⲥ ⲛ̀ⲁⲣⲭⲓⲉⲡⲓⲥⲕⲟⲡⲟⲥ ⲛ̀ϣⲉⲃⲓⲱ ⲙ̀ⲫⲏⲉⲧⲁϥⲉⲛⲕⲟⲧ. ⲧⲟⲧⲉ ⲁϥⲣⲁϣⲓ ⲉⲙⲁϣⲱ ⲛ̀ϫⲉ Ⲑⲉⲟⲇⲱⲥⲓⲟⲥ ⲡⲟⲩⲣⲟ ⲉϫⲉⲛ ⲡⲁⲓϩⲱⲃ ⲟⲩⲟϩ ⲥⲁⲧⲟⲧϥ ⲁϥⲟⲩⲱⲣⲡ ⲛ̀ⲟⲩⲙⲁⲅⲓⲥⲧⲣⲓⲁⲛⲟⲥ ⲛ̀ⲥⲱϥ ⲛⲉⲙ ⲕⲉ ⲙ̀ⲙⲁⲧⲟⲓ ⲉⲁϥⲥϧⲉ ⲡⲓⲉⲡⲁⲣⲭⲟⲥ ⲛ̀ⲧⲉ ϯⲤⲩⲣⲓⲁ ϫⲉ ϩⲓⲛⲁ ⲛ̀ⲧⲉϥⲧⲁϩⲉ ⲛⲓⲁⲅⲓⲟⲥ ⲛ̀ⲧⲉϥⲣⲱⲓⲥ ⲉⲣⲱⲟⲩ ϣⲁⲧⲟⲩⲑⲱⲟⲩϯ ⲛ̀ⲛⲓⲉⲡⲓⲥⲕⲟⲡⲟⲥ ⲛ̀ⲧⲉ ⲛⲓⲉⲡⲁⲣⲭⲓⲁ.

47. ⲉⲧⲁⲩⲫⲟϩ ⲇⲉ ⲉⲡⲓⲉⲡⲁⲣⲭⲟⲥ ⲛ̀ϫⲉ ⲡⲓⲙⲁⲅⲓⲥⲧⲣⲓⲁⲛⲟⲥ ⲛⲉⲙ ⲛⲓⲙⲁⲧⲟⲓ ⲟⲩⲟϩ ⲉⲧⲁⲩϯ ⲛⲁϥ ⲛ̀ⲛⲓⲥϧⲁⲓ ⲛ̀ⲧⲉ ⲡⲟⲩⲣⲟ ⲁϥⲣⲁϣⲓ ⲡⲉϫⲁϥ ⲛⲱⲟⲩ ϫⲉ ⲙⲁⲣⲉⲛⲉⲣⲁⲣⲓⲥⲧⲟⲛ ⲙ̀ⲫⲟⲟⲩ ⲇⲉ ⲁⲣⲉⲧⲉⲛⲏⲓⲥⲓ ϩⲓ ⲡⲓⲙⲱⲓⲧ ⲟⲩⲟϩ ⲣⲁⲥϯ ⲧⲉⲛⲛⲁⲉⲛⲟⲩ ϧⲉⲛ ⲫⲟⲩⲱϣ ⲙ̀Ⲫϯ. ⲕⲁⲧⲁ ⲟⲩⲟⲓⲕⲟⲛⲟⲙⲓⲁ ⲟⲩⲛ ⲛ̀ⲧⲉ Ⲫϯ ⲉⲧⲁⲥⲉⲙⲓ ⲉⲫⲁⲓ ⲛ̀ϫⲉ ϯⲥϩⲓⲙⲓ ⲙ̀ⲡⲓⲉⲡⲁⲣⲭⲟⲥ ⲁⲥⲙⲟⲕⲙⲉⲕ ϫⲉ ⲁⲣⲉ ⲡⲟⲩⲣⲟ ⲛⲁⲱⲗⲓ ⲛ̀ⲛⲁⲓⲁⲅⲓⲟⲥ ⲉⲔⲱⲥⲧⲁⲛⲧⲓⲛⲟⲩⲡⲟⲗⲓⲥ ⲁⲥⲉⲣⲙⲕⲁϩⲛ̀ϩⲏⲧ ⲉⲙⲁϣⲱ ϫⲉ ⲟⲩⲏⲓ ⲟⲩⲟⲛ ⲛ̀ⲧⲁⲥ ⲙ̀ⲙⲁⲩ ⲛ̀ⲟⲩⲛⲓϣϯ ⲛ̀ⲛⲁϩϯ ⲉϧⲟⲩⲛ ⲉⲣⲱⲟⲩ ⲟⲩⲟϩ ⲥⲁⲧⲟⲧⲥ ⲁⲥⲟⲩⲱⲣⲡ ⲛ̀ⲛⲉⲥϣⲏⲣⲓ ⲛ̀ⲭⲱⲡ ⲛⲉ ⲕⲉⲥⲓⲟⲟⲩⲣ ⲛ̀ⲧⲁⲥ ⲙ̀ⲡⲓⲉⲭⲱⲣϩ ⲁⲥⲧⲁⲙⲉ ⲛⲓⲁⲅⲓⲟⲥ ϫⲉ ⲓⲥ ⲡⲟⲩⲣⲟ ⲁϥⲟⲩⲱⲣⲡ ⲛ̀ⲥⲱⲧⲉⲛ ⲉⲑⲉⲗ ⲑⲏⲛⲟⲩ ⲉⲔⲱⲥⲧⲁⲛⲧⲓⲛⲟⲩⲡⲟⲗⲓⲥ. ⲗⲟⲓⲡⲟⲛ ⲓⲥϫⲉ ⲧⲉⲧⲉⲛⲟⲩⲱϣ ⲁⲣⲓⲁⲛⲭⲱⲣⲓⲛ ⲛⲱⲧⲉⲛ.

48. Ⲉⲧⲁⲩⲥⲱⲧⲉⲙ ⲇⲉ ⲉⲛⲁⲓⲥⲁϫⲓ ⲛ̀ϫⲉ ⲛⲓⲁⲅⲓⲟⲥ ⲁⲩϫⲱⲗⲉⲙ ⲙ̀ⲙⲱⲟⲩ ⲥⲁⲧⲟⲧⲟⲩ ⲁⲩⲓ ⲉⲃⲟⲗϧⲉⲛ ⲡⲓⲙⲟⲛⲁⲥⲧⲏⲣⲓⲟⲛ ⲉⲩϫⲱ ⲙ̀ⲙⲟⲥ ϫⲉ ⲫⲁⲓ ⲡⲉ ⲡⲓⲛⲁⲩ ⲉⲧⲁ Ⲫϯ ⲟⲩⲱϣ ⲉⲟⲗⲧⲉⲛ ⲉⲫⲙⲁ ⲙ̀ⲡⲉⲛⲓⲱⲧ ⲁⲃⲃⲁ Ⲙⲁⲕⲁⲣ ⲡⲓⲣⲱⲙⲓ ⲛ̀ⲧⲉ Ⲫϯ ϧⲉⲛ ⲟⲩⲙⲉⲑⲙⲏⲓ ϩⲱⲥ ⲇⲉ ⲉⲩⲙⲟϣⲓ ⲛ̀ϫⲉ ⲛⲁⲓⲁⲅⲓⲟⲥ ⲁⲩϫⲓⲙⲓ ⲛ̀ⲟⲩϧⲉⲗⲗⲟ ⲙ̀ⲙⲁⲛⲉⲥⲱⲟⲩ ⲉϥϩⲉⲙⲥⲓ ϧⲉⲛ ⲟⲩⲕⲁⲗⲓⲃⲓ ϧⲉⲛ ⲟⲩⲙⲁⲛⲉⲣⲏⲙⲟⲥ ⲁⲩⲭⲟⲡⲟⲩ ϧⲁⲧⲟⲧϥ.

49. ⲉⲡⲉϥⲣⲁⲥϯ ϫⲉ ⲁⲡⲓⲙⲁⲅⲓⲥⲧⲣⲓⲁⲛⲟⲥ ⲛⲉⲙ ⲛⲏⲉⲑⲛⲉⲙⲁϥ ϣⲉⲛⲱⲟⲩ ⲉⲡⲓⲙⲟⲛⲁⲥⲧⲏⲣⲓⲟⲛ ⲉⲩⲕⲱϯ ⲛ̀ⲥⲁ ⲛⲓⲙⲁⲕⲁⲣⲓⲟⲥ ⲟⲩⲟϩ ⲙ̀ⲡⲟⲩϫⲉⲙⲟⲩ. ⲧⲟⲧⲉ ⲁⲡⲓⲉⲡⲁⲣⲭⲟⲥ ⲟⲩⲁϩⲥⲁϩⲛⲓ ⲉⲕⲱϯ ⲛ̀ⲥⲱⲟⲩ ϧⲉⲛ ⲟⲩⲧⲁϫⲣⲟ ϧⲉⲛ ⲙⲁⲓ ⲛⲓⲃⲉⲛ ⲛ̀ⲧⲉ ϯⲤⲩⲣⲓⲁ ⲛⲉⲙ ϯⲠⲁⲗⲉⲥⲧⲓⲛⲏ ⲉⲑⲃⲉ ⲫⲁⲓ ⲛⲁⲣⲉ ⲛⲁⲓⲁⲅⲓⲟⲥ

APPENDIX 2

ⲭⲏⲡ ⲡⲉ ⲛ̇ϩⲁⲛⲙⲏϣ ⲛ̇ⲉϩⲟⲟⲩ ⲟⲩⲟϩ ⲛⲁⲩϣⲟⲩⲱⲛϩ ⲙ̇ⲙⲱⲟⲩ ⲉⲃⲟⲗ ⲁⲛ ⲉⲡⲧⲏⲣϥ ⲡⲉ ⲉⲑⲃⲉ ϫⲉ ⲛⲁⲩⲥⲱⲟⲩⲛ ⲙ̇ⲙⲱⲟⲩ ⲡⲉ ϩⲓⲧⲉⲛ ⲟⲩⲟⲛ ⲛⲓⲃⲉⲛ ⲛ̇ⲧⲉ †ⲤⲨⲢⲒⲀ ⲛⲉⲙ ⲛⲏⲉⲧⲭⲏ ⲙ̇ⲡⲉⲥⲕⲱ†. ⲙⲉⲛⲉⲛⲥⲁ ⲛⲁⲓ ⲁⲩⲧⲱⲟⲩⲛ ϧⲉⲛ ⲟⲩⲥⲟϭⲛⲓ ⲛ̇ⲧⲉ Ⲫ† ⲛ̇ϫⲉ ⲛⲁⲓⲙⲁⲕⲁⲣⲓⲟⲥ ⲁⲩⲃⲁϣⲟⲩ ⲛ̇ⲛⲓϩⲃⲱⲥ ⲙ̇ⲙⲟⲛⲁⲭⲟⲥ ⲁⲩⲑⲏⲓⲧⲟⲩ ⲉϧⲣⲏⲓ ⲉϩⲁⲛⲥⲟⲕ ⲁⲩⲉⲣⲫⲟⲣⲓⲛ ⲛ̇ϩⲁⲛϩⲃⲱⲥ ⲛ̇ⲕⲟⲥⲙⲓⲕⲟⲛ ⲟⲩⲟϩ ⲁⲩⲙⲟⲩⲣ ⲛ̇ϩⲁⲛⲫⲁⲥⲕⲓⲁ ⲛ̇ⲛⲟⲩⲁⲫⲏⲟⲩⲓ ϫⲉ ϩⲓⲛⲁ ⲛ̇ⲧⲟⲩϣⲧⲉⲙⲥⲱⲟⲩⲛⲟⲩ. ⲧⲟⲧⲉ ⲁⲩⲓ ⲉⲃⲟⲗ ⲗⲟⲓⲡⲟⲛ ⲉⲣⲉ ⲡⲓⲕⲟⲩϫⲓ ⲛ̇ⲥⲟⲕ ⲧⲁⲗⲏⲟⲩⲧ ⲉⲣⲱⲟⲩ ⲉⲣⲉ ⲫⲟⲩⲁⲓ ⲫⲟⲩⲁⲓ ⲉⲣⲫⲟⲣⲓⲛ ⲛ̇ⲛⲓϩⲃⲱⲥ ⲛ̇ⲕⲟⲥⲙⲓⲕⲟⲛ ⲕⲁⲧⲁ ⲛⲓⲥⲩⲣⲟⲥ ⲟⲩⲟϩ ⲛⲁⲩⲙⲟϣⲓ ⲉⲩⲧⲱⲃϩ ⲙ̇Ⲫ† ⲉⲩⲭⲱ ⲙ̇ⲙⲟⲥ ϫⲉ Ⲫ† ⲙ̇ⲡⲉⲛⲓⲱⲧ ⲁⲃⲃⲁ Ⲙⲁⲕⲁⲣⲓⲟⲥ ⲉⲕⲉϭⲓⲙⲱⲓⲧ ϧⲁϫⲱⲛ ⲛ̇ⲧⲉⲕⲟⲗⲧⲉⲛ ϣⲁⲣⲟϥ ϧⲉⲛ ⲟⲩϩⲓⲣⲏⲛⲏ.

50. Ⲉⲧⲁⲩⲙⲟϣⲓ ⲇⲉ ⲛ̇ⲉϩⲟⲟⲩ Ⲃ̅ ⲉϫⲉⲛ ⲛⲉⲛⲥⲫⲟⲧⲟⲩ ⲙ̇ⲫⲓⲟⲙ ⲡⲉϫⲉ ⲡⲓⲕⲟⲟⲩϫⲓ ⲙ̇ⲡⲓⲛⲓϣ† ϧⲉⲛ ⲟⲩⲛⲓϣ† ⲙ̇ⲙⲉⲧⲭⲁⲣϩⲏⲧ ϫⲉ ϫⲉⲙⲛⲟⲙ† ⲡⲁⲟ̅ⲥ̅ ⲛ̇ⲥⲟⲛ ϫⲉ ϧⲉⲛ ⲫⲟⲩⲱϣ ⲙ̇ⲡⲉⲛⲟ̅ⲥ̅ Ⲓⲏ̅ⲥ̅ Ⲡⲭ̅ⲥ̅ ⲡⲉⲛⲛⲟⲩ† ⲛ̇ⲧⲁⲫⲙⲏ ⲛⲉⲙ ⲛⲓⲧⲱⲃϩ ⲛ̇ⲧⲉ ⲡⲓⲁⲅⲓⲟⲥ ⲁⲃⲃⲁ Ⲙⲁⲕⲁⲣ ⲫⲏⲉⲧⲁϥⲛⲁⲩ ⲉⲣⲟϥ ⲡⲓϩⲟⲣⲁⲙⲁ ⲛ̇ϫⲉ ⲡⲉⲛⲙⲁⲕⲁⲣⲓⲟⲥ ⲛ̇ⲓⲱⲧ Ⲁⲅⲁⲡⲟⲥ ⲉⲁϥϫⲟⲥ ⲛⲁϥ ϫⲉϩⲟⲛϩⲉⲛ ⲉⲧⲟⲧⲟⲩ ⲛ̇ⲛⲉⲕϣⲏⲣⲓ ⲙⲉⲛⲉⲛⲥⲱⲕ ⲛ̇ⲧⲟⲩⲓ ⲉϧⲣⲏⲓ ⲉⲭⲏⲙⲓ ⲛ̇ⲧⲟⲩϣⲱⲡⲓ ϧⲁⲧⲟⲧ. ⲧⲉⲛⲛⲁϩ† ϫⲉ ⲛⲉϥϣⲗⲏⲗ ⲛⲁϭⲓⲙⲱⲓⲧ ⲛⲁⲛ ϣⲁⲧⲉⲛϩⲱⲗ ⲉⲣⲁⲕⲟ† ⲉⲡⲉϥⲙⲁ. ⲙⲁⲣⲉⲙⲟϣⲓ ⲇⲉ ⲟⲩⲛ ⲡⲁⲥⲟⲛ ⲉϫⲉⲛ ⲡⲁⲓⲥⲫⲟⲧⲟⲩ ⲛ̇ⲣⲏⲥ ⲛ̇ⲧⲉ ⲫⲓⲟⲙ ϧⲉⲛ ⲟⲩⲙⲟⲩⲛ ⲉⲃⲟⲗ ϣⲁⲧⲉⲛϩⲱⲗ ⲉⲣⲁⲕⲟ† ⲙⲏ ⲙ̇ⲡⲉⲕⲥⲱⲧⲉⲙ ⲉⲡⲓⲡⲣⲁⲅⲙⲁⲧⲉⲩⲧⲏⲥ ⲉⲧⲁϥϫⲟⲥ ⲛⲁⲛ ⲙ̇ⲡⲓⲥⲛⲟⲩ ϫⲉ ⲉⲛϣϩⲏⲣ ⲥⲁ ⲡⲁⲓⲥⲫⲟⲧⲟⲩ ⲛⲉⲣⲏⲥ ⲛ̇ⲧⲉ ⲫⲓⲟⲙ ϣⲁⲧⲉⲛϩⲱⲗ ⲉⲣⲁⲕⲟ† ⲟⲩⲟϩ ⲡⲉϫⲉ ⲡⲓⲛⲓϣ† ϫⲉ ⲟⲩⲟϩ ⲁⲛⲛⲁϫⲉⲙ ⲙⲱⲟⲩ ⲛ̇ⲑⲱⲛ ⲛ̇ⲧⲉⲛⲥⲱ. ⲡⲉϫⲉ ⲡⲓⲕⲟⲩϫⲓ ⲛⲁϥ ϧⲉⲛ ⲟⲩⲣⲁϣⲓ ⲛⲉⲙ ⲟⲩϩⲉⲗⲡⲓⲥ ⲉⲥⲧⲁϫⲣⲏⲟⲩⲧ ϫⲉ ⲱ ⲡⲁϭⲟⲓⲥ Ⲓⲏⲥⲟⲩⲥ Ⲡⲓⲭⲣⲓⲥⲧⲟⲥ ⲛ̇ⲧⲉϥⲫⲱⲛϩ ⲙ̇ⲡⲁⲓⲙⲱⲟⲩ ⲛⲉⲙ ⲛⲁⲓⲡⲉⲧⲣⲁ ⲛ̇ϩⲁⲛⲕⲩⲙⲏⲛ ⲙ̇ⲙⲱⲟⲩ. ⲡⲉϫⲉ ⲡⲓⲛⲓϣ† ⲛⲁϥ ϫⲉ ⲥⲉ ⲡⲁϭⲟⲓⲥ †ⲛⲁϩ† ϫⲉ ⲟⲩⲟⲛϣϫⲟⲙ ⲙ̇ⲙⲟϥ ϧⲉⲛ ϩⲱⲃ ⲛⲓⲃⲉⲛ ⲁⲗⲗⲁ ⲭⲱ ⲛⲏⲓ ⲉⲃⲟⲗ ⲡⲁⲥⲟⲛ ϫⲉ ⲁⲓϣⲟϥⲧ ϩⲱ ϩⲱⲥ ⲣⲱⲙⲓ.

51. ⲙⲉⲛⲉⲛⲥⲁ ⲛⲁⲓⲥⲁϫⲓ ⲇⲉ ⲛⲁⲩⲙⲟϣⲓ ⲡⲉ ϧⲉⲛ ⲟⲩⲣⲁϣⲓ ⲛⲉⲙ ⲟⲩⲣⲱⲟⲩⲧϥ ⲛ̇ϩⲏⲧ ⲉⲩⲑⲉⲗⲏⲗ ⲟⲩⲟϩ ⲉⲩⲥⲙⲟⲩ ⲉⲪ† ⲟⲩⲟϩ ⲛⲁⲩ†ⲛⲟⲙ† ⲛ̇ⲛⲟⲩⲉⲣⲏⲟⲩ ⲡⲉ ϧⲉⲛ ⲟⲩⲙⲟⲩⲛ ⲉⲃⲟⲗ. Ⲫ† ⲇⲉ ⲉⲧⲁϥϭⲓⲙⲱⲓⲧ ⲙ̇ⲡⲓⲥ̅ⲁ̅ ⲙ̇ⲡⲓⲥⲛⲟⲩ ϩⲓ ⲡϣⲁϥⲉ ⲛⲉⲙ ϧⲉⲛ ⲫⲓⲟⲙ ⲛ̇ⲑⲟϥ ⲟⲛ ⲡⲉ ⲉⲧⲁϥϭⲓⲙⲱⲓⲧ

ⲛ̅ⲛⲁⲓⲕⲉⲁⲅⲓⲟⲥ ⲟⲩⲟϩ ⲉϣⲱⲡ ⲁⲩϣⲁⲛⲓⲃⲓ ⲛⲉϣⲁϣⲉⲛϣⲟⲩ ⲉϥⲓⲟⲙ
ⲛ̅ⲧⲟⲩⲥⲱ ⲉⲃⲟⲗⲛ̅ϧⲏⲧϥ ϣⲁⲩⲭⲉⲙϥ ⲉϥϩⲟⲗϫ ⲟⲩⲟϩ ⲛⲁϥϣⲓⲛⲓ
ⲛ̅ⲛⲟⲩⲉⲣⲛⲟⲩ ⲁⲛ ⲡⲉ ⲉⲑⲃⲉ ⲫⲁⲓ ϫⲉ ϥϩⲟⲗϫ ⲓⲉ ϥⲉⲛϣⲁϣⲓ.

52. Ⲉⲧⲁⲩⲙⲟϣⲓ ⲇⲉ ⲁⲩⲓ ⲉϫⲉⲛ ⲟⲩⲕⲟϩ ⲙ̅ⲡⲉⲧⲣⲁ ⲉϥⲟⲓ ⲛ̅ⲭⲁϫⲣⲓⲛ
ϩⲱⲥⲧⲉ ⲛ̅ⲧⲟⲩⲙⲟϣⲓ ϩⲓϫⲉⲛ ⲛⲟⲩϫⲓϫ ⲛⲉⲙ ⲛⲟⲩϭⲁⲗⲁⲩϫ ⲛ̅ⲟⲩⲙⲏϣ
ⲛ̅ⲥⲟⲡ ⲥⲉⲟϣ ⲅⲁⲣ ⲛ̅ϫⲉ ⲛⲓϩⲓⲥⲓ ⲉⲧⲁⲩϣⲟⲡⲟⲩ ⲛ̅ϫⲉ ⲛⲁⲓⲙⲁⲕⲁⲣⲓⲟⲥ ϧⲉⲛ
ⲛⲓⲡⲉⲧⲣⲁ ⲉⲧϭⲟⲥⲓ ⲉⲧⲙⲙⲁⲩ ⲕⲉ ⲅⲁⲣ ⲛⲁⲩⲥⲱⲟⲩⲛ ⲁⲛ ⲡⲉ ϫⲉ ⲉⲩⲛⲁ
ⲉⲑⲱⲛ ⲁⲗⲗⲁ ⲡⲓⲣⲱⲟⲩⲧϥ ⲛ̅ϩⲏⲧ ⲛ̅ⲧⲉ Ⲡⲭ̅ⲥ̅ ⲛⲉⲙ ϯϩⲉⲗⲡⲓⲥ ⲉⲧϧⲉⲛ
ⲡⲟⲩϩⲏⲧ ⲛⲁϥⲉⲣ ⲙ̅ⲡⲓϩⲓⲥⲓ ⲉⲁⲥⲓⲁⲓ ⲛⲁϩⲣⲉⲛ ⲡⲉ. ⲟⲩⲟϩ ⲕⲁⲧⲁ ϯϩⲉ
ⲉⲧⲁⲩϫⲟⲥ ⲛⲏⲓ ⲛ̅ⲑⲱⲟⲩ ⲛⲁⲓⲙⲁⲕⲁⲣⲓⲟⲥ ⲉⲧⲁⲩⲙⲟϣⲓ ϣⲁ ⲑ̅ ⲛ̅ⲉϩⲟⲟⲩ
ⲁⲩϩⲓⲥⲓ ⲉⲙⲁϣⲱ ⲉⲑⲃⲉ ⲡⲧϩⲉⲙⲕⲟ ⲛ̅ⲛⲟⲩϭⲁⲗⲁⲩϫ ⲉⲑⲃⲉ ϫⲉ ϩⲁⲛⲣⲱⲙⲓ
ⲛⲉ ⲉⲩⲭⲏⲛ ϧⲉⲛ ⲛⲟⲩⲥⲱⲙⲁ ⲛ̅ⲥⲉⲕⲉϩ ⲁⲛ ⲉⲛⲁⲓϩⲓⲥⲓ ⲙ̅ⲡⲁⲓⲥⲙⲟⲧ. ϩⲟⲧⲉ
ⲟⲩⲛ ⲡⲉϫⲱⲟⲩ ⲉⲧⲁⲛⲁⲗⲏⲓ ⲉϩⲣⲏⲓ ⲉϫⲉⲛ ⲟⲩⲡⲉⲧⲣⲁⲛ ⲉⲥϭⲟⲥⲓ ⲉⲡϩⲟⲩⲟ
ⲙ̅ⲡⲉⲛϣϫⲉⲙϫⲟⲙ ⲗⲟⲓⲡⲟⲛ ⲉⲙⲁϣⲓ ϫⲉ ⲁⲗⲗⲁ ⲁⲛ ϣⲑⲛⲟⲩⲧ ⲡⲉ ⲉϫⲉⲛ
ϯⲡⲉⲧⲣⲁ.

53. ⲉⲛϧⲟⲥⲓ ⲉⲉⲙⲁϣⲱ ⲁⲧⲉⲧⲉⲛⲛⲁⲛⲁⲩ ⲉⲑⲙⲉⲧϫⲱⲣⲓ ⲛ̅ⲛⲁⲓⲅⲱⲛⲓⲥⲧⲏⲥ
ⲟⲩⲟϩ ⲛ̅ⲁⲑⲗⲏⲧⲏⲥ ⲛ̅ⲧⲉ Ⲡⲭ̅ⲥ̅ ⲛⲁⲓⲉⲧⲁⲩⲉⲣ ⲃ̅ ⲁⲧϭⲛⲉ ⲫⲉⲛⲥⲛⲟϥ
ⲉⲃⲟⲗϩⲓⲧⲉⲛ ⲛⲁⲓⲙⲏϣ ⲛ̅ϩⲓⲥⲓ ⲉⲧⲁⲩϣⲟⲡⲟⲩ. ⲗⲟⲓⲡⲟⲛ ⲛⲉ ⲁⲩⲉⲣⲕⲉ ⲉ̅
ⲛ̅ⲉϩⲟⲟⲩ ⲡⲉ ⲉⲩϭⲛϯ ⲉⲃⲟⲗϩⲓϫⲉⲛ ϯⲡⲉⲧⲣⲁ ⲉⲧⲉⲙⲙⲁⲩ ⲛ̅ⲁⲑⲟⲩⲱⲙ ⲟⲩⲟϩ
ⲛ̅ⲁⲧⲥⲱ ⲉⲩⲣⲟϫⲡ ⲙ̅ⲫⲣⲏϯ ⲛ̅ϩⲁⲛⲣⲉϥⲙⲱⲟⲩⲧ. Ⲫϯ ⲇⲉ ⲫⲛⲉⲑⲙⲟϩⲉⲙ
ⲛ̅ⲛⲉⲧⲉⲣϩⲉⲗⲡⲓⲥ ⲉⲣⲟϥ ⲛ̅ⲥⲏⲟⲩ ⲛⲓⲃⲉⲛ ⲉϥⲧⲟⲩϫⲟ ⲙ̅ⲙⲱⲟⲩ ⲉⲃⲟⲗϧⲉⲛ
ⲛⲓⲑⲗⲓⲯⲓⲥ ⲧⲏⲣⲟⲩ ⲫⲛⲉⲧⲉⲣⲫⲙⲉⲩⲓ ⲛ̅Ⲇⲁⲛⲓⲏⲗ ⲙ̅ⲡⲓⲥⲛⲟⲩ ⲁϥⲛⲁϩⲙⲉϥ
ⲉⲃⲟⲗϧⲉⲛ ⲣⲱⲟⲩ ⲛ̅ⲛⲓⲙⲟⲩⲓ ⲟⲩⲟϩ ⲁϥⲛⲟϩⲉⲙ ⲛ̅Ⲓⲱⲛⲁ ⲉⲃⲟⲗϧⲉⲛ ⲑⲛⲉϫⲓ
ⲛ̅ⲧⲉ ⲡⲓⲕⲏⲧⲟⲥ ⲟⲩⲟϩ ⲉⲧⲁϥⲧⲟⲩϫⲟ ⲛ̅Ⲥⲟⲩⲥⲁⲛⲛⲁ ⲉⲃⲟⲗϧⲉⲛ ⲡⲓϩⲓⲟⲩⲓ
ⲉⲡϩⲁⲡ ⲛ̅ⲧⲉ ⲫⲙⲟⲩ ⲛ̅ⲑⲟϥ ⲟⲛ ⲁϥⲛⲟϩⲉⲙ ⲛ̅ⲛⲉϥⲉⲃⲓⲁⲓⲕ ⲛ̅ⲣⲱⲙⲉⲟⲥ
ⲉⲃⲟⲗϧⲉⲛ ⲣⲱⲟⲩ ⲛ̅ⲛⲓⲁⲅⲣⲓⲟⲛ ⲛ̅ⲧⲉ ⲡⲓⲙⲁ ⲉⲧⲉⲙⲙⲁⲩ ⲛⲉⲙ ⲛⲓϩⲁⲗⲁϯ
ⲛ̅ⲉⲩⲉⲙⲥⲁⲣⲝ ⲉⲧϩⲓϫⲉⲛ ⲛⲉⲛⲥⲫⲟⲧⲟⲩ ⲙ̅ⲫⲓⲟⲙ.

54. Ⲫϯ ⲛ̅ⲧⲉ ⲛⲓϫⲟⲙ ⲫⲛⲉⲧⲁϥⲟⲩⲱⲧⲉⲃ ⲛ̅Ⲉⲛⲱⲭ ⲉⲃⲟⲗ
ⲉϥⲧⲉⲙⲑⲣⲉϥⲛⲁⲩ ⲉⲫⲙⲟⲩ ⲟⲩⲟϩ ⲉⲧⲁϥⲟⲩⲱⲣⲡ ⲛ̅ϩⲁⲛϩⲁⲣⲙⲁ ⲛ̅ⲭⲣⲱⲙ
ϣⲁⲧⲟⲩϣⲓⲗⲓ ⲉⲡϣⲱⲓ ⲛ̅Ⲏⲗⲓⲁⲥ ⲫⲛⲉⲧⲁϥⲧⲁⲟⲩⲟ ⲙ̅ⲡⲉϥⲁⲅⲅⲉⲗⲟⲥ
ⲁϥϥⲁⲓ ⲛ̅ⲁⲃⲃⲁⲕⲟⲩⲙ ⲉⲃⲟⲗϧⲉⲛ ⲡⲓⲁⲏⲣ ⲁⲧϭⲛⲉϩⲓⲥⲓ ϣⲁⲧⲉϥϭⲓⲧϥ

APPENDIX 2   131

ⲉⲑⲂⲁⲃⲩⲗⲱⲛ ⲉϫⲉⲛ ⲡⲓⲗⲁⲕⲕⲟⲥ ⲛ̀ⲧⲉ ⲛⲓⲙⲟⲩⲓ ⲉⲁϥϯ ⲙ̀ⲡⲁⲣⲓⲥⲧⲟⲛ ⲛ̀Ⲇⲁⲛⲓⲏⲗ ⲟⲩⲟϩ ⲡⲁⲗⲓⲛⲁϥⲧⲁⲥⲑⲟϥ ⲉϯⲒⲟⲩⲇⲉⲁ ⲛ̅ⲅ̅ ⲛ̀ⲁⲃⲟⲧ ⲙ̀ⲙⲟϥⲓ ⲛ̀ⲑⲟϥ ⲟⲛ ⲡ̅ⲟ̅ⲥ̅ ⲁϥⲟⲩⲱⲣⲡ ⲙ̀ⲡⲉϥⲁⲅⲅⲉⲗⲟⲥ ⲁϥⲧⲱⲟⲩⲛ ⲛ̀ⲛⲁⲓⲁⲅⲓⲟⲥ ϧⲉⲛ ⲡⲓⲁⲏⲣ ⲁⲧϭⲛⲉϧⲓⲥⲓ ϣⲁⲧⲉϥⲉⲛⲟⲩ ⲉⲘ̀ϣⲓϩⲧ ⲛ̀ⲧⲉϥⲭⲁⲩ ϩⲓϫⲉⲛ ϯⲛⲓϣϯ ⲙ̀ⲡⲉⲧⲣⲁ ⲉⲧⲉ ⲡⲓⲭⲟϣϫⲉϣ ⲙ̀ⲙⲱⲟⲩ ⲥⲁⲣⲏⲥ ⲙ̀ⲙⲟⲥ. ⲑⲁⲓ ⲅⲁⲣ ⲁⲟⲩⲙⲏⲓⲛⲓ ⲛ̀ⲧⲉ Ⲫϯ ϣⲱⲡⲓ ⲛ̀ϩⲏⲧⲥ ⲁϥⲟⲩⲱⲛϩ ⲉⲃⲟⲗ ⲉⲁⲡⲓⲃⲱⲕ ⲛ̀ⲧⲉ Ⲫϯ ⲁⲃⲃⲁ ⲙⲁⲕⲁⲣ ⲙⲟⲩϯ ⲉⲣⲟⲥ ϯⲡⲉⲧⲣⲁ ⲛ̀ⲕⲟⲩⲛⲛⲉϫⲓ ϣⲁ ⲉϧⲟⲩⲛ ⲉⲫⲟⲟⲩ.

55. Ⲙⲁⲑⲏⲧⲉⲩⲉⲛ ⲉⲣⲟⲓ ϧⲉⲛ ⲟⲩϯϩⲑⲏϥ ⲛ̀ⲧⲉⲧⲉⲛⲥⲱⲧⲉⲙ ⲉⲧⲁⲓϣⲫⲏⲣⲓ ⲉⲧⲁⲥϣⲱⲡⲓ ⲛ̀ⲛⲁⲓⲙⲁⲕⲁⲣⲓⲟⲥ ⲕⲁⲧⲁ ⲫⲣⲏϯ ⲉⲧⲁⲩⲧⲁⲙⲟⲓ ⲛ̀ⲱⲟⲩ. ⲁⲥϣⲱⲡⲓ ⲅⲁⲣ ϧⲉⲛ ⲡⲓⲉϫⲱⲣϩ ⲉⲧⲁ Ⲫϯ ⲓⲛⲓ ⲛ̀ⲛⲁⲓⲙⲁⲕⲁⲣⲓⲟⲥ ⲉⲘ̀ϣⲓϩⲧ ⲁⲩⲛⲁⲩ ϧⲉⲛ ⲡⲓⲉϫⲱⲣϩ ⲉⲟⲩⲣⲱⲙⲓ ⲛ̀ⲟⲩⲱⲓⲛⲓ ⲉϥⲭⲏ ϧⲉⲛ ⲧⲟⲩⲙⲏϯ ⲉϥⲁⲙⲟⲛⲓ ⲛ̀ⲧⲟⲩϫⲓϫ ⲉϥⲥⲱⲕ ⲛⲉⲙⲱⲟⲩ ϧⲉⲛ ⲡⲓⲁⲏⲣ ϣⲁⲧⲉϥⲉⲛⲟⲩ ⲉϩⲣⲏⲓ ⲉϫⲉⲛ ϯⲡⲉⲧⲣⲁ ⲉⲧⲁⲛⲉⲣϣⲟⲣⲡ ⲙ̀ⲫⲓⲣⲓ ⲉⲣⲟⲥ.

56. ϩⲟⲧⲉ ⲡⲉϫⲱⲟⲩ ⲉⲧⲁⲛⲧⲱⲟⲩⲛ ϩⲁⲛⲁⲧⲟⲟⲩⲓ ⲟⲩⲛ ⲕⲁⲧⲁ ϯϫⲟⲙ ⲉⲧⲁ Ⲡ̅ⲭ̅ⲥ̅ ⲟⲩⲁϩ ⲉⲣⲟⲛ ⲁⲛϫⲉⲙⲧⲉⲛ ϩⲓϫⲉⲛ ϯⲡⲉⲧⲣⲁ ϧⲉⲛ Ⲙ̀ϣⲓϩⲧ ⲟⲩⲟϩ ⲉⲧⲁⲛϫⲟⲩϣⲧ ⲉⲃⲟⲗ ⲉϫⲉⲛ ⲡⲓⲧⲱⲟⲩ ⲁⲛⲛⲁⲩ ⲉⲡⲓϩⲉⲗⲟⲥ ⲙ̀ⲙⲱⲟⲩ ⲛⲉⲙ ϩⲁⲛⲕⲟⲩϫⲓ ⲛ̀ⲥⲓⲗⲟⲩⲕⲓ ⲙ̀ⲃⲉⲛⲓ ⲉⲩⲣⲏⲧ ⲛⲉⲙ ϯⲑⲉⲱⲣⲓⲁ ⲛ̀ⲧⲉ ⲡⲓⲧⲱⲟⲩ ⲁⲛⲉⲣϣⲫⲏⲣⲓ ⲟⲩⲟϩ ⲁⲛⲉⲣ ⲙ̀ⲫⲣⲏϯ ⲉⲁⲡⲉⲛϩⲏⲧ ⲥⲓϣⲓ ⲁⲛⲙⲟⲕⲙⲉⲕ ⲉⲃⲟⲗ ⲉⲑⲃⲉ ⲫⲏⲉⲧⲁϥϣⲱⲡⲓ ⲙ̀ⲙⲟⲛ ϫⲉ ⲣⲟⲩϩⲓ ⲙⲉⲛ ⲛⲁⲛⲉⲛⲕⲟⲧ ⲡⲉ ϧⲉⲛ ⲟⲩⲙⲉⲧϫⲱⲃ ϩⲓϫⲉⲛ ⲡⲓⲭⲣⲟ ⲛ̀ⲧⲉ ⲫⲓⲟⲙ ⲉⲛⲥⲱⲧⲉⲙ ⲉⲡⲡⲓϣⲑⲟⲣⲧⲉⲣ ⲛ̀ⲧⲉ ⲛⲓϩⲱⲓⲙⲓ ⲙ̀ⲫⲟⲟⲩ ⲇⲉ ϩⲱϥ ⲧⲉⲛⲟϩⲓ ⲉⲣⲁⲧⲉⲛ ϧⲉⲛ ⲟⲩⲭⲁⲙⲏ ⲉⲛϫⲉⲙⲛⲟⲙϯ ⲟⲩⲟϩ ⲉⲛⲛⲁⲩ ⲉϩⲁⲛⲥⲓⲗⲟⲩⲕⲓ ⲙ̀ⲃⲉⲛⲓ ⲛⲉⲙ ϩⲁⲛϣⲏⲓ ⲙ̀ⲙⲱⲟⲩ ⲛⲉⲙ ϩⲁⲛⲕⲉϫⲓⲛⲛⲁⲩ ⲙ̀ⲡⲁⲓⲣⲏϯ ⲛ̀ϩⲱⲃ ⲛ̀ϣⲫⲏⲣⲓ.

57. ⲓⲧⲁ ⲙⲉⲛⲉⲛⲥⲁ ⲟⲩⲕⲟⲩϫⲓ ⲇⲉ ⲉⲛⲥⲟⲙⲥ ⲉⲙⲛⲏ ⲛⲉⲙ ⲙⲛⲁⲓ ⲟⲩⲟϩ ⲉⲧⲁ ϥ̀ⲛⲁⲩ ⲛ̀ⲁⲭⲡ̅ ϣⲱⲡⲓ ⲁⲛⲛⲁⲩ ⲉⲟⲩⲣⲱⲙⲓ ⲉϥⲥⲱⲛ ϧⲁϫⲱⲟⲩ ⲛ̀ϩⲁⲛⲭⲁⲙⲟⲩⲗ ϧⲉⲛ ϯⲃⲉⲗⲗⲟⲧ ⲉⲧϩⲓ ⲫⲣⲏⲥ ⲙ̀ⲙⲟⲛ ⲁⲛⲣⲁϣⲓ ⲉⲙⲁϣⲱ ⲁⲛϫⲉⲙⲛⲟⲙϯ ϧⲉⲛ ⲡⲉⲛϩⲏⲧ ⲛⲉⲙ ⲛⲉⲛⲯⲩⲭⲏ ⲟⲩⲟϩ ⲉⲧⲁⲛⲓ ⲉⲡⲉⲥⲏⲧ ⲉⲃⲟⲗ ϩⲓϫⲉⲛ ϯⲡⲉⲧⲣⲁ ⲛⲁⲛϧⲱⲛⲧ ⲙ̀ⲙⲟⲛ ⲉⲣⲟϥ ⲡⲉ ϫⲉ ⲛ̀ⲧⲉⲛϣⲉⲛϥ ϫⲉ ⲡⲁⲓⲙⲁⲑⲱⲛ ⲡⲉ. ϩⲟⲧⲉ ⲟⲩⲛ ⲉⲧⲁϥⲛⲁⲩ ⲉⲣⲟⲛ ⲉⲣⲉ ⲛⲓϩⲃⲱⲥ ⲛ̀ⲍⲉⲛⲓⲕⲟⲥ ⲧⲟⲓ ϩⲓⲱⲧⲉⲛ ⲟⲩⲟϩ ⲉⲣⲉ ⲡⲓⲗⲉⲛⲧⲓⲟⲛ ⲙⲏⲣ ⲉϫⲉⲛ ⲛⲉⲛⲁⲫⲏⲟⲩⲓ ⲁϥⲉⲣϩⲟϯ ⲉⲙⲁϣⲱ ⲟⲩⲟϩ ⲁϥⲉⲣϩⲏⲧⲥ ⲙ̀ⲫⲱⲧ ⲁϥⲭⲁ ⲛⲓⲧⲉⲃⲛⲱⲟⲩⲓ

ⲉⲃⲟⲗ ϫⲉ ⲁⲛϯⲙⲉⲧⲁⲛⲟⲓⲁ ϣⲁⲧⲉϥⲟϩⲓ ⲉⲣⲁⲧϥ. ⲉⲧⲁⲛϩⲱⲛⲧ ⲇⲉ ⲉⲡⲓⲣⲱⲙⲓ ⲁⲛⲥⲁϫⲓ ⲛⲉⲙⲁϥ ⲡⲉ ⲉⲛϣⲓⲛⲓ ⲙ̄ⲙⲟϥ ⲛ̄ⲑⲟϥ ⲇⲉ ⲙ̄ⲡⲉϥⲉⲙⲓ ⲉⲧⲉⲛϫⲓⲛⲥⲁϫⲓ ⲟⲩⲇⲉ ⲁⲛⲟⲛ ϩⲱⲛ ⲙ̄ⲉⲛⲉⲙⲓ ⲉⲑⲱϥ. ⲉⲡϩⲁⲉ ⲇⲉ ⲡⲉϫⲁϥ ⲛⲁⲛ ⲉϥϭⲱⲣⲉⲙ ⲉⲣⲟⲛ ϫⲉ ⲁⲙⲱⲓⲛⲓ ⲛ̄ⲧⲁⲉⲗ ⲑⲏⲛⲟⲩ ⲉϥⲙⲁ ⲛ̄ⲁⲃⲃⲁ ⲙⲁⲕⲁⲣ. ⲁⲛⲣⲁϣⲓ ⲟⲩⲟϩ ⲁⲛϫⲉⲙⲛⲟⲙϯ ⲉⲙⲁϣⲱ ⲟⲩⲟϩ ⲡⲁⲓⲣⲏϯ ⲁⲛⲟⲩⲁϩⲧⲉⲛ ⲛ̄ⲥⲁ ⲡⲓⲣⲱⲙⲓ ⲉⲛϣⲉⲡϩⲙⲟⲧ ⲛ̄ⲧⲉⲛ ⲫϯ ⲟⲩⲟϩ ⲉⲛϯⲱⲟⲩ ⲛⲁϥ ϫⲉ ⲁϥϭⲓⲙⲱⲓⲧ ϧⲁϫⲱⲛ ⲉϥⲙⲁ ⲙ̄ⲡⲉϥⲃⲱⲕ.

58. ϩⲟⲧⲉ ⲟⲩⲛ ⲉⲧⲁⲛⲫⲟϩ ϣⲁ ⲡⲓⲡⲣⲟⲫⲏⲧⲏⲥ ⲛ̄ⲧⲉ ⲫϯ ⲁϥϣⲟⲡⲧⲉⲛ ⲉⲣⲟϥ ϧⲉⲛ ⲟⲩⲙⲉⲧⲣⲉⲙⲣⲁⲩϣⲟⲩϩ ⲁϥϣⲓⲛⲓ ⲙ̄ⲙⲟⲛ ϫⲉ ⲁⲣⲉⲧⲉⲛⲓ ⲉⲡⲁⲓⲙⲁ ⲉⲑⲃⲉ ⲟⲩ ⲛ̄ϩⲱⲃ. ⲁⲛⲟⲛ ⲇⲉ ⲁⲛⲉⲣⲟⲩⲱ ⲉⲛϫⲱ ⲙ̄ⲙⲟⲥ ϫⲉ ⲁⲛⲥⲱⲧⲉⲙ ⲉⲑⲃⲉ ⲛⲉⲕⲁⲣⲉⲧⲉⲛ ⲛⲉⲙ ϣⲓϩⲏⲧ ⲁⲛⲓ ϫⲉ ⲛ̄ⲧⲉⲛϣⲱⲡⲓ ϧⲁ ⲡⲉⲕⲥⲕⲉⲡⲓ ⲛ̄ⲧⲉⲕⲁⲓⲧⲉⲛ ⲙ̄ⲙⲟⲛⲁⲭⲟⲥ. ⲛ̄ⲑⲟϥ ⲇⲉ ⲉϥϯⲛⲓⲁⲧϥ ⲙ̄ⲙⲟⲛ ⲛ̄ⲕⲁⲗⲱⲥ ⲡⲉϫⲁϥ ⲛⲁⲛ ϫⲉ ⲧⲉⲛⲛⲁϣϫⲉⲙϫⲟⲙ ⲁⲛ ⲉⲟϩⲓ ϧⲉⲛ ⲡⲁⲓⲙⲁ ϫⲉ ⲟⲩϣⲁϥⲉ ⲡⲉ ⲉϥⲃⲟⲥⲓ. ⲁⲛⲟⲛ ⲇⲉ ⲁⲛϯⲙⲉⲧⲁⲛⲟⲓⲁ ⲛⲁϥ ⲉⲛϫⲱ ⲙ̄ⲙⲟⲥ ϫⲉ ⲉϣⲱⲡ ⲁⲛϣⲧⲉⲙϫⲉⲙϫⲟⲙ ⲛ̄ϩⲉⲙⲥⲓ ⲙ̄ⲡⲁⲓⲙⲁ ⲧⲉⲛⲛⲁϩⲱⲗ ⲉⲕⲉⲙⲁ ⲙⲟⲛⲟⲛ ⲉⲑⲃⲉ ⲫϯ ⲙ̄ⲡⲉⲣϩⲓⲧⲧⲉⲛ ⲉⲃⲟⲗϩⲁⲣⲟⲕ ⲡⲉⲛⲓⲱⲧ ⲉⲑⲛⲁⲛⲉϥ. ⲁϥⲉⲣⲟⲩⲱ ⲇⲉ ⲕⲁⲗⲱⲥ ⲓⲥϫⲉ ⲡⲁⲓⲣⲏϯ ⲡⲉ ⲁⲙⲱⲓⲛⲓ ⲛ̄ⲧⲁⲧⲁⲙⲉ ⲑⲏⲛⲟⲩ ⲉⲡⲓⲙⲁ ⲉⲧⲉⲧⲉⲛⲛⲁϣⲱⲡⲓ ⲙ̄ⲙⲁⲩ. ⲟⲩⲟϩ ⲉⲧⲁϥϭⲓⲧⲧⲉⲛ ⲁϥⲉⲛⲧⲉⲛ ⲉϫⲉⲛ ⲟⲩⲡⲉⲧⲣⲁ. ⲁϥⲧⲁⲙⲟⲛ ⲉⲡⲓⲣⲏϯ ⲛ̄ⲕⲱⲧ ⲙ̄ⲡⲓⲥⲡⲏⲗⲉⲟⲛ ⲛⲉⲙ ⲡⲓϩⲱⲃ ⲛ̄ϫⲓϫ ⲕⲁⲧⲁ ϣⲓϩⲏⲧ.

59. ⲛⲁⲓ ⲇⲉ ⲧⲏⲣⲟⲩ ⲁⲛⲁⲓⲙⲁⲕⲁⲣⲓⲟⲥ ϫⲟⲧⲟⲩ ⲛⲏⲓ ⲁⲩϣⲱⲡⲓ ⲙ̄ⲙⲱⲟⲩ ⲉⲟⲓⲇⲏ ⲁⲛⲟⲕ ⲟⲩⲣⲉⲙⲧⲁⲓⲡⲟⲗⲓⲥ ⲛ̄ⲟⲩⲱⲧ ⲛⲉⲙⲱⲟⲩ ⲕⲱⲥⲧⲁⲛⲧⲓⲛⲟⲩⲡⲟⲗⲓⲥ ⲟⲩⲟϩ ϧⲉⲛ ⲛⲁⲩ ⲇⲉ ⲛ̄ⲟⲩⲙⲏϣ ⲛ̄ⲥⲟⲡ ⲉⲩϩⲟⲛϩⲉⲛ ⲉⲧⲟⲧ ϫⲉ ⲙ̄ⲡⲉⲣϫⲉ ϩⲗⲓ ϧⲉⲛ ⲛⲏⲉⲧⲁⲛⲧⲁⲙⲟⲕ ⲉⲣⲱⲟⲩ ⲉⲧⲓ ⲉⲛⲟⲛϧ ⲕⲉ ⲅⲁⲣ ⲉⲛⲉ ⲙ̄ⲡⲓⲉⲣϣⲟⲣⲡ ⲛ̄ⲥⲟⲩⲟⲛⲟⲩ ⲡⲉ ⲛⲁⲩⲛⲁϫⲉ ϩⲗⲓ ϧⲉⲛ ⲛⲁⲓ ⲛⲏⲓ ⲁⲛ ⲡⲉ ⲁⲗⲗⲁ ⲁⲓⲥⲟⲩⲟⲛⲟⲩ ⲁⲛⲟⲕ ⲟⲩⲟϩ ⲛ̄ⲑⲱⲟⲩ ϩⲱⲟⲩ ⲁⲩⲥⲟⲩⲟⲛⲧ.

60. ⲉⲡⲓⲇⲏ ⲟⲩⲛ ⲁⲡⲓⲡⲣⲟⲫⲏⲧⲏⲥ ⲛ̄ⲧⲉ ⲡ̅ⲟ̅ⲥ̅ ⲁⲃⲃⲁ ⲙⲁⲕⲁⲣ ⲥⲱⲕ ϧⲁϫⲱⲟⲩ ⲛ̄ⲛⲉϥϣⲏⲣⲓ ⲙ̄ⲡⲣⲟⲫⲏⲧⲏⲥ ⲙⲁⲗⲗⲟⲛ ⲇⲉ ⲛ̄ϩⲟⲩⲟ ⲡⲣⲟⲫⲏⲧⲏⲥ ⲁϥⲉⲛⲟⲩ ⲉϯⲡⲉⲧⲣⲁ ⲁϥⲧⲁⲙⲱⲟⲩ ⲉⲡⲓⲙⲁ ⲛ̄ⲭⲁϫⲱⲛⲓ ⲟⲩⲟϩ ⲁϥϯ ⲛϣⲟⲩ ⲛ̄ⲛⲓⲥⲕⲉⲩⲟⲥ ⲛ̄ϣⲓⲕⲓ ⲟⲩⲟϩ ⲁϥⲧⲥⲁⲃⲱⲟⲩ ⲉⲧⲁⲣⲭⲏ ⲛ̄ϭⲛⲉⲃϯ ⲛⲉⲙ ⲡⲓⲣⲏϯ ⲛ̄ϣⲱⲗⲕ ⲟⲩⲟϩ ⲁϥϯ ⲉⲧⲟⲧⲟⲩ ⲛ̄ⲛⲓⲕⲉⲉⲛⲧⲟⲗⲏ ⲧⲏⲣⲟⲩ ⲉⲁⲩⲧⲁⲥⲑⲟ ⲉⲡⲉϥⲙⲁⲛϣⲱⲡⲓ ϧⲉⲛ ⲟⲩϩⲓⲣⲏⲛⲏ. ⲛⲓⲁⲅⲓⲟⲥ ⲇⲉ ⲁⲩⲱⲗⲓ

ⲉⲃⲟⲗ ϩⲓϫⲱⲟⲩ ⲛ̅ⲛⲓϩⲃⲱⲥ ⲛ̅ⲝⲉⲛⲓⲕⲟⲥ ⲛ̅ⲧⲉ ϯⲥⲩⲣⲓⲁ ⲁⲩⲉⲣⲫⲟⲣⲓⲛ ⲙ̅ⲡⲓⲥⲭⲏⲙⲁ ⲛ̅ⲧⲉ ⲛⲓⲙⲟⲛⲁⲭⲟⲥ ⲛ̅ⲧⲉ ⲡⲓⲙⲁ ⲉⲧⲉⲙⲙⲁⲩ ⲟⲩⲟϩ ⲛⲁⲩⲭⲱ ⲙ̅ⲙⲟⲥ ⲛ̅ⲛⲟⲩⲉⲣⲏⲟⲩ ϫⲉ ⲁⲛⲁⲩ ⲙ̅ⲡⲉⲛⲑⲣⲉ ϩⲗⲓ ⲉⲙⲓ ⲙ̅ⲡⲉⲛⲣⲁⲛ ⲟⲩⲇⲉ ϫⲉ ⲛⲁⲛⲟⲓ ⲙ̅ⲙⲟⲛⲁⲭⲟⲥ ⲛ̅ϣⲟⲣⲡ ϫⲉ ⲟⲩⲏⲓ ⲡⲁⲓⲙⲁ ϧⲉⲛ ⲡⲟⲩϩⲟ ⲉϩⲟⲧⲉ ϯⲥⲩⲣⲓⲁ.

61. ⲗⲟⲓⲡⲟⲛ ⲁⲩⲓⲣⲓ ⲛ̅ⲧⲟⲩⲥⲡⲟⲩⲇⲏ ⲧⲏⲣⲥ ⲡⲉ ⲉϣⲧⲉⲙⲥⲁϫⲓ ⲛⲉⲙ ϩⲗⲓ ⲛ̅ⲣⲱⲙⲓ ⲟⲩⲇⲉ ⲉϩⲓⲕⲟⲧ ⲉⲟⲩⲟⲛ ⲉⲡⲧⲏⲣϥ ⲥⲁⲃⲟⲗ ⲙ̅ⲡⲟⲩⲙⲁⲛϣⲱⲡⲓ ⲛⲉⲙ ϯⲉⲕⲕⲗⲏⲥⲓⲁ. ⲧⲟⲩⲧⲣⲟⲫⲏ ⲇⲉ ⲛⲉ ⲡⲓⲱⲕ ⲡⲉ ⲛⲉⲙ ⲡⲓϩⲙⲟⲩ ⲛ̅ⲥⲛⲟⲩ ⲛⲓⲃⲉⲛ ⲓⲥϫⲉⲛ ⲉⲧⲁⲩⲓ ⲉϧⲟⲩⲛ ⲉϥⲃⲓⲟⲥ ⲛ̅ϯⲙⲉⲧⲙⲟⲛⲁⲭⲟⲥ ⲙ̅ⲡⲟⲩϫⲉⲙϯⲡⲓ ⲛ̅ⲟⲩⲁϥ ⲉⲡⲧⲏⲣϥ ⲟⲩⲇⲉ ⲟⲩⲏⲣⲡ ⲟⲩⲇⲉ ⲧⲉⲃⲧ ⲟⲩⲟϩ ⲛⲁⲩⲥⲉⲕ ⲃ̄ⲃ̄ ⲛ̅ⲥⲛⲟⲩ ⲛⲓⲃⲉⲛ. ⲟⲩⲟϩ ⲛⲁⲩⲓⲣⲓ ⲛ̅ϩⲁⲛⲧⲱⲃϩ ⲉⲩⲟϣ ⲛⲁⲩⲭⲱ ⲇⲉ ⲛ̅ⲛⲟⲩⲯⲁⲗⲙⲟⲥ ⲕⲁⲧⲁ ⲝ̄ⲝ̄ ⲛ̅ⲗⲉⲝⲓⲥ ⲛⲉⲙ ⲟⲩⲥⲧⲁⲩⲣⲟⲥ ⲕⲁⲧⲁ ⲡⲉⲑⲟⲥ ⲛ̅ⲛⲁϯⲥⲩⲣⲓⲁ.

62. ⲁⲩϣⲱⲡⲓ ⲇⲉ ϧⲉⲛ ⲱⲓϩⲏⲧ ⲙ̅ⲡⲟⲩⲛⲁⲩ ⲉⲡϩⲟ ⲛ̅ϩⲗⲓ ⲛ̅ⲣⲱⲙⲓ ⲉⲡⲧⲏⲣϥ ⲓⲙⲏϯ ⲉⲟⲩϧⲉⲗⲗⲟ ⲛ̅ⲟⲩⲣⲓⲧ ⲉϥⲣⲱⲓⲥ ⲉⲛⲓϩⲟⲥⲉⲙ ⲉϥⲱⲗⲓ ⲙ̅ⲡⲟⲟⲩϩⲱⲃ ⲛ̅ϫⲓϫ ⲟⲩⲟϩ ⲉϥⲓⲛⲓ ⲛⲱⲟⲩ ⲙ̅ⲡⲓⲕⲟⲩϫⲓ ⲛ̅ⲱⲓⲕ ⲫⲁⲓ ⲣⲱ ⲟⲛ ⲛⲁϥⲉⲣⲇⲓⲁⲕⲟⲛⲓⲛ ⲡⲉ ⲉⲡⲓⲕⲉⲁⲃⲃⲁ ⲙⲁⲕⲁⲣ ⲉⲑⲃⲉ ϫⲉ ⲛⲁϥⲥⲱⲟⲩⲛ ⲙ̅ⲙⲟϥ ⲣⲱ ⲡⲉ ⲓⲥϫⲉⲛ ϣⲟⲣⲡ ⲉϥϩⲁⲗ ϣⲁⲣⲟϥ ⲛ̅ⲟⲩⲙⲏϣ ⲛ̅ⲥⲟⲡ ⲉϥϭⲓ ⲙ̅ⲡⲉϥⲥⲙⲟⲩ.

63. ⲉϣⲱⲡ ⲇⲉ ⲁⲣⲉϣⲁⲛ ⲛⲁⲓⲁⲅⲓⲟⲥ ⲓ ⲉϯⲉⲕⲕⲗⲏⲥⲓⲁ ⲛⲁⲩϥⲁⲓ ⲛ̅ⲛⲟⲩⲃⲁⲗ ⲉⲡϣⲱⲓ ⲁⲛ ⲉⲡⲧⲏⲣϥ ⲉⲛⲁⲩ ⲉⲡϩⲟ ⲛ̅ϩⲗⲓ ⲁⲗⲗⲁ ⲁⲣⲉ ⲡⲟⲩϩⲟ ⲫⲁϧⲧ ⲉⲡⲉⲥⲏⲧ ⲉϥⲙⲏⲛ ϣⲁⲧⲟⲩϩⲱⲗ ⲉⲡⲓⲥⲡⲏⲗⲉⲟⲛ ϧⲉⲛ ⲟⲩⲭⲱⲗⲉⲙ ⲛⲉⲙ ⲟⲩϯϩⲑⲏϥ ⲕⲉ ⲅⲁⲣ ⲁⲗⲏⲑⲱⲥ ⲁⲕϣⲁⲛⲛⲁⲩ ⲉⲣⲱⲟⲩ ϧⲉⲛ ⲧⲁⲓⲕⲁⲧⲁⲥⲧⲁⲥⲓⲥ ⲙ̅ⲡⲁⲓⲣⲏϯ ⲭⲛⲁϫⲟⲥ ϫⲉ ⲟⲛⲧⲱⲥ ⲫϯ ϣⲟⲡ ϧⲉⲛ ⲛⲁⲓⲣⲱⲙⲓ ⲕⲉ ⲅⲁⲣ ⲁⲗⲏⲑⲱⲥ ϥϣⲟⲡ ⲛ̅ϧⲏⲧⲟⲩ ⲙ̅ⲫⲣⲏϯ ⲛ̅ⲏⲗⲓⲁⲥ ⲛⲉⲙ ⲓⲱ̄ⲁ̄ ⲡⲁⲓⲣⲏϯ ϩⲱⲟⲩ ⲛⲁⲓⲁⲅⲓⲟⲥ ⲛⲁⲣⲉ ⲡⲓⲭⲣⲱⲙ ⲛ̅ⲧⲉ ⲡⲓⲡ̄ⲛ̄ⲁ̄ ⲉ̄ⲑ̄ⲩ̄ ϣⲟⲡ ⲛ̅ϩⲣⲏⲓ ⲛ̅ϧⲏⲧⲟⲩ ⲡⲉ ⲉϥⲣⲱⲕϩ ⲛ̅ⲛⲓⲉⲛⲉⲣⲅⲓⲁ ⲉⲧϩⲱⲟⲩ ⲛ̅ⲧⲉ ⲡⲓⲡ̄ⲛ̄ⲁ̄ ⲙ̅ⲡⲟⲛⲏⲣⲟⲛ ⲛⲁⲓⲉⲧⲉⲣⲡⲟⲗⲉⲙⲓⲛ ⲛⲉⲙ ⲡⲉⲛϣⲗⲟⲗ ⲛ̅ⲥⲛⲟⲩ ⲛⲓⲃⲉⲛ ϧⲉⲛ ⲟⲩⲙⲉⲧⲁⲧϣⲓⲡⲓ

64. ⲁⲛⲟⲕ ⲅⲁⲣ ⲁⲛ ⲡⲉ ⲉⲧϫⲱ ⲙ̅ⲙⲟⲥ ⲁⲗⲗⲁ ⲁⲃⲃⲁ Ⲙⲁⲕⲁⲣ ⲡⲉ ⲡⲓⲡ̅ⲛ̅ⲁ̅ⲧⲟⲫⲟⲣⲟⲥ. ϩⲟⲧⲉ ⲡⲉϫⲁϥ ⲉⲧⲁⲓϩⲓⲕⲟⲧ ⲉⲣⲱⲟⲩ ⲙⲉⲛⲉⲛⲥⲁ Ⲅ̅ⲧ̅ ⲛ̅ⲣⲟⲙⲡⲓ ϩⲓⲛⲁ ⲛ̅ⲧⲁⲉⲙⲓ ⲉⲡⲟⲩϫⲓⲛϩⲉⲙⲥⲓ ⲟⲩⲟϩ ⲉⲧⲁ ⲣⲟⲩϩⲓ ϣⲱⲡⲓ ⲡⲉϫⲱⲟⲩ ⲛⲏⲓ ϫⲉ ⲭⲛⲁϩⲱⲗ. ⲁⲛⲟⲕ ⲇⲉ ⲡⲉϫⲏⲓ ⲛⲱⲟⲩ ϫⲉ ⲙ̅ⲙⲟⲛ ⲁⲗⲗⲁ ⲁⲓⲛⲁⲉⲛⲕⲟⲧ ⲙ̅ⲡⲁⲓⲙⲁ ⲟⲩⲟϩ ⲁⲩϫⲱ ⲛⲏⲓ ⲉϩⲣⲏⲓ ⲛ̅ⲟⲩⲑⲟⲙ ⲥⲁⲟⲩⲥⲁ ⲛ̅ⲧⲉ ⲡⲓⲥⲡⲏⲗⲉⲟⲛ ⲟⲩⲟϩ ⲁⲩⲉⲛⲕⲟⲧ ϩⲓ ⲟⲩⲙⲁ ⲟⲩⲟϩ ⲁⲩⲱⲗⲓ ⲛ̅ⲛⲟⲩⲃⲱⲕ ⲙ̅ⲡⲁⲙⲑⲟ ⲁⲩⲭⲁⲩ ⲉϩⲣⲏⲓ ⲟⲩⲟϩ ⲛⲁⲩⲭⲱ ⲛ̅ⲣⲱⲟⲩ ⲡⲉ

65. ⲉⲧⲁⲩⲉⲣ ⲫⲁⲓ ⲅⲁⲣ ⲉⲑⲃⲉ ⲁϣ ⲛ̅ⲉⲧⲓⲁ ⲉⲡⲓⲇⲏ ⲅⲁⲣ ⲡⲓⲥⲭⲏⲙⲁ ⲛ̅ⲧⲉ ⲛⲁϯⲤⲩⲣⲓⲁ ⲟⲩⲟⲛ ⲙⲁⲣϭⲛⲁϩ ⲉⲣⲱⲟⲩ ⲁⲛ ⲁⲗⲗⲁ ϩⲁⲛϩⲃⲱⲥ ⲛ̅ⲭⲁⲙⲉ ⲉⲡ ⲉⲧⲟⲩⲉⲣⲭⲟⲣⲓⲛ ⲙ̅ⲙⲱⲟⲩ. ϩⲟⲧⲉ ⲗⲟⲓⲡⲟⲛ ⲉⲧⲁ ⲛⲁⲓⲙⲁⲕⲁⲣⲓⲟⲥ ⲛⲁⲩ ⲉⲡⲟⲩⲓⲱⲧ ⲙ̅ⲡ̅ⲛ̅ⲁ̅ⲧⲟⲫⲟⲣⲟⲥ ⲁⲃⲃⲁ Ⲙⲁⲕⲁⲣ ⲉϥⲉⲣⲫⲟⲣⲓⲛ ⲙ̅ⲡⲓⲃⲱⲕ ⲛⲉⲙ ϯⲙⲁⲣϭⲛⲁϩ ⲁⲩⲟⲩⲱϣ ϩⲱⲟⲩ ⲉⲙⲟϣⲓ ⲕⲁⲧⲁ ⲡⲟⲩⲓⲱⲧ ⲉⲑⲣⲟⲩⲙⲟⲣⲟⲩ ⲕⲁⲧⲁ ⲡⲉϥⲥⲙⲟⲧ ⲉⲑⲃⲉ ⲫⲁⲓ ⲁⲩⲓⲛⲓ ⲛ̅ⲟⲩⲃⲱⲕ ⲙ̅ⲡⲉϥⲙⲑⲟ ⲉⲃⲟⲗ ⲁⲩⲭⲁⲩ ⲉⲡⲉⲥⲏⲧ ⲉⲩⲓⲣⲓ ⲇⲉ ⲙ̅ⲫⲁⲓ ⲉⲑⲣⲉϥϣⲗⲏⲗ ⲉϫⲱⲟⲩ ϩⲓⲛⲁ ⲁⲩϣⲁⲛⲧⲱⲟⲩⲛⲟⲩ ⲛ̅ⲧⲟⲩⲙⲟⲣⲟⲩ ⲙ̅ⲙⲱⲟⲩ ⲥⲁⲧⲟⲧϥ ϫⲉ ⲁϥⲉⲙⲓ ⲉⲫⲁⲓ ϩⲓⲧⲉⲛ ⲡⲓⲡ̅ⲛ̅ⲁ̅ ⲙ̅ⲡⲣⲟⲫⲏⲧⲓⲕⲟⲛ ⲉⲧϣⲟⲡ ⲛ̅ϧⲏⲧϥ ⲛ̅ϫⲉ ⲫⲏⲉ̅ⲑ̅ⲩ̅ ⲁⲃⲃⲁ Ⲙⲁⲕⲁⲣ ⲟⲩⲟϩ ⲁϥϣⲗⲏⲗ ⲉϫⲱⲟⲩ.

66. ⲁⲓⲧⲱⲃϩ ⲇⲉ ⲙ̅Ⲫϯ ⲡⲉϫⲁϥ ϩⲓⲛⲁ ⲛ̅ⲧⲉϥϭⲱⲣⲡ ⲛⲏⲓ ⲉⲃⲟⲗ ⲛ̅ⲧⲟⲩϫⲓⲛⲉⲣϩⲱⲃ ⲁⲥⲟⲩⲱⲛ ⲛ̅ϫⲉ ϯⲟⲩⲁϩⲥⲟⲓ ⲟⲩⲟϩ ⲁϥϣⲱⲡⲓ ⲛ̅ϫⲉ ⲟⲩⲱⲓⲛⲓ ⲙ̅ⲫⲣⲏϯ ⲙ̅ⲡⲓⲉϩⲟⲟⲩ. ⲛ̅ⲑⲱⲟⲩ ⲇⲉ ⲛⲁⲩⲛⲁⲩ ⲁⲛ ⲡⲉ ⲉⲡⲓⲟⲩⲱⲓⲛⲓ. ϩⲱⲥ ⲉⲓⲙⲉⲩⲓ ⲛ̅ⲑⲱⲟⲩ ϫⲉ ⲛⲁⲓⲉⲛⲕⲟⲧ ⲡⲉ ⲁⲡⲓⲛⲓϣϯ ⲕⲓⲙ ⲉⲡⲓⲕⲟⲩϫⲓ ⲁⲩⲧⲱⲟⲩⲛⲟⲩ ⲁⲩⲙⲟⲣⲟⲩ ⲁⲛⲟⲕ ⲙⲉⲛ ⲛⲁⲓⲛⲁⲩ ⲉⲣⲱⲟⲩ ⲡⲉ ⲛ̅ⲑⲱⲟⲩ ⲛⲁⲩⲛⲁⲩ ⲉⲣⲟⲓ ⲁⲛ ⲡⲉ ⲁⲩϭⲱⲗⲕ ⲛ̅ⲛⲟⲩϫⲓϫ ⲉⲡϣⲱⲓ ⲉⲧⲫⲉ ⲟⲩⲟϩ ⲁⲓⲛⲁⲩ ⲉⲛⲓⲇⲉⲙⲱⲛ ⲉⲩⲛⲏⲟⲩ ⲉϫⲉⲛ ⲡⲓⲕⲟⲩϫⲓ ⲙ̅ⲫⲣⲏϯ ⲛ̅ϩⲁⲛⲁϥ ϩⲁⲛⲟⲩⲟⲛ ⲙⲉⲛ ⲉⲩⲛⲏⲟⲩ ⲉϫⲉⲛ ⲛⲉϥⲃⲁⲗ ⲛⲉⲙ ⲣⲱϥ ⲟⲩⲟϩ ⲁⲓⲛⲁⲩ ⲉⲟⲩⲁⲅⲅⲉⲗⲟⲥ ⲛ̅ⲧⲉ ⲡ̅ⲟ̅ⲥ̅. ⲉⲣⲉ ⲟⲩⲟⲛ ⲟⲩⲥⲏϥⲓ ⲛ̅ⲭⲣⲱⲙ ⲛ̅ⲧⲟⲧϥ ⲉϥⲧⲁⲕⲧⲉϭⲗⲟ ⲉⲣⲱϥ ⲉϥϭⲟϫⲓ ⲛ̅ⲥⲁ ⲛⲓⲇⲉⲙⲱⲛ ⲛⲁⲩϣⲉⲣⲧⲟⲗⲙⲁⲛ ⲁⲛ ⲡⲉ ⲉϧⲱⲛⲧ ⲉⲡⲓⲛⲓϣϯ ⲉⲡⲧⲏⲣϥ.

67. ⲉⲣⲉ ϣⲱⲣⲡ ⲇⲉ ⲛⲁϣⲱⲡⲓ ⲁⲩⲭⲁⲩ ⲉϩⲣⲏⲓ ⲟⲛ ϩⲱⲥ ϫⲉ ⲉⲩⲛⲁⲉⲛⲕⲟⲧ. ⲁⲛⲟⲕ ⲇⲉ ϩⲱ ⲁⲓⲁⲓⲧ ⲙ̅ⲫⲣⲏϯ ϫⲉ ⲉⲓϩⲟⲣⲡ ⲛ̅ⲑⲱⲟⲩ ϩⲱⲟⲩ ⲙ̅ⲡⲁⲓⲣⲏϯ. ⲟⲩⲟϩ ⲁⲡⲓⲛⲓϣϯ ϫⲱ ⲙ̅ⲡⲁⲓⲥⲁϫⲓ ⲛ̅ⲟⲩⲱⲧ ⲛⲏⲓ ϫⲉ ⲭⲟⲩⲱϣ ⲛ̅ⲧⲉⲛϫⲱ ⲙ̅ⲡⲓⲃ̅ ⲙ̅ⲯⲁⲗⲙⲟⲥ. ⲡⲉϫⲏⲓ ϫⲉ ⲥⲉ ⲟⲩⲟϩ ⲁⲡⲡⲓⲕⲟⲟⲩϫⲓ ϫⲱ ⲛ̅Ⲋ̅

APPENDIX 2 135

ⲙ̅ⲯⲁⲗⲙⲟⲥ ⲛ̅ⲋ̅ ⲋ̅ ⲛ̅ⲗⲉⲝⲓⲥ ⲫⲟⲩⲁⲓ ⲛⲉⲙ ⲟⲩⲁⲗ ⲟⲩⲟϩ ⲕⲁⲧⲁ ⲗⲉⲝⲓⲥ ⲛⲁϥⲛⲏⲟⲩ ⲉⲃⲟⲗϧⲉⲛ ⲣⲱϥ ⲛ̅ϫⲉ ⲟⲩϫⲁϩ ⲛ̅ⲭⲣⲱⲙ ⲟⲩⲟϩ ⲛⲁϥⲛⲁ ⲉⲡϣⲱⲓ ⲉⲧⲫⲉ. ⲡⲁⲓⲣⲏϯ ⲟⲛ ⲡⲓⲛⲓϣϯ ϩⲱⲥⲧⲉ ⲉⲧⲁⲛⲟⲩⲱⲛ ⲛ̅ⲣⲱϥ ⲉⲉⲣⲯⲁⲗⲓⲛ ⲛⲁϥⲛⲏⲟⲩ ⲉⲃⲟⲗϧⲉⲛ ⲣⲱϥ ⲙ̅ⲫⲣⲏϯ ⲛ̅ⲟⲩⲛⲟϩ ⲛ̅ⲭⲣⲱⲙ ⲟⲩⲟϩ ⲉϥⲛⲁ ⲛ̅ⲟⲩⲕⲟⲩϫⲓ ⲛ̅ⲁⲡⲟ ⲉⲡϣⲱⲓ ⲉⲧⲫⲉ.

68. ⲁⲛⲟⲕ ⲇⲉ ϩⲱ ⲁⲓϫⲱ ⲛ̅ⲟⲩⲕⲟⲩϫⲓ ⲛ̅ⲁⲡⲟⲥⲧⲏⲑⲥ ⲉⲧⲁⲓⲛⲁⲩ ⲇⲉ ⲉⲧⲟⲩⲕⲁⲧⲁⲥⲧⲁⲥⲓⲥ ⲛⲉⲙ ⲧⲟⲩϫⲓⲛⲉⲣϩⲱⲃ ⲉⲑⲛⲁⲛⲉⲥ ⲛⲉⲙ ⲡⲓⲛⲓϣϯ ⲛ̅ϩⲙⲟⲙ ⲉⲧϣⲟⲡ ⲛ̅ϧⲏⲧⲟⲟⲩ ⲉϧⲟⲩⲛ ⲉⲫϯ ⲁⲓϫⲉⲙϩⲟⲩ ⲉⲣⲱⲟⲩ ⲉⲙⲁϣⲱ ⲟⲩⲟϩ ⲥⲉⲛⲏⲟⲩ ⲉⲃⲟⲗ ⲁⲓϫⲟⲥ ϫⲉ ⲧⲱⲃϩ ⲉϫⲱⲓ. ⲛ̅ⲑⲱⲟⲩ ⲇⲉ ⲁⲩϩⲟ ⲉⲣⲟⲓ ⲉⲑⲣⲓϯ ⲉϫⲱⲟⲩ ⲙ̅ⲡⲓⲥⲭⲏⲙⲁ ⲟⲩⲟϩ ⲡⲁⲓⲣⲏϯ ⲁⲓⲑⲉⲧ ⲡⲟⲩϩⲏⲧ ⲁⲓⲧⲛⲓϥ ⲉϫⲱⲟⲩ ⲁⲓⲓ ⲉⲃⲟⲗ ϩⲓⲧⲟⲧⲟⲩ ϧⲉⲛ ⲟⲩϩⲓⲣⲏⲛⲏ.

69. ⲓⲥ ϩⲏⲡⲡⲉ ⲟⲩⲛ ⲁⲛⲥⲱⲧⲉⲙ ⲉⲡⲓⲛⲓϣϯ ⲁⲃⲃⲁ ⲙⲁⲕⲁⲣ ⲉϥⲧⲁⲙⲟ ⲙ̅ⲙⲟⲛ ⲣⲏⲧⲱⲥ ϫⲉ ⲁⲛⲁⲓⲙⲁⲕⲁⲣⲓⲟⲥ ⲉⲣⲡⲉⲙⲡϣⲁ ⲙ̅ⲡⲓϩⲙⲟⲧ ⲛ̅ⲧⲉ ⲡⲓⲡ̅ⲛ̅ⲁ̅ ⲙ̅ⲡⲁⲣⲁⲕⲗⲏⲧⲟⲛ ⲙ̅ⲫⲣⲏϯ ⲛ̅ⲟⲩⲭⲣⲱⲙ ⲅⲁⲣ ϧⲉⲛ ⲟⲩⲙⲉⲑⲙⲏⲓ ⲉϣⲱⲡ ⲛ̅ⲧⲁϩⲓⲧⲟⲧ ⲉϫⲉⲛ ⲛⲏⲉⲧⲁ ⲡⲓⲛⲓϣϯ ⲉⲧⲉⲙⲙⲁⲩ ϫⲟⲧⲟⲩ ⲛⲏⲓ ⲉⲑⲃⲏⲧⲟⲩ ⲛⲉⲙ ⲛⲏⲉⲧⲁⲩⲛⲁⲩ ⲉⲣⲱⲟⲩ ϩⲱ ϧⲉⲛ ⲛⲁⲃⲁⲗ ⲡⲓⲥⲁϫⲓ ⲛⲁϥⲁϣⲁⲓ ⲉⲡϩⲟⲩⲟ ⲉⲑⲃⲉ ⲫⲁⲓ ⲁⲓϫⲱ ⲛ̅ⲥⲱⲓ ⲙ̅ⲡⲓϩⲟⲩⲟ ⲉⲑⲃⲉ ⲛⲏⲉⲧⲟⲓ ⲛ̅ⲕⲟⲩϫⲓ ϧⲉⲛ ⲡⲓⲛⲁϩϯ ⲛ̅ⲧⲟⲩϣⲧⲉⲙⲉⲣⲓ ⲉⲧⲙⲉⲑⲙⲏⲓ ϫⲉ ⲟⲩⲙⲉⲑⲛⲟⲩϫ ⲧⲉ ϯⲛⲁϫⲱ ⲛ̅ϩⲁⲛⲕⲟⲩϫⲓ ⲉⲃⲟⲗϧⲉⲛ ϩⲁⲛⲙⲏϣ ⲛ̅ⲧⲁϥ ⲑⲱϣ ⲉⲡⲓⲥⲁϫⲓ.

70. ⲡⲓϧⲉⲗⲗⲟ ⲅⲁⲣ ⲛ̅ⲣⲱⲙⲓ ⲱⲧⲁⲛⲉⲣϣⲟⲣⲡ ⲙ̅ⲫⲓⲣⲓ ⲉⲣⲟϥ ϫⲉ ϥⲉⲣⲇⲓⲁⲕⲟⲛⲓⲛ ⲉⲛⲁⲓⲁⲅⲓⲟⲥ ⲛⲉ ⲟⲩⲙⲁⲓⲛⲟⲩϯ ⲡⲉ ⲉⲡϩⲟⲩⲟ ⲟⲩⲟϩ ⲛⲉ ⲟⲩⲟⲛ ⲛ̅ⲧⲁϥ ⲛ̅ⲟⲩⲛⲓϣϯ ⲛ̅ⲛⲁϩϯ ⲉϧⲟⲩⲛ ⲉⲣⲱⲟⲩ ⲫⲁⲓ ⲟⲩⲛ ⲉⲧⲁ ⲟⲩⲙⲁⲧⲟⲓ ⲱⲗⲓ ⲛ̅ⲛⲉϥϭⲁⲙⲟⲩⲗ ⲛ̅ⲟⲩⲥⲟⲡ ⲛ̅ⲭⲃⲁ ⲟⲩⲟϩ ⲉⲧⲁ ⲡⲓⲙⲁⲧⲟⲓ ⲉⲣⲉⲡⲓⲭⲣⲓⲛ ⲉⲡⲓϧⲉⲗⲗⲟ ⲁϥⲥⲱⲟⲩⲧⲉⲛ ⲁϥϯ ⲛ̅ⲟⲩⲕⲟⲩⲣ ϧⲉⲛ ⲧⲉϥⲟⲩⲟϫⲓ ⲛ̅ⲟⲩⲓⲛⲁⲙ ⲡⲓϧⲉⲗⲗⲟ ⲇⲉ ⲙ̅ⲙⲁⲓⲛⲟⲩϯ ⲥⲁⲧⲟⲧϥ ⲁϥⲫⲱⲛϩ ⲛ̅ϯⲭⲉⲧ ⲉⲣⲟϥ ⲉϥϫⲱⲕ ⲉⲃⲟⲗ ⲛ̅ϯⲉⲛⲧⲟⲗⲏ ⲛ̅ⲧⲉ ⲡⲓⲉⲩⲁⲅⲅⲉⲗⲓⲟⲛ. ⲧⲟⲧⲉ ⲡⲓⲧⲩⲣⲁⲛⲟⲥ ⲙ̅ⲙⲁⲧⲟⲓ ⲁϥⲟⲩⲁϩⲧⲟⲧϥ ⲁϥⲥⲱⲟⲩⲧⲉⲛ ϧⲉⲛ ⲡⲓⲥⲕⲉⲩⲟⲥ ⲉⲧϧⲉⲛ ⲧⲉϥϫⲓϫ ⲉϧⲟⲩⲛ ϧⲉⲛ ⲡⲣⲟ ⲙ̅ⲡⲓϧⲉⲗⲗⲟ ⲁϥⲫⲱⲣⲕ ⲙ̅ⲡⲉϥⲃⲁⲗ ⲛ̅ϫⲁϭⲉ. ⲡⲓϧⲉⲗⲗⲟ ⲇⲉ ⲁϥϣⲉⲡϩⲙⲟⲧ ⲛ̅ⲧⲉⲛ ⲫϯ ϫⲉ ⲁϥⲙ̅ⲡϣⲁ ⲣⲱ ⲁⲩϣⲁϥ ⲙ̅ⲡⲉϥⲃⲁⲗ ⲉⲑⲃⲉ ϯⲉⲛⲧⲟⲗⲏ ⲛ̅ⲧⲉ ⲡⲓⲉⲩⲁⲅⲅⲉⲗⲓⲟⲛ ⲛ̅ⲧⲉ ⲡⲉⲛⲟ̅ⲥ̅ ⲓ̅ⲏ̅ⲥ̅ ⲡ̅ⲭ̅ⲥ̅.

71. ⲁⲥϣⲱⲡⲓ ⲇⲉ ⲛⲁϥ ⲟⲛ ⲛ̅ⲟⲩⲥⲟⲡ ⲉⲑⲣⲉϥϣⲁⲗ ⲛ̅ⲛⲓⲕⲟⲩϫⲓ ⲛ̅ϩⲱⲃ ⲛ̅ϫⲓϫ ⲛ̅ⲧⲉ ⲛⲁⲓⲙⲁⲕⲁⲣⲓⲟⲥ ⲉⲭⲏⲙⲓ. ϫⲉ ϩⲓⲛⲁ ⲛ̅ⲧⲉϥⲑⲁⲙⲓⲟ ⲙ̅ⲡⲓⲕⲟⲟⲩϫⲓ

ǸⲰⲓⲕ ⲚⲰⲞⲨ ⲕⲀⲦⲀ ⲦⲈϤⲤⲨⲚⲎⲐⲒⲀ ⲪⲀⲒ ⲆⲈ ⲚⲈ ⲞⲨⲢⲈⲘϪⲈⲠⲢⲞⲘⲈⲚⲤⲒⲚ ϦⲈⲚ ⲠⲐⲰϢ ⲀⲢⲂⲀⲦ ⲈϤϢⲞⲠ ϦⲈⲚ ⲠⲒϮⲘⲒ ⲈⲦⲞⲨⲘⲞⲨϮ ⲈⲢⲞϤ ϪⲈ Ⲡⲓⲛⲟⲩⲃ. ⲘⲈⲚⲈⲚⲤⲀ ⲐⲢⲈϤⲐⲀⲘⲒⲞ ⲆⲈ Ⲙ̀ⲠⲒⲔⲞⲨϪⲒ Ǹⲱⲓⲕ Ǹⲧⲉ ⲚⲒⲀⲄⲒⲞⲤ ⲀϤⲈⲠⲦ ⲚⲒϪⲀⲘⲞⲨⲖ ⲀϤⲒ ⲈϢⲰϨⲦ ⲈⲦⲀϤϤⲞⲢ ⲆⲈ ⲈⲠⲒⲘⲀⲚⲒ ⲈⲠⲈⲤⲚⲦ ⲈϦⲢⲎⲒ ⲈⲠⲒϨⲈⲖⲞⲤ ⲞⲨⲞϨ ϨⲰⲤ ⲈϤⲘⲞϢⲒ ⲚⲈⲘ ⲠⲒϪⲀⲘⲞⲨⲖ ⲀϤϨⲞⲢ ⲈⲞⲨⲘⲀ ⲈϤⲞⲒ Ǹ̀ϨⲀⲖⲘⲒ ⲞⲨⲞϨ ⲔⲀⲦⲀ ⲞⲨⲤⲨⲚⲀⲚⲦⲎⲘⲀ Ǹ̀ⲦⲈ ⲠⲒϪⲀϪⲒ Ⲙ̀ⲘⲞⲤϤ ⲠⲈⲐⲚⲀⲚⲈϤ ⲚⲒⲂⲈⲚ ⲀϤⲤⲖⲀϮ Ǹ̀ϪⲈ ⲠⲒϪⲀⲘⲞⲨⲖ ⲀϤϨⲈⲒ ⲞⲨⲞϨ ⲀⲦⲈϤⲪⲀⲦ Ⲃ̅ ϮⲔⲰϢ ⲈⲠⲒϢⲀⲢ Ⲙ̀ⲘⲀⲨⲀⲦϤ ⲈⲐⲘⲞⲚⲒ.

72. ϦⲈⲚ ⲠϪⲒⲚⲐⲢⲈ ⲪⲀⲒ ϢⲰⲠⲒ ⲀⲠⲒϦⲈⲖⲖⲞ ⲢⲒⲘⲒ ϦⲈⲚ ⲞⲨⲈⲚϢⲀϢⲒ ⲚⲈⲘ ⲞⲨⲚⲒϢϮ Ǹ̀ⲘⲔⲀϨ Ǹ̀ϨⲎⲦ ϨⲰⲤⲦⲈ Ǹ̀ⲦⲈϤⲪⲰϦ Ǹ̀ⲚⲈϤϨⲂⲰⲤ ⲞⲨⲞϨ Ǹ̀ⲦⲈϤⲦⲀⲖⲈ ⲔⲀϨⲒ ⲈϪⲈⲚ ⲦⲈϤⲀⲪⲈ ⲈⲐⲂⲈ ϪⲈ ⲚⲈ ⲠⲒϪⲀⲘⲞⲨⲖ ⲪⲰϤ ⲀⲚ ⲠⲈ ⲈⲐⲂⲈ ⲪⲀⲒ ⲀϤⲈⲢⲘⲔⲀϨ Ǹ̀ϨⲎⲦ ⲞⲨⲞϨ ⲀϤⲢⲒⲘⲒ. ⲒⲦⲀ ⲀϤϢⲈⲠϨⲘⲞⲦ Ǹ̀ⲦⲈⲚ Ⲫ̀Ϯ ⲈϤϪⲰ Ⲙ̀ⲘⲞⲤ ϪⲈ ϮϢⲈⲠϨⲘⲞⲦ Ǹ̀ⲦⲞⲦⲔ ⲠⲀϬⲞⲒⲤ Ⲓⲏⲥⲟⲩⲥ Ⲡⲓⲭⲣⲓⲥⲧⲟⲥ Ⲫ̀Ϯ Ǹ̀ⲚⲒⲀⲄⲒⲞⲤ. ⲞⲨⲞϨ ⲈⲦⲀϤⲬⲀ ⲠⲒϪⲀⲘⲞⲨⲖ ⲆⲈ ⲈϤⲤⲚⲦ ⲈⲂⲞⲖ ϨⲒϪⲈⲚ ⲠⲔⲀϨⲒ ⲀϤϨⲰⲖ ⲈⲠⲒⲤⲠⲎⲖⲈⲞⲚ Ǹ̀ⲦⲈ ⲚⲀⲒⲘⲀⲔⲀⲢⲒⲞⲤ ⲀϤⲦⲀⲘⲰⲞⲨ ⲈⲪⲚⲈⲦⲀϤϢⲰⲠⲒ Ⲙ̀ⲘⲞϤ ⲚⲈⲘ ⲠⲒϪⲀⲘⲞⲨⲖ. ⲈⲠⲒⲆⲎ ⲞⲨⲚ Ⲙ̀ⲠⲞⲨⲈⲘⲒ ⲈⲠⲦⲀϪⲢⲞ Ⲙ̀ⲠⲒⲤⲀϪⲒ ⲀⲖⲖⲀ ϦⲈⲚ ⲠⲠⲒϪⲒⲚⲐⲢⲞⲨⲚⲀⲨ ⲈⲢⲞϤ ⲈϤⲈⲢⲦⲀⲖⲈⲠⲰⲢⲒⲚ ⲀⲨⲘⲞϢⲒ ⲚⲈⲘⲀϤ.

73. ⲈⲦⲀⲨϤⲞⲢ ⲈⲠⲒⲘⲀ ⲈⲦⲒ ⲈⲨϨⲒ ⲪⲞⲨⲈⲒ Ⲙ̀ⲠⲒϪⲀⲘⲞⲨⲖ Ǹ̀ⲞⲨⲔⲞⲨϪⲒ ⲀⲠⲒϦⲈⲖⲖⲞ ⲢⲒⲘⲒ ⲈⲀϤⲚⲀⲨ ⲈⲢⲞϤ. Ǹ̀ⲐⲰⲞⲨ ⲆⲈ ϨⲰⲞⲨ ⲚⲎⲈⲐⲞⲨⲀⲂ ϦⲈⲚ ⲠϪⲒⲚⲐⲢⲞⲨⲚⲀⲨ ⲈⲠⲒϪⲀⲘⲞⲨⲖ ⲈϤⲢⲀϦⲦ ⲈⲠⲈⲤⲚⲦ ϨⲒϪⲈⲚ ⲠⲔⲀϨⲒ ⲀⲨⲞϨⲒ ⲈⲢⲀⲦⲞⲨ ⲀⲨⲦⲰⲂϨ Ⲙ̀Ⲫ̀Ϯ ⲞⲨⲞϨ ϦⲈⲚ ⲠϪⲒⲚⲐⲢⲞⲨϨⲰⲚⲦ ⲈⲢⲞϤ ⲀϤⲈⲢϨⲞϮ ⲀϤⲈϢϨⲢⲰⲞⲨ ⲈⲂⲞⲖ ⲀϤⲦⲈⲘⲢⲰϤ ⲈⲠⲒⲔⲀϨⲒ ϨⲰⲤ ⲈϤⲞⲨⲰϢⲦ Ǹ̀ⲚⲒⲀⲄⲒⲞⲤ ⲠⲈϪⲰⲞⲨ ⲆⲈ Ⲙ̀ⲠⲒϪⲀⲘⲞⲨⲖ ϪⲈ Ⲙ̀ⲠⲈⲢⲈⲢϨⲞϮ ⲀⲖⲖⲀ ⲦⲰⲚⲔ ⲞϨⲒ ⲈⲢⲀⲦⲔ ϦⲈⲚ ϮϪⲞⲘ Ǹ̀ⲦⲈ ⲪⲎⲈⲦⲀϤⲦⲰⲚϤ ⲈⲂⲞⲖ ϦⲈⲚ ⲚⲎⲈⲐⲘⲰⲞⲨⲦ Ⲓⲏⲥⲟⲩⲥ Ⲡⲓⲭⲣⲓⲥⲧⲟⲥ Ⲫ̀Ϯ Ǹ̀ⲚⲒⲬⲢⲒⲤⲦⲒⲀⲚⲞⲤ.

74. ⲞⲨⲞϨ ⲪⲀⲒ ⲈⲦⲀⲨϪⲞϤ ⲀⲨϤⲀⲒ Ǹ̀ⲚⲞⲨⲂⲀⲖ ⲈⲠϢⲰⲒ ⲈⲦⲪⲈ ⲈⲨϪⲰ Ⲙ̀ⲘⲞⲤ ϪⲈ Ⲫ̀Ϯ Ⲙ̀ⲠⲈⲚⲒⲰⲦ ⲀⲂⲂⲀ Ⲙⲁⲕⲁⲣ ⲤⲰⲦⲈⲘ ⲈⲢⲞⲚ ⲈⲚⲦⲰⲂϨ Ⲙ̀ⲘⲞⲔ ⲠⲒⲘⲀⲒⲢⲰⲘⲒ ϦⲈⲚ ⲞⲨⲈⲬⲀⲠⲒⲚⲀ ⲆⲈ ⲀϤϤⲞϪϤ ⲈⲠϢⲰⲒ Ǹ̀ϪⲈ ⲠⲒϪⲀⲘⲞⲨⲖ ⲈϤⲞϨⲒ ⲈⲢⲀⲦϤ ⲈϪⲈ ⲚⲈϤϬⲀⲖⲀⲨϪ ⲈϤⲞⲨⲞϪ Ⲙ̀Ⲫ̀ⲢⲎϮ ⲒⲤϪⲈⲔ Ⲙ̀ⲠⲈϤϨⲈⲒ ⲈⲠⲦⲎⲢϤ ⲠⲒϦⲈⲖⲖⲞ ⲆⲈ ⲈϤⲞⲨⲰϢⲦ Ǹ̀ⲚⲒⲀⲄⲒⲞⲤ ⲈϤϪⲰ Ⲙ̀ⲘⲞⲤ ϪⲈ Ϥ̀ⲤⲘⲀⲢⲰⲞⲨⲦ Ǹ̀ϪⲈ Ⲓ̅ⲏ̅ⲥ̅ Ⲡ̅ⲭ̅ⲥ̅ ⲪⲎⲈⲦϢⲞⲠ ϦⲈⲚ ⲐⲎⲚⲞⲨ.

APPENDIX 2   137

75. ⲟⲩⲟϩ ⲉⲧⲓ ⲉⲩⲙⲟϣⲓ ⲉⲡⲓⲙⲁⲛϣⲱⲡⲓ ⲉⲩⲥⲟⲡ ⲁ ⲫⲛⲉⲑⲩ Ⲇⲟⲙⲉⲧⲓⲟⲥ ⲛⲁⲩ ⲉⲡϩⲟ ⲙ̄ⲡⲓϩⲉⲗⲗⲟ ⲉϥⲙⲉϩ ⲛ̄ⲓⲧⲉⲛ ⲉⲑⲃⲉ ⲡⲓⲛⲁⲩ ⲉⲧⲁϥⲧⲁⲗⲉ ⲕⲁϩⲓ ⲉϫⲉⲛ ⲧⲉϥⲁⲫⲉ ϧⲉⲛ ⲡϫⲓⲛⲉⲣⲉ ⲡⲓϫⲁⲙⲟⲩⲗ ϩⲉⲓ ⲛ̄ⲧⲟⲧϥ. ⲁⲡⲓⲁⲅⲓⲟⲥ Ⲇⲟⲙⲉⲧⲓⲟⲥ ⲁⲙⲟⲛⲓ ⲙ̄ⲡⲓⲗⲁⲕϩ ⲛ̄ⲧⲉ ⲡⲓⲫⲣⲟⲕ ⲉⲧⲧⲟⲓ ⲉⲭⲱϥ ϩⲱⲥ ⲉϥϭⲱϯ ⲛ̄ⲥⲁ ⲡϩⲟ ⲙ̄ⲡⲓϩⲉⲗⲗⲟ ⲛ̄ⲑⲟϥ ⲇⲉ ϩⲱϥ ⲉⲃⲟⲗϩⲓⲧⲉⲛ ⲡⲉϥⲛⲓϣϯ ⲛ̄ⲛⲁϩϯ ⲉϧⲟⲩⲛ ⲉⲣⲱⲟⲩ ⲛⲉⲙ ϯϣⲫⲏⲣⲓ ⲉⲧⲁⲩⲛⲁⲩ ⲉⲣⲟⲥ ⲉⲧⲁⲥϣⲱⲡⲓ ⲉⲃⲟⲗϩⲓⲧⲉⲛ ⲛⲓⲁⲅⲓⲟⲥ ⲉ̅ⲑ̅ⲩ̅ ⲁϥⲁⲙⲟⲛⲓ ⲛ̄ϫⲓϫ ⲙ̄ⲡⲓⲙⲁⲕⲁⲣⲓⲟⲥ ⲁϥⲭⲁⲥ ⲉϫⲉⲛ ⲡⲉϥⲃⲁⲗ ⲉⲑⲙⲟⲕϩ ϩⲱⲥ ⲉϥⲛⲁϭⲓ ⲉⲡⲉϥⲥⲙⲟⲩ ⲟⲩⲟϩ ⲉⲧⲁ ⲧϫⲓϫ ⲙ̄ⲫⲛⲉ̅ⲑ̅ⲩ̅ ϭⲟϩ ⲉⲡⲉϥⲃⲁⲗ ⲥⲁⲧⲟⲧϥ ⲁϥⲛⲁⲩ ⲙ̄ⲃⲟⲗ.

76. Ⲡⲓϩⲉⲗⲗⲟ ⲇⲉ ⲛ̄ⲟⲩⲣⲓⲧ ⲉⲧⲉ ⲡⲓⲙⲁⲛϫⲁⲙⲟⲩⲗ ⲡⲉ ⲁϥⲉⲣϣⲫⲏⲣⲓ ⲙ̄ⲫⲏⲉⲧⲁϥϣⲱⲡⲓ ⲟⲩⲙⲟⲛⲟⲛ ϫⲉ ⲁⲩⲧⲟⲩϫⲉ ⲡⲓϫⲁⲙⲟⲩⲗ ⲁⲗⲗⲁ ϫⲉ ⲁϥⲛⲁⲩ ⲙ̄ⲃⲟⲗ ⲥⲁⲧⲟⲧϥ ϧⲉⲛ ⲡϫⲓⲛⲑⲣⲉϥϩⲓ ⲧϫⲓϫ ⲙ̄ⲡⲓⲁⲅⲓⲟⲥ ⲉϫⲉⲛ ⲡⲉϥⲃⲁⲗ ⲟⲩⲟϩ ⲁϥϯⲱⲟⲩ ⲙ̄ⲫϯ ⲉⲙⲁϣⲱ ⲉϩⲣⲏⲓ ϯⲇⲱⲣⲉⲁ ⲉⲧⲁⲥⲧⲁϩⲟϥ ⲉⲩϫⲱ ⲙ̄ⲙⲟⲥ ϫⲉ ⲁⲛⲁⲩ ⲙ̄ⲡⲉⲣⲧⲁⲙⲉ ϩⲗⲓ ⲉⲫⲁⲓ ⲟⲩⲟϩ ⲟⲛ ⲡⲉϫⲱⲟⲩ ⲛⲁϥ ϫⲉ ⲙ̄ⲡⲉⲣⲙⲉⲩⲓ ϫⲉ ⲉⲧⲁ ⲡⲓⲟⲩϫⲁⲓ ⲧⲁϩⲟⲕ ⲉⲑⲃⲏⲧⲉⲛ ⲁⲛⲟⲛ ⲅⲁⲣ ⲁⲛⲟⲛ ϩⲁⲛⲣⲱⲙⲓ ⲛ̄ⲣⲉϥⲉⲣⲛⲟⲃⲓ ⲁⲗⲗⲁ ⲉⲧⲁ ⲫⲁⲓ ϣⲱⲡⲓ ⲉⲃⲟⲗϩⲓⲧⲉⲛ ⲧϫⲟⲙ ⲙ̄ⲡ̅ⲭ̅ⲥ̅.

77. ⲛ̄ⲑⲟϥ ⲇⲉ ⲉⲛⲁϥ ⲟⲩⲟϩ ⲛⲓⲕⲟⲩϫⲓ ⲛ̄ⲱⲓⲕ ⲉⲃⲟⲗ ⲛⲱⲟⲩ ⲁϥⲧⲁⲥⲑⲟ ⲙ̄ⲡⲉϥⲙⲁⲛⲉⲣϩⲱⲃ ϧⲉⲛ ⲡⲓϩⲟⲥⲉⲙ ⲟⲩⲟϩ ⲉⲧⲁ ⲛⲉϥϣⲫⲏⲣ ⲛⲁⲩ ⲉⲣⲟϥ ⲉⲧⲁ ⲡⲉϥⲃⲁⲗ ⲟⲩⲱⲛ ⲁⲩⲉⲣϣⲫⲏⲣⲓ ⲉⲙⲁϣⲱ ⲟⲩⲟϩ ⲛⲁⲩϣⲓⲛⲓ ⲙ̄ⲙⲟϥ ⲡⲉϫⲉ ⲡⲱⲥ ⲁⲕⲛⲁⲩ ⲙ̄ⲃⲟⲗ. ⲛ̄ⲑⲟϥ ⲇⲉ ⲁϥⲧⲁⲙⲱⲟⲩ ϫⲉ ⲛⲓⲙⲁⲑⲏⲧⲏⲥ ⲛ̄ⲧⲉ ⲁⲃⲃⲁ Ⲙⲁⲕⲁⲣ ⲛⲉ ⲉⲧⲁⲩⲧⲁⲗϭⲟⲓ ⲟⲩⲟϩ ⲟⲩⲟⲛ ⲛⲓⲃⲉⲛ ⲉⲧⲁⲩⲥⲱⲧⲉⲙ ⲁⲩϯⲱⲟⲩ ⲙ̄ⲫϯ.

78. ⲁⲛⲟⲕ ⲅⲁⲣ ϩⲱ ϧⲉⲛ ⲡϫⲓⲛⲑⲣⲓⲥⲱⲧⲉⲙ ⲉⲡⲁⲓⲥⲁϫⲓ ⲙⲉⲛⲉⲛⲥⲁ ⲑⲣⲟⲩⲕⲏⲛ ⲉⲙⲧⲟⲛ ⲙ̄ⲙⲱⲟⲩ ⲁⲓϣⲓⲛⲓ ⲛ̄ⲧⲟⲧϥ ⲙ̄ⲡⲓⲛⲓϣϯ ⲁⲃⲃⲁ Ⲙⲁⲕⲁⲣ ϩⲓⲛⲁ ⲛ̄ⲧⲁⲉⲙⲓ ⲉⲡⲓⲧⲁϫⲣⲟ ⲉⲓϫⲱ ⲙ̄ⲙⲟⲥ ⲛⲁϥ ⲙ̄ⲡⲁⲓⲣⲏϯ ϫⲉ ⲡⲁⲓⲱⲧ ⲉ̅ⲑ̅ⲩ̅ ⲁⲓⲥⲱⲧⲉⲙ ⲉⲑⲃⲉ ⲛⲁⲓⲙⲁⲕⲁⲣⲓⲟⲥ ϫⲉ ⲁⲩⲟⲩⲱⲛ ⲙ̄ⲫⲃⲁⲗ ⲛ̄ⲟⲩⲃⲉⲗⲗⲉ ⲁⲛ ⲧⲁⲫⲙⲏ ⲧⲉ ⲡⲉϫⲁϥ ⲛⲏⲓ ϫⲉ ⲁϩⲁ ⲟⲩⲙⲉⲑⲙⲏⲓ ⲡⲉ. ⲁⲛⲟⲕ ⲇⲉ ⲡⲉϫⲏⲓ ⲛⲁϥ ϩⲱⲥ ⲉⲓⲉⲣϣⲫⲏⲣⲓ ϫⲉ ⲟⲛⲧⲱⲥ ⲡⲁⲓϩⲱⲃ ⲟⲩⲛⲓϣϯ ⲡⲉ ⲁϥⲉⲣⲟⲩⲱ ⲇⲉ ⲡⲉϫⲁϥ ⲛⲏⲓ ϫⲉ ⲙ̄ⲙⲟⲛ ⲡⲁϣⲏⲣⲓ ⲫⲁⲓ ⲟⲩⲛⲓϣϯ ⲛ̄ϩⲱⲃ ⲡⲉ ⲕⲁⲧⲁ ⲑⲙⲁⲓⲏ ⲙ̄ⲡⲓⲛⲓϣϯ ⲛ̄ϩⲙⲟⲧ ⲉⲧⲁⲩϭⲓⲧϥ ⲉⲃⲟⲗϩⲓⲧⲉⲛ Ⲫϯ ⲕⲉ ⲅⲁⲣ ⲁⲩⲉⲣⲡⲉⲙⲡϣⲁ ⲛ̄ϯϫⲟⲙ ⲉⲧⲭⲏ ⲛⲉⲙ Ⲏⲗⲓⲁⲥ ⲛⲉⲙ Ⲓⲱ̅ⲁ̅

ⲁⲠⲭ̄ⲥ̄ ϯⲙⲡⲉϥⲉⲣϣⲓϣⲓ ⲛ̀ⲱⲟⲩ ⲙ̀ⲫⲣⲏϯ ⲛ̀ⲛⲉⲇⲁⲡⲟⲥⲧⲟⲗⲟⲥ ⲉⲑⲃⲉ ϫⲉ ⲙ̀ⲡⲟⲩⲕⲱϯ ⲛ̀ⲥⲁ ⲡϣⲟⲩ ⲧⲏⲣϥ ⲛ̀ⲧⲉ ⲡⲁⲓⲕⲟⲥⲙⲟⲥ ⲉⲑⲛⲁⲧⲁⲕⲟ

79. ⲉⲑⲃⲉ ⲡϣⲟⲩ ⲙ̀ⲫⲏⲉⲧⲁⲩⲉⲣϩⲉⲗⲡⲓⲥ ⲉⲣⲟϥ Ⲡⲭ̄ⲥ̄ ⲕⲉ ⲅⲁⲣ ⲁⲩⲉⲣ ⲙ̀ⲫⲣⲏϯ ⲛ̀ⲟⲩϣⲁϩ ⲛ̀ⲭⲣⲱⲙ ⲉϥϯⲙⲟⲩⲉ ⲉⲙⲁϣⲱ ϩⲱⲥ ⲇⲉ ϣⲁ ⲉϧⲣⲏⲓ ⲉⲡⲓⲕⲉⲛⲓϥⲓ ⲉⲑⲛⲏⲟⲩ ⲉⲃⲟⲗϧⲉⲛ ⲣⲱⲟⲩ ⲟⲩⲭⲣⲱⲙ ⲉϥⲙⲟϩ ⲡⲉ ϩⲱⲥⲧⲉ ⲁⲩϣⲁⲛⲟⲩⲱⲛ ⲛ̀ⲣⲱⲟⲩ ⲉⲉⲣⲡⲣⲟⲥⲉⲩⲭⲉⲥⲑⲉ ⲉⲣⲉ ⲡⲓϣⲁϩ ⲛⲏⲟⲩ ⲉⲃⲟⲗϧⲉⲛ ⲣⲱⲟⲩ ⲙ̀ⲫⲣⲏϯ ⲛ̀ⲟⲩⲥⲉⲧⲉⲃⲣⲏϫ ⲉϥⲉⲣⲟⲩⲱⲓⲛⲓ ϣⲁ ⲉϩⲣⲏⲓ ⲉⲧⲫⲉ. ⲗⲟⲓⲡⲟⲛ ⲡⲁϣⲏⲣⲓ ⲙ̀ⲡⲉⲣⲉⲣⲁⲑⲛⲁϩϯ ⲉⲛⲏ ⲧⲏⲣⲟⲩ ⲉⲧⲁⲕⲥⲟⲑⲙⲟⲩ ⲉⲑⲃⲏⲧⲟⲩ. ⲁⲛⲟⲕ ⲇⲉ ⲁⲟⲩⲱϣⲧ ⲛ̀ⲛⲉϥϫⲓϫ ⲉⲑ̄ⲩ̄ ⲉⲓϯⲱⲟⲩ ⲙ̀Ⲡⲭ̄ⲥ̄ ⲫⲏⲉⲧⲓⲣⲓ ⲛ̀ⲛⲓϣⲫⲏⲣⲓ ϧⲉⲛ ⲛⲏⲉⲧⲓⲣⲓ ⲙ̀ⲡⲉϥⲟⲩⲱϣ.

80. Ⲓⲧⲁ ⲙⲉⲛⲉⲛⲥⲁ ⲛⲁⲓ ⲁⲥⲣⲁⲛⲁⲥ ⲛ̀ϯⲙⲉⲧⲙⲁⲓⲣⲱⲙⲓ ⲛ̀ⲧⲉ Ⲫϯ ⲉϯⲙ̀ⲧⲟⲛ ⲛ̀ⲛⲉϥⲉⲃⲓⲁⲓⲕ ⲟⲩⲟϩ ⲉⲟⲩⲟⲑⲃⲟⲩ ⲉⲃⲟⲗϧⲉⲛ ⲡⲁⲓⲕⲟⲥⲙⲟⲥ ⲛ̀ⲉⲫⲗⲏⲟⲩ ⲛⲉⲙ ⲛⲉϥϩⲟϫϩⲉϫ ⲙ̀ⲡⲣⲟⲥⲟⲩⲥⲛⲟⲩ ⲟⲩⲟϩ ⲛ̀ⲧⲉϭⲓⲧⲟⲩ ⲉϧⲟⲩⲛ ⲉⲛⲓⲙⲁ ⲙ̀ⲙⲧⲟⲛ ⲛ̀ⲉⲡⲟⲩⲣⲁⲛⲓⲟⲛ ⲉⲑⲟⲩⲟϣⲥ ⲉⲃⲟⲗ ϧⲉⲛ ⲡⲓⲟⲩⲛⲟϥ ⲛⲉⲙ ⲡⲓⲑⲉⲗⲏⲗ ⲡⲓⲙⲁ ⲉⲧⲁϥⲫⲱⲧ ⲉⲃⲟⲗⲛ̀ϧⲏⲧϥ ⲛ̀ϫⲉ ⲛⲓⲙⲕⲁϩⲛ̀ϩⲏⲧ ⲛⲉⲙ ϯⲗⲩⲡⲏ ⲛⲉⲙ ⲡⲓϥⲓⲁϩⲟⲙ.

81. ϧⲉⲛ ⲡⲓⲉϩⲟⲟⲩ ⲟⲩⲛ ⲉⲑ̄ⲩ̄ ⲛ̀ⲧⲉ ⲡϣⲁⲓ ⲛ̀ⲧⲉ ⲡⲓⲫⲁⲛⲓⲁ ⲉⲧⲉ ⲡⲁϣⲁⲓ ⲛ̀Ⲧⲱⲃⲓ ⲡⲉ ⲁϥⲉⲣϩⲏⲧⲥ ⲛ̀ϫⲉ ⲡⲓⲙⲁⲕⲁⲣⲓⲟⲥ Ⲙⲁⲝⲓⲙⲟⲥ ⲛ̀ⲉⲛⲕⲟⲧ ⲁϥϣⲱⲛⲓ ⲁϥⲁⲙⲟⲛⲓ ⲙ̀ⲙⲟϥ ⲛ̀ϫⲉ ⲟⲩϧⲙⲟⲙ ⲉϥⲟϣ ϩⲟⲧⲉ ⲟⲩⲛ ⲉⲧⲁϥϩⲣⲟϣ ϧⲉⲛ ⲡⲓϣⲱⲛⲓ ⲡⲉϫⲁϥ ϫⲉ ⲁⲣⲓ ϯⲁⲅⲁⲡⲏ ⲙⲟⲩϯ ⲛⲏⲓ ⲉⲡⲉⲛⲓⲱⲧ ⲁⲃⲃⲁ Ⲙⲁⲕⲁⲣ. ⲁⲛⲟⲕⲇⲉ ⲁⲓϣⲉⲛⲏⲓ ⲁⲓⲙⲟⲩϯ ⲉⲣⲟϥ. ⲓⲧⲁ ⲙⲉⲛⲉⲛⲥⲁ ⲑⲣⲉϥϣⲱⲡⲓ ⲛ̀ϫⲉ ⲫⲣⲏ ⲡⲉϫⲁϥ ⲛⲁⲛ ϫⲉ ⲁϣⲛ̀ⲛⲁⲩⲡⲉ ⲫⲁⲓ. ⲁⲛⲟⲛ ⲇⲉ ⲁⲛⲧⲁⲙⲟϥ ϫⲉ ⲡϫⲱⲕ ⲙ̀ⲡⲓⲉϩⲟⲟⲩ ⲡⲉ. ⲛ̀ⲑⲟϥ ⲇⲉ ⲡⲉϫⲁϥ ⲛⲁⲛ ϫⲉ ⲉⲧⲓ ⲕⲉⲕⲟⲩϫⲓ ϯⲛⲁϣⲉⲛⲏⲓ ⲉⲡⲁⲙⲁⲙⲧⲟⲛ.

82. ⲉⲣⲉ ⲡⲓⲉϫⲱⲣϩ ⲇⲉ ⲛⲁϣⲱⲡⲓ ⲡⲉϫⲉ ⲡⲉⲛⲓⲱⲧ ⲁⲃⲃⲁ Ⲙⲁⲕⲁⲣ ⲛⲁⲛ ϫⲉ ϭⲉⲣⲟ ⲡⲓϧⲏⲃⲥ ⲟⲩⲟϩ ⲁⲛⲑⲉⲣⲱϥ. ⲧⲟⲧⲉ ⲡⲓⲙⲁⲕⲁⲣⲓⲟⲥ Ⲙⲁⲝⲓⲙⲟⲥ ⲁϥϩⲱⲗⲉⲙ ⲡⲉϥⲛⲟⲩⲥ ⲉϩⲣⲏⲓ ⲉⲧⲫⲉ ⲟⲩⲟϩ ⲛⲁϥϫⲱ ⲙ̀ⲙⲟⲥ ⲡⲉϫⲉ ⲟⲩⲱⲣⲡ ⲙ̀ⲡⲉⲕⲟⲩⲱⲓⲛⲓ ⲛⲉⲙ ⲧⲉⲕⲙⲉⲑⲙⲏⲓ ⲱ ⲡⲁⲛⲟⲩϯ ⲛ̀ⲧⲟⲩϭⲓⲙⲱⲓⲧ ϧⲁϫⲱⲓ ϩⲓ ⲡⲓⲙⲱⲓⲧ ϫⲉ ⲟⲩⲏⲓ ϯⲛⲁϩϯ ϫⲉ ⲛⲁⲥⲟⲩⲧⲉⲛ ⲡⲁⲙⲱⲓⲧ ⲟⲩⲟϩ ⲛ̀ⲧⲉⲕⲛⲁϩⲙⲉⲧ ⲛ̀ⲧⲟⲧⲟⲩ ⲛ̀ⲧⲉ ⲛⲓϫⲟⲩⲥⲓⲁ ⲛ̀ⲧⲉ ⲡⲭⲁⲕⲓ ⲙ̀ⲡⲁⲏⲣ ⲛ̀ⲧⲉ ⲛⲓⲡ̄ⲛ̄ⲁ̄. ⲥⲟⲃϯ ⲛ̀ⲛⲁⲛⲁⲩⲃⲉⲛ ϩⲓ ⲡⲉⲕⲙⲱⲓⲧ ⲡⲁⲛⲟⲩϯ ϩⲓⲛⲁ ⲛ̀ⲧⲁⲓ ϣⲁⲣⲟⲕ ⲁⲧϭⲛⲉ ⲕⲱⲗⲩⲥⲓⲥ ϣⲱⲡⲓ ⲛⲏⲓ ⲛ̀ⲟⲩϩⲉⲗⲡⲓⲥ ⲛ̀ⲧⲉ ⲟⲩϫⲟⲙ Ⲓⲏ̄ⲥ̄

ⲡⲁⲛⲟⲩϯ ϫⲉ ⲛⲑⲟⲕ ⲡⲉ ⲡⲁⲟⲩⲱⲓⲛⲓ ⲛⲉⲙ ⲡⲁⲛⲟϩⲉⲙ ⲁⲓⲛⲁⲉⲣϩⲟϯ ⲁⲛⲟⲕ ϧⲁⲧϩⲏ ⲛ̀ⲛⲓⲙ.

83. ⲙⲉⲛⲉⲛⲥⲁ ⲛⲁⲓ ⲁϥⲭⲁⲣⲱϥ ⲛ̀ⲟⲩⲕⲟⲩϫⲓ ⲟⲩⲟϩ ⲡⲁⲗⲓⲛ ⲡⲁϫϥ ϫⲉ ⲧⲉⲛⲑⲏⲛⲟⲩ ⲙⲁⲣⲟⲛ ⲉⲃⲟⲗ ⲧⲁⲓ ϩⲏⲡⲡⲉ ⲓⲥ ⲛⲓⲁⲡⲟⲥⲧⲟⲗⲟⲥ ⲛⲉⲙ ⲛⲓⲡⲣⲟⲫⲏⲧⲏⲥ ⲁⲩⲓ ⲉⲟⲗⲧ ⲉⲃⲟⲗ ⲧⲁⲓ. ⲗⲟⲓⲡⲟⲛ ⲁϥⲭⲁⲣⲱϥ ⲙⲉⲛⲉⲛⲥⲁ ⲕⲉⲕⲟⲩϫⲓ ⲁϥⲛⲉⲑⲩ ⲁⲃⲃⲁ Ⲙⲁⲕⲁⲣ ⲛⲁⲩ ⲉⲡⲭⲱⲣⲁ ⲛ̀ⲧⲉ ⲛⲏⲉⲑⲩ ⲁⲩⲓ ⲛ̀ⲥⲱϥ ⲥⲁⲧⲟⲧϥ ⲁϥⲧⲱⲛϥ ⲛ̀ϫⲉ ⲁⲃⲃⲁ Ⲙⲁⲕⲁⲣ ⲁϥⲟϩⲓ ⲉⲣⲁⲧϥ ⲉϥⲭⲱ ⲛ̀ⲣⲱϥ.

84. Ⲉⲧⲁⲓⲛⲁⲩ ⲇⲉ ⲟⲛ ⲉⲡⲓϩⲛⲃⲥ ⲛ̀ⲭⲉⲇⲟⲛ ⲁϥϭⲉⲛⲟ ⲡⲉϫⲏⲓ ⲙ̀ⲡⲓϧⲉⲗⲗⲟ ⲁⲃⲃⲁ Ⲙⲁⲕⲁⲣ ϫⲉ ⲭⲟⲩⲱϣ ⲛ̀ⲧⲁⲑⲁⲙⲓⲟ ⲡⲓϩⲛⲃⲥ ⲕⲁⲗⲱⲥ. ⲡⲉϫⲁϥ ⲛⲏⲓ ⲙ̀ⲙⲟⲛ ⲁⲗⲗⲁ ⲭⲁϥ ⲙ̀ⲡⲁⲓⲣⲏϯ. ⲁⲛⲟⲕ ⲇⲉ ⲁⲓϯϩⲟ ⲉⲣⲟϥ ⲉⲓⲭⲱ ⲙ̀ⲙⲟⲥ ϫⲉ ⲁⲣⲓ ϯⲁⲅⲁⲡⲏ ⲡⲁⲓⲱⲧ ⲙⲟⲧⲛ ⲙ̀ⲙⲟⲕ ⲉϫⲉⲛ ϯϭⲗⲟⲃⲓ ⲛ̀ⲟⲩⲕⲟⲟⲩϫⲓ ⲛⲑⲟϥ ⲇⲉ ⲁϥⲉⲣⲟⲩⲱ ϫⲉ ⲭⲁⲣⲱⲕ ⲡⲁϣⲏⲣⲓ ϫⲉ ⲡⲥⲛⲟⲩ ⲛ̀ⲥⲁϫⲓ ⲁⲛ ⲡⲉ ⲁⲗⲗⲁ ⲙⲁⲗⲗⲟⲛⲟⲩⲥⲛⲟⲩ ⲛ̀ⲭⲁⲣⲱϥ ⲡⲉ.

85. ⲟⲩⲟϩ ⲛⲁⲣⲉ ⲡⲓⲙⲁⲕⲁⲣⲓⲟⲥ Ⲙⲁⲍⲓⲙⲟⲥ ⲥⲁϫⲓ ⲛⲉⲙ ⲟⲩⲁⲓ ϧⲉⲛ ⲛⲏⲉⲑⲩ ⲉϥϣⲓⲛⲓ ⲙ̀ⲙⲟϥ ⲉϥⲣⲁⲛ ⲛ̀ⲛⲓⲁⲅⲓⲟⲥ ⲉⲧⲉ ⲙ̀ⲡⲉϥⲕⲱϯ ⲁⲛⲟⲛ ⲇⲉ ⲙ̀ⲡⲉⲛⲉⲙⲓ ⲉⲫⲛⲉⲧⲉϥϫⲱ ⲙ̀ⲙⲟϥ ⲁⲗⲗⲁ ⲡⲓⲡ̅ⲛ̅ⲁ̅ⲧⲟⲫⲟⲣⲟⲥ ⲁⲃⲃⲁ Ⲙⲁⲕⲁⲣ ⲁϥⲧⲁⲙⲟⲛ ϫⲉ ⲛⲁⲩⲧⲁⲙⲟ ⲙ̀ⲙⲟϥ ⲡⲉ ⲉϥⲣⲁⲛ ⲛ̀ⲛⲓⲁⲅⲓⲟⲥ ⲉⲧⲉ ⲙ̀ⲡⲉϥⲕⲱϯ ⲟⲩⲟϩ ⲉⲧⲁⲥⲉⲣϩⲩⲇⲟⲛⲉⲥⲑⲉ ⲛ̀ϫⲉ ⲧⲉϥⲯⲩⲭⲏ ⲉⲧⲡⲁⲣⲟⲩⲥⲓⲁ ⲛ̀ⲛⲏⲉⲑⲩ ⲥⲁⲧⲟⲧⲥ ⲁϥϫⲟⲥ ⲉⲃⲟⲗϧⲉⲛ ⲡⲓⲥⲱⲙⲁ ϧⲉⲛ ⲟⲩⲣⲁϣⲓ. ⲫⲁⲓ ⲡⲓⲣⲏϯ ⲉⲧⲁϥϫⲱⲕ ⲉⲃⲟⲗ ⲛ̀ϫⲉ ⲡⲁⲓⲙⲁⲕⲁⲣⲓⲟⲥ ϧⲉⲛ ⲟⲩϩⲓⲣⲏⲛⲏ ⲉⲁϥⲙⲧⲟⲛ ⲙ̀ⲙⲟϥ ⲛⲉⲙ ⲛⲏⲉⲑⲩ ⲧⲏⲣⲟⲩ ⲛ̀ⲥⲟⲩⲓ̅ⲇ̅ ⲛ̀Ⲧⲱⲃⲓ.

86. ϩⲟⲧⲉ ⲟⲩⲛ ⲉⲧⲁⲛⲑⲱⲙⲥ ⲙ̀ⲡⲉϥⲁⲅϣⲁⲛⲟⲛ ⲉⲑⲩ ⲟⲩⲟϩ ⲉⲧⲁⲛⲓ ⲉⲡⲉϥⲣⲁⲥϯ ⲁϥⲉⲛⲕⲟⲧ ⲛ̀ϫⲉ ⲡⲉϥⲙⲁⲕⲁⲣⲓⲟⲥ ⲛ̀ⲥⲟⲛ Ⲇⲟⲙⲉⲧⲓⲟⲥ ⲁϥⲁⲙⲟⲛⲓ ⲉϫⲱϥ ⲛ̀ϫⲉ ⲟⲩⲛⲓϣϯ ⲛ̀ϧⲙⲟⲙ. ⲉⲧⲁϥⲛⲁⲩⲇⲉ ⲉⲣⲟϥ ⲛ̀ϫⲉ ⲡⲓⲛⲓϣϯ ⲁⲃⲃⲁ Ⲙⲁⲕⲁⲣ ϫⲉ ⲁϥϣⲱⲛⲓ ⲡⲉϫⲁϥ ⲛⲏⲓ ϫⲉ ϩⲉⲙⲥⲓ ⲡⲁϣⲏⲣⲓ ⲛ̀ⲧⲉⲕϣⲉⲙϣⲓ ⲙ̀ⲡⲓⲥⲟⲛ ϣⲁⲧⲉⲕϭⲓ ⲙ̀ⲡⲉϥⲥⲙⲟⲩ. ⲁⲛⲟⲕ ⲇⲉ ⲁⲓⲧϥⲓ ⲉⲛⲉϥϭⲁⲗⲁⲩϫ ⲉⲓⲭⲱ ⲙ̀ⲙⲟⲥ ⲛⲁϥ ϫⲉ ⲧⲱⲃϩ ⲉϫⲱⲓ ⲡⲁⲓⲱⲧ ⲉⲑⲩ.

87. ⲉⲡⲉϥⲣⲁⲥϯ ⲇⲉ ⲁϥϩⲣⲱϣ ϧⲉⲛ ⲡⲓϣⲱⲛⲓ ⲛ̀ϫⲉ ⲡⲓⲁⲅⲓⲟⲥ Ⲇⲟⲙⲉⲧⲓⲟⲥ ⲟⲩⲟϩ ⲉⲧⲁϥⲫⲟϩ ⲉⲡⲓⲉⲭⲱⲣϩ ⲙ̀ⲙⲁϩⲅ̅ ⲁⲓⲛⲁⲩ ⲉⲣⲟϥ ⲉϥϩⲟⲥⲓ ⲡⲉϫⲏⲓ ⲛⲁϥ ϫⲉ ⲭⲟⲩⲱϣ ⲛ̀ⲧⲁⲙⲟⲩϯ ⲉⲡⲉⲛⲓⲱⲧ ⲁⲃⲃⲁ Ⲙⲁⲕⲁⲣ. ⲡⲉϫⲁϥ ϫⲉ

ⲥⲉ. ⲁⲛⲟⲕ ⲇⲉ ⲁⲓϣⲉⲛⲏⲓ ⲁⲓⲙⲟⲟⲩϯ ⲉⲣⲟϥ ⲟⲩⲟϩ ⲉⲧⲓ ⲉⲓⲙⲟϣⲓ ⲛⲉⲙⲁϥ
ϩⲓ ⲡⲓⲙⲱⲓⲧ ⲁϥⲟϩⲓ ⲉⲣⲁⲧϥ ⲛ̀ⲟⲩⲛⲓϣϯ ⲛ̀ⲛⲁⲩ ⲉϥϫⲟⲩϣⲧ ⲉⲡⲥⲁ
ⲙ̀ⲡⲓⲥⲡⲏⲗⲉⲟⲛ. ⲟⲩⲟϩ ⲙⲉⲛⲉⲛⲥⲱⲥ ⲁϥⲫⲟⲛϩϥ ⲉⲡⲥⲁ ⲛ̀ϯⲁⲛⲁⲧⲗⲟⲛ.
ⲛⲁⲓⲙⲉⲩⲓ ⲁⲛⲟⲕ ⲡⲉϫⲉ ⲁⲣⲏⲟⲩ ⲉϥⲧⲱⲃϩ ⲁⲗⲁ ⲛⲁϥⲥⲟⲙⲥ ⲉⲡⲭⲱⲣⲟⲥ
ⲛ̀ⲛⲏⲉⲑⲩ ⲉⲩⲥⲱⲕ ϩⲁϫⲱⲥ ⲛ̀ϯⲙⲁⲕⲁⲣⲓⲟⲥ ⲙ̀ⲯⲩⲭⲏ ⲛ̀ⲧⲉ ⲡⲓⲁⲅⲓⲟⲥ
Ⲇⲟⲙⲉⲧⲓⲟⲥ. ⲁϥⲥⲟⲙⲥ ⲇⲉ ⲉⲡϣⲱⲓ ⲉⲧⲫⲉ ⲁϥϥⲓⲁϩⲟⲙ ⲟⲩⲟϩ ⲁϥⲣⲓⲙⲓ
ⲉϥⲕⲱⲗϩ ⲙ̀ⲙⲟⲥ ϫⲉ ⲟⲩⲟⲓ ⲛⲏⲓ ⲁⲛⲟⲕ ϫⲉ ⲙ̀ⲡⲉⲣⲙⲟⲛⲁⲭⲟⲥ ⲉⲡⲧⲏⲣϥ
ⲛⲁⲓⲓ ⲅⲁⲣ ⲛⲉⲙ ⲛⲓⲙⲟⲛⲁⲭⲟⲥ ⲛ̀ⲧⲁⲫⲙⲏ ϫⲉ ϧⲉⲛ ⲟⲩⲕⲟⲩϫⲓ ⲛ̀ⲥⲏⲟⲩ
ⲛ̀ϩⲓⲭⲣⲉϫ ⲁⲩϫⲓⲙⲓ ⲙ̀ⲡⲓⲙⲱⲓⲧ ⲛ̀ⲭⲱⲗⲉⲙ.

88. ⲁⲛⲟⲕ ⲇⲉ ⲉⲧⲁⲓⲛⲁⲩ ⲉⲣⲟϥ ⲉϥⲣⲓⲙⲓ ⲙ̀ⲡⲁⲓⲣⲏϯ ⲁⲓⲧⲱⲙⲧ ⲟⲩⲟϩ
ⲡⲉϫⲏⲓ ⲛⲁϥ ϫⲉ ⲟⲩ ⲡⲉ ⲉⲧϣⲟⲡ ⲱ ⲡⲁⲓⲱⲧ ⲉⲑⲩ ⲛⲑⲟϥ ⲇⲉ ⲡⲉϫⲁϥ
ⲛⲏⲓ ϫⲉ ⲙⲁⲣⲟⲛ ⲡⲁϣⲏⲣⲓ ϫⲉ ⲁⲡⲓⲁⲅⲓⲟⲥ Ⲇⲟⲙⲉⲧⲓⲟⲥ ⲁϥⲙⲟⲧⲛ ⲙ̀ⲙⲟϥ.
ⲉⲧⲁⲛⲓ ⲇⲉ ⲉϧⲟⲩⲛ ⲉⲡⲓⲥⲡⲏⲗⲉⲟⲛ ⲁⲛϫⲉⲙϥ. ⲉϥϩⲉⲙⲥⲓ ⲉϥⲟⲩⲉϩ ⲉϧⲟⲩⲛ
ⲉⲧϫⲟⲟⲓ ⲉⲣⲉ ⲧⲉϥϫⲓϫ ⲃ̄ ϭⲟⲗⲕ ⲉϩⲣⲏⲓ ⲉⲧⲫⲉ. ⲉⲧⲁϥϫⲱⲕ ⲉⲃⲟⲗ
ⲙ̀ⲡⲁⲓⲣⲏϯ ⲛ̀ⲥⲟⲩⲓ︦ⲍ︦ ⲛ̀ⲧⲱⲃⲓ ⲁⲛϭⲓ ⲙ̀ⲡⲉϥⲥⲱⲙⲁ ⲉⲑⲩ ⲁⲛϣⲟⲧϥ ⲉϫⲉⲛ
ϯϭⲗⲟⲃⲓ ⲁϥⲛⲉⲑⲩ ⲁⲃⲃⲁ Ⲙⲁⲕⲁⲣ ⲉⲣⲙⲉⲑⲣⲉ ⲛ̀ⲁⲃⲃⲁ Ⲓⲥⲏⲇⲱⲣⲟⲥ ϫⲉ
ⲛⲓⲧⲁⲝⲓⲥ ⲉⲧⲁⲩⲓ ⲛ̀ⲥⲁ ⲧⲯⲩⲭⲏ ⲙ̀ⲡⲓⲛⲓϣϯ ⲛⲁⲓ ⲟⲛ ⲛⲉ ⲉⲧⲁⲩⲓ ⲛ̀ⲥⲁ ⲧⲯⲩⲭⲏ
ⲙ̀ⲡⲉϥⲥⲟⲛ ⲉⲩⲭⲏ ⲛⲉⲙⲱⲟⲩ ϩⲱϥ.

89. Ⲓⲥ ϩⲏⲡⲡⲉ ⲟⲩⲛ ⲁⲛⲧⲁⲙⲱⲧⲉⲛ ⲉⲡⲓⲣⲏϯ ⲉⲧⲁ ⲛⲁⲓⲙⲁⲕⲁⲣⲓⲟⲥ
ϫⲱⲕ ⲉⲃⲟⲗ ⲙ̀ⲡⲟⲩⲇⲣⲟⲙⲟⲥ ϧⲉⲛ ⲟⲩⲃⲓⲟⲥ ⲛ̀ⲁⲅⲅⲉⲗⲓⲕⲟⲛ ⲉⲁⲩⲙⲉⲛⲣⲉ
ⲛⲓϧⲓⲥⲓ ⲛ̀ⲧⲉ ⲛⲓⲡⲟⲗⲓⲧⲓⲁ ⲛⲉⲙ ⲛⲓϩⲟϫϩⲉϫ ⲙ̀ⲡⲣⲟⲥⲟⲩⲥⲏⲟⲩ ⲁⲩⲁⲙⲟⲛⲓ
ⲛ̀ⲧⲟⲧⲟⲩ ϧⲉⲛ ϯϩⲩⲡⲟⲙⲟⲛⲏ. ⲉⲁⲩⲉⲣⲁⲅⲱⲛⲓⲍⲉⲥⲑⲉ ⲛ̀ⲕⲁⲗⲱⲥ ⲉⲩϭⲟϫⲓ
ϧⲉⲛ ⲡⲓⲥⲧⲁⲇⲓⲟⲥ ⲛ̀ⲧⲉ ϯⲁⲣⲉⲧⲏ ⲉⲩⲥⲱⲟⲩⲧⲉⲛ ⲙ̀ⲙⲱⲟⲩ ⲉⲛⲁⲧϩⲏ
ⲕⲁⲧⲁ ⲡⲥⲁϫⲓ ⲙ̀ⲫⲛⲉⲑⲩ ⲛ̀ⲁⲡⲟⲥⲧⲟⲗⲟⲥ Ⲡⲁⲩⲗⲟⲥ ϣⲁⲛⲧⲟⲩϣⲱⲡⲓ ⲛⲉⲙ
ⲫⲛⲉⲧⲟⲩϭⲓϣϣⲱⲟⲩ ⲙ̀ⲙⲟϥ Ⲡ̅ⲭ̅ⲥ̅ ⲛ̀ⲟⲩⲁⲅⲱⲛⲟⲑⲉⲧⲏⲥ ⲙ̀ⲙⲏⲓ ⲉⲁⲩⲙⲉⲥⲧⲉ
ⲡϣⲟⲩ ⲛ̀ⲧⲉ ⲡⲁⲓⲕⲟⲥⲙⲟⲥ ⲙ̀ⲡⲣⲟⲥⲟⲩⲥⲏⲟⲩ ⲛⲉⲙ ⲛⲓⲁⲡⲟⲗⲁⲩⲥⲓⲥ ⲧⲏⲣⲟⲩ
ⲛ̀ⲉⲫⲗⲏⲟⲩ ⲉⲑⲛⲁⲕⲱⲣϥ ⲁⲩⲟⲡⲟⲩ ⲉϩⲁⲛⲗⲉⲃϣ ⲟⲩⲟϩ ⲁⲩϣⲱⲡⲓ ⲉⲩⲙⲟⲥϯ
ⲙ̀ⲡⲁⲓⲕⲟⲥⲙⲟⲥ ⲙ̀ⲫⲣⲏϯ ⲛ̀ⲟⲩϣⲧⲉⲕⲟ.

90. ⲁⲥϣⲱⲡⲓ ⲇⲉ ⲛ̀ⲟⲩⲥⲟⲡ ϩⲱⲥ ⲉⲓⲥⲓ ⲛ̀ϩⲣⲁⲓ ⲛⲉⲙⲱⲟⲩ ⲡⲉϫⲏⲓ
ⲛⲱⲟⲩ ϫⲉ ⲛⲁⲣⲉⲧⲉⲛⲭⲏ Ⲕⲱⲥⲧⲁⲛⲓⲛⲟⲩⲡⲟⲗⲓⲥ ⲡⲉ ⲛⲁⲓⲟϯ ⲡⲟⲗⲗⲁⲕⲓⲥ
ⲧⲉⲧⲉⲛⲁϫⲉⲙ ⲑⲏⲛⲟⲩ ⲡⲉ ⲉⲣⲉⲧⲉⲛⲟⲓ ⲛ̀ⲟⲩⲣⲟ ϯⲛⲟⲩ ⲡⲉ ⲛⲑⲱⲟⲩ ⲇⲉ
ⲁⲩⲕⲉⲧ ⲡⲟⲩϩⲟ ⲉⲣⲟⲓ ⲡϫⲉϣⲱⲟⲩ ⲛⲏⲓ ϧⲉⲛ ⲟⲩⲙⲉⲧⲣⲉⲙⲣⲁⲩϣ ϫⲉ ⲁⲣⲉ

ⲡⲉⲕⲛⲟⲩⲥ ⲭⲏ ⲛⲑⲱⲛ ⲱ ⲡⲓⲥⲟⲛ ⲉⲧⲁⲕϫⲉ ⲡⲁⲓⲥⲁϫⲓ ⲫⲁⲓ ⲁⲣⲏⲟⲩ
ⲡⲁⲛⲧⲱⲥ ⲉϥϩⲉⲛ ⲡⲓⲙⲁ ⲉⲧⲁⲕϥⲓⲣⲓ ⲉⲣⲟϥ. ⲁⲛⲟⲩⲱ ⲉⲛϫⲱ ⲙ̀ⲙⲟⲥ ⲛⲁⲕ
ⲛ̀ⲟⲩⲙⲏϣ ⲛ̀ⲥⲟⲡ ⲱ ⲡⲓⲥⲟⲛ Ⲡⲁϣⲟⲓ ϫⲉ ⲉⲕⲣⲉⲙⲥⲓ ⲛⲉⲙⲁⲛ ⲓⲧⲉ ⲉⲕⲭⲏ ϧⲉⲛ
ⲟⲉⲕⲙⲁⲛϣⲱⲡⲓ ⲁⲙⲟⲛⲓ ⲙ̀ⲡⲓⲣⲁⲛ ⲛ̀ⲟⲩϫⲁⲓ ⲛ̀ⲧⲉ ⲡⲉⲛⲟ̅ⲥ̅ Ⲓⲏ̅ⲥ̅ Ⲡⲭ̅ⲥ̅ ϧⲉⲛ
ⲟⲩⲙⲉⲧⲁⲑⲙⲟⲩⲛⲕ ⲕⲉ ⲅⲁⲣ ⲁⲗⲏⲑⲱⲥ ⲉⲛⲁⲣⲉ ⲡⲓⲣⲁⲛ ⲉ̅ⲑ̅ⲩ̅ ϧⲉⲛ ⲡⲉⲕϩⲏⲧ
ⲡⲉ ⲛⲁⲕⲛⲁϫⲉ ⲡⲁⲓⲥⲁϫⲓ ⲁⲛ ⲡⲉ ⲉⲧⲁⲕϫⲟⲧⲟⲩ. ⲗⲟⲓⲡⲟⲛ ⲙⲁⲑⲏⲛⲕ ⲉⲣⲟⲕ
ϧⲉⲛ ⲟⲩⲧⲁϫⲣⲟ ⲙ̀ⲡⲉⲣⲉⲣⲁⲙⲗⲉⲥ ⲉⲡⲡⲓⲣⲁⲛ ⲛ̀ⲟⲟⲩϫⲁⲓ ⲛ̀ⲧⲉ ⲡⲉⲛⲟ̅ⲥ̅
Ⲓⲏ̅ⲥ̅ Ⲡⲭ̅ⲥ̅ ⲁⲗⲗⲁ ⲁⲙⲟⲛⲓ ⲙ̀ⲙⲟϥ ϧⲉⲛ ⲡⲉⲕϩⲏⲧ ⲧⲏⲣϥ ϧⲉⲛ ⲟⲩⲙⲟⲩⲛ
ⲉⲃⲟⲗϧⲉⲛ ⲟⲩⲙⲉⲧⲣⲉϥϣⲉⲡϩⲓⲥⲓ ϫⲉ ⲟⲩⲏⲓ ⲉϣⲱⲡ ⲛ̀ⲧⲉⲛⲉⲣⲁⲙⲉⲗⲏⲥ
ⲉⲫⲁⲓ ⲓⲉ ⲁⲛⲙⲏⲛ ⲧⲉⲛⲙϣⲟⲩⲧ ϧⲉⲛ ⲛⲉⲛⲡⲁⲣⲁⲡⲧⲱⲙⲁ.

91. ⲗⲟⲓⲡⲟⲛ ⲙ̀ⲡⲉⲛⲑⲣⲉⲙⲉⲛⲣⲉ ϯⲡⲁⲣⲣⲏⲥⲓⲁ ⲛⲉⲙ ⲡⲓϭⲓϩⲣⲁϥ ⲛⲉⲙ
ⲛⲓⲥⲁϫⲓ ⲛ̀ⲉⲫⲗⲏⲟⲩ ⲛⲁⲓ ⲛⲉ ⲉⲧⲧⲁⲕⲟ ⲙ̀ⲡⲟⲩⲧⲁϩ ⲧⲏⲣϥ ⲙ̀ⲡⲓⲙⲟⲛⲁⲭⲟⲥ
ⲕⲁⲧⲁ ϯϩⲉ ⲉⲧⲁⲛⲉⲙⲓ ⲉⲫⲁⲓ ⲉⲧⲓ ⲉⲛϣⲟⲡ ϧⲉⲛ ϯⲤⲩⲣⲓⲁ ϩⲟⲧⲉ ⲉⲧⲁ
ϯⲙⲉⲧⲣⲱⲙⲓ ⲁⲓⲧⲉⲛ ⲛ̀ϭⲓϩⲣⲁϥ ⲙ̀ⲡⲟⲟⲩⲭⲁⲛ ⲉⲉⲣⲫⲙⲉⲩⲓ ⲛ̀ⲛⲉⲛⲟⲃⲓ
ϯⲙⲉⲧϣⲉⲙⲙⲟ ⲇⲉ ⲛⲉⲙ ⲡⲓⲭⲁⲣⲱϥ ϧⲉⲛ ⲟⲩⲉⲙⲓ ⲛⲉⲙ ⲡⲓϩⲟϫϩⲉϫ
ϩⲁⲛⲥⲓⲉⲃⲁⲓ ⲛ̀ⲧⲉ ⲡⲉⲛϣⲗⲟⲗ ⲛⲉ ⲡⲓϩⲟϫϩⲉϫ ⲉⲧⲙⲓⲥⲓ ⲙ̀ⲡⲓⲧⲱⲃϩ ϧⲉⲛ
ⲟⲩⲧⲟⲩⲃⲟ ⲡⲓⲧⲱⲃϩ ⲉⲑⲙⲓⲥⲓ ⲛ̀ϯϩⲟϯ ⲛ̀ⲧⲉ Ⲫϯ ⲛⲉⲙ ϯⲁⲅⲁⲡⲏ ⲟⲩⲟϩ ⲛⲁⲓ
ⲛⲉ ⲉⲑⲙⲓⲥⲓ ⲙ̀ⲡⲓⲣⲱⲙⲓ ϫⲉ ⲟⲩⲏⲓ ⲙ̀ⲙⲟⲛ ⲁⲝⲓⲱⲙⲁ ⲟⲩⲇⲉ ⲙⲉⲧⲣⲁⲙⲁⲟ
ⲟⲩⲇⲉ ⲙⲉⲧϫⲱⲣⲓ ⲧⲁⲓⲏⲟⲩⲧ ϧⲁⲧⲉⲛ Ⲫϯ ⲁⲗⲗⲁ ⲟⲩⲯⲩⲭⲏ ⲉⲥⲟⲩⲁⲃ ⲧⲉ
ⲉⲧⲉϥⲕⲱϯ ⲛ̀ⲥⲱⲥ ⲟⲩⲟϩ ⲧⲉϥⲑⲩⲥⲓⲁ ⲛⲉⲙ ⲡⲉϥϭⲗⲓⲗ ⲡⲉ ⲡⲉⲛⲟⲩϫⲁⲓ.
ⲁⲛⲟⲕ ⲁⲓϣⲉⲡ ⲛⲟⲩⲥⲁϫⲓ ⲉⲣⲟⲓ ϧⲉⲛ ⲟⲩⲣⲱⲟⲩⲧϥ ⲛ̀ϩⲏⲧ ⲉⲁⲓϯⲙⲉⲧⲁⲛⲟⲓⲁ
ⲉⲓϫⲱ ⲙ̀ⲙⲟⲥ ϫⲉ ⲭⲱ ⲛⲏⲓ ⲉⲃⲟⲗ ⲛⲁⲓⲟϯ ⲧⲱⲃϩ ⲉϫⲱⲓ.

92. ⲗⲟⲓⲡⲟⲛ ⲙⲉⲛⲉⲛⲥⲁ ⲟⲩⲣⲟⲙⲡⲓ ⲛ̀ⲉϩⲟⲟⲩ ⲛ̀ⲧⲉ ⲫⲟⲩⲱⲧⲉⲃ ⲉⲃⲟⲗ
ⲛⲁⲓⲙⲁⲕⲁⲣⲓⲟⲥ ⲁⲡⲓϣⲁϥⲉ ϫⲱⲣϫ ⲛ̀ⲕⲁⲗⲱⲥ ⲓⲧⲉ ⲛ̀ⲧⲉ ⲡⲓⲧⲱⲟⲩ ⲛ̀ⲧⲉ
Ⲡⲉⲣⲛⲟⲩϫ ⲓⲧⲉ ⲛ̀ⲧⲉ ⲙⲟⲩⲛϣⲟⲩⲓ ⲉⲧⲥⲏⲣ ⲉⲃⲟⲗϧⲉⲛ ⲭⲏⲙⲓ ⲁⲡⲁⲝ
ⲁⲡⲗⲱⲥ ⲁⲡⲓϣⲁϥⲉ ϫⲱⲣϫ ⲁⲩⲕⲱⲧ ⲛⲱⲟⲩ ⲛ̀ⲟⲩⲛⲓϣϯ ⲛ̀ⲉⲕⲕⲗⲥⲓⲁ
ⲟⲩⲟϩ ⲁⲩⲛⲁϣ ⲛ̀ⲁⲃⲃⲁ Ⲓⲥⲏⲇⲱⲣⲟⲥ ⲙ̀ⲡⲣⲉⲥⲃⲩⲧⲉⲣⲟⲥ. ⲁⲛⲟⲕ ⲇⲉ ϩⲱ
ϩⲁ ⲡⲁⲧⲉⲙⲡϣⲁ ⲁⲩⲁⲓⲧ ⲛ̀ⲇⲓⲁⲕⲱⲛ. ⲙⲉⲛⲉⲛⲥⲁ ⲛⲁⲓ ⲁⲡⲓⲛⲓϣϯ ⲁⲃⲃⲁ
Ⲙⲁⲕⲁⲣ ⲙⲟⲩϯ ⲉⲃⲟⲗϧⲉⲛ ϯⲉⲕⲕⲗⲏⲥⲓⲁ ⲉϥⲥⲟϩⲣⲉⲛ ⲉϥϫⲱ ⲙ̀ⲙⲟⲥ ϫⲉ
ⲙⲟⲩϯ ⲉⲡⲁⲓⲧⲟⲡⲟⲥ ϫⲉ ⲟⲩⲣⲁⲟⲩⲏ ⲛ̀ⲛⲓⲣⲱⲙⲉⲟⲥ.

93. ⲁⲩⲉⲣⲟⲩⲱ ⲛ̀ϫⲉ ⲅ̅ ⲛ̀ⲛⲓϣϯ ⲛ̀ϧⲉⲗⲗⲟ ⲛ̀ⲧⲉ ⲡⲧⲱⲟⲩ ⲙ̀Ⲡⲉⲣⲛⲟⲩϫ
ⲉⲧⲁⲩϣⲱⲡⲓ ϧⲁⲧⲟⲧⲉⲛ ⲉⲧⲉ ⲁⲡⲁ Ⲡⲁⲙⲱ ⲡⲱ ⲁⲡⲁ Ⲡⲓϩⲱⲣ ⲛⲉⲙ ⲁⲡⲁ

ⲁⲑⲣⲉ ⲡⲉϫⲱⲟⲩ ⲙ̀ⲡⲓⲉⲑⲟⲩⲁⲃ ⲁⲃⲃⲁ Ⲙⲁⲕⲁⲣ ϫⲉ ⲙ̀ⲡⲉⲕⲉⲙⲓ ⲉⲛⲟⲩⲣⲁⲛ
ⲡⲉⲛⲓⲱⲧ ⲉⲧⲥⲙⲁⲣⲱⲟⲩⲧ ⲡⲉϫⲁϥ ⲛⲱⲟⲩ ϫⲉ ⲁϩⲁ ⲁⲗⲗⲁ ⲡⲉⲧⲉϣⲉ
ⲁⲛ ⲡⲉ ⲉⲑⲣⲉⲛⲙⲟⲩϯ ⲉϥⲣⲁⲛ ⲛ̀ⲟⲩⲁⲓ ⲛ̀ϧⲏⲧⲟⲩ ⲉϫⲉⲛ ⲡⲓⲧⲟⲡⲟⲥ
ⲛ̀ⲧⲉⲛⲭⲁ ⲡⲓⲟⲩⲁⲓ ⲉⲡⲓⲇⲏ ⲁⲩϫⲱⲕ ⲉⲃⲟⲗϧⲉⲛ ⲟⲩϩⲩⲡⲟⲙⲟⲛⲏ ⲛ̀ⲟⲩⲱⲧ
ⲛ̀ϧⲏⲧϥ ⲛⲉⲙ ⲛⲟⲩⲉⲣⲏⲟⲩ ⲟⲩⲟϩ ⲟⲛ ϫⲉ ϩⲁⲛⲥⲛⲏⲟⲩ ⲛⲉ ⲉⲑⲃⲉ ⲫⲁⲓ
ⲁⲛⲛⲁⲉⲣⲟⲛⲟⲙⲁⲍⲓⲛ ⲙ̀ⲙⲱⲟⲩ ⲉⲩⲥⲟⲡ ⲛⲉⲙ ⲛⲟⲩⲉⲣⲏⲟⲩ ⲛ̀ⲧⲉⲛⲙⲟⲩϯ
ⲉⲡⲟⲩⲧⲟⲡⲟⲥ ϫⲉ ⲡⲓⲣⲱⲙⲉⲟⲥ ⲙⲉⲛⲉⲛⲥⲁ ⲡⲟⲩϫⲱⲕ ⲉⲃⲟⲗ. ⲡⲁⲓⲣⲏϯ ⲣⲱ
ⲟⲛ ⲡⲉ ⲉⲧⲁⲩⲑⲣⲟⲩϭϩⲉ ⲛⲟⲩⲣⲁⲛ ⲉⲡⲓⲇⲏ ⲧⲓⲭⲟⲛ ϫⲉ ⲛⲉⲛⲓⲟϯ ⲛ̀ⲣⲱⲙⲉⲟⲥ
ϣⲁ ⲉϧⲟⲩⲛ ⲉⲫⲟⲟⲩ ⲕⲁⲧⲁ ⲫⲣϯ ⲉⲧⲁⲩⲟⲩⲁϩⲥⲁϩⲛⲓ ⲛⲁϥ ⲉⲃⲟⲗϩⲓⲧⲉⲛ
Ⲫϯ.

94. ⲁϥⲉⲣⲙⲉⲑⲣⲉ ⲇⲉ ⲛⲁⲛ ⲟⲛ ⲙ̀ⲫⲁⲓ ⲛ̀ϫⲉ ⲁⲃⲃⲁ Ⲡⲁⲫⲛⲟⲩϯ ⲡⲓⲙⲁⲑⲏⲧⲏⲥ
ⲛ̀ⲧⲉ ⲁⲃⲃⲁ Ⲙⲁⲕⲁⲣ ⲫⲏⲉⲧⲁϥⲉⲣⲓⲱⲧ ⲛ̀ϣ̀ϩⲏⲧ ⲙⲉⲛⲉⲛⲥⲱⲥ ϫⲉ ϩⲟⲧⲉ
ⲡⲉϫⲁϥ ⲉⲧⲁⲛⲕⲱⲧ ⲉϯⲉⲕⲕⲗⲏⲥⲓⲁ ⲁⲫϯ ⲟⲩⲁϩⲥⲁϩⲛⲓ ⲙ̀ⲡⲉⲛⲓⲱⲧ ϩⲓⲧⲉⲛ
ⲟⲩⲭⲉⲣⲟⲩⲃⲓⲙ ⲛ̀ⲟⲩⲱⲓⲛⲓ ϫⲉ ⲙⲟⲩϯ ⲉⲡⲁⲓⲙⲁ ⲑⲣⲁⲟⲩⲏ ⲛ̀ⲛⲓⲣⲱⲙⲉⲟⲥ
ⲟⲩⲟϩ ⲛ̀ⲑⲟⲕ ϩⲱⲕ ⲡⲉϫⲁϥ ⲟⲩⲁϩⲕ ⲛ̀ⲥⲱⲓ ⲛ̀ⲧⲁⲧⲁⲙⲟⲕ ⲉⲡⲓⲙⲁ
ⲉⲧⲟⲩⲙⲟⲩϯ ⲉⲡⲉⲕⲣⲁⲛ ⲉϩⲣⲏⲓ ⲉϫⲱⲕ

95. ⲗⲟⲓⲡⲟⲛ ⲁ ⲡⲓⲭⲉⲣⲟⲩⲃⲓⲙ ⲥⲱⲕ ϧⲁϫⲱϥ ⲁϥⲉⲛϥ ⲙ̀ⲡⲓⲁⲗⲟⲕ ⲛⲉⲣⲏⲥ ⲛ̀ⲧⲉ
ⲡⲓϩⲉⲗⲟⲥ ⲉϥⲙⲁ ⲙ̀ⲡⲓϣⲏⲓ ⲁϥⲟϩⲓ ⲉⲣⲁⲧϥ ⲉϫⲉⲛ ϯⲡⲉⲧⲣⲁ ⲉⲧⲥⲁⲡⲉⲙⲉⲛⲧ
ⲁϥϣⲱ ⲉϥϫⲱ ⲙ̀ⲙⲟⲥ ϫⲉ ⲫⲁⲓ ⲡⲉ ⲡⲓⲙⲁ ⲉⲧⲟⲩⲛⲁⲙⲟⲩϯ ⲙ̀ⲡⲉⲕⲣⲁⲛ
ⲉϩⲣⲏⲓ ⲉϫⲱϥ ⲡⲓⲙⲁ ⲉⲧⲏⲏ ⲉⲧⲁⲕⲕⲟⲧϥ ⲁⲩⲛⲁⲧⲓϥ ⲛ̀ⲛⲓⲣⲱⲙⲉⲟⲥ
ϣⲁ ⲉⲛⲉϩ ⲉⲑⲃⲉ ϫⲉ ⲛⲑⲱⲟⲩ ⲛⲉ ⲛⲓϣⲟⲣⲡ ⲉⲧⲁⲩⲭⲁ ⲥⲱⲙⲁ ⲉϩⲣⲏⲓ ϧⲉⲛ
ⲡⲁⲓⲧⲱⲟⲩ ⲉ̅ⲑ̅ⲩ̅ ⲉⲁⲩϣⲱⲡⲓ ⲛ̀ϣⲟⲣⲡ ⲛ̀ⲁⲡⲁⲣⲭⲏ ⲛ̀ⲧⲉ ⲛⲉⲕϧⲓⲥⲓ ϧⲉⲛ
ⲡⲁⲓⲁϩⲁⲗⲟⲗⲓ ⲛ̀ⲧⲉ Ⲡ̅ⲟ̅ⲥ̅ ⲥⲁⲃⲁⲱⲑ ⲫⲁⲓ ⲉⲧⲁⲩⲑⲁϣⲕ ⲛ̀ⲟⲩⲱⲓ ⲉⲣⲟϥ
ⲟⲩⲟϩ ⲛ̀ⲁⲣⲭⲓⲅⲟⲥ ⲉⲧⲉ ⲫⲁⲓ ⲡⲉ ⲡⲓϣⲗⲟⲗ ⲉⲧⲧⲁⲓⲏⲟⲩⲧ ⲛ̀ⲧⲉ ⲛⲓⲙⲟⲛⲁⲭⲟⲥ
ⲡⲓⲗⲁⲟⲥ ⲉⲧⲓⲣⲓ ⲙ̀ⲫⲟⲩⲱϣ ⲙ̀Ⲫϯ ⲟⲩⲟϩ ⲉⲧⲥⲱⲕ ⲛ̀ⲛⲉϥⲙⲉⲧϣⲉⲛϩⲏⲧ
ⲉϩⲣⲏⲓ ⲉϫⲉⲛ ⲡⲅⲉⲛⲟⲥ ⲛ̀ⲛⲓⲣⲱⲙⲓ ⲉⲑⲃⲉ ⲛⲟⲩⲡⲁⲗⲏⲧⲓⲁ ⲛⲉⲙ ⲛⲟⲩϣⲗⲏⲗ
ⲛⲉⲙ ⲛⲟⲩⲉⲣⲙⲱⲟⲩⲓ ⲉⲧⲟⲩⲫⲱⲛ ⲙ̀ⲙⲱⲟⲩ ⲉⲃⲟⲗ ⲙ̀ⲡⲓⲉϩⲟⲟⲩ ⲛⲉⲙ
ⲡⲓⲉϫⲱⲣϩ ϧⲉⲛ ⲟⲩⲙⲉⲧⲁⲑⲙⲟⲩⲛⲕ ⲉⲑⲃⲉ ⲛⲓⲣⲉϥⲉⲣⲛⲟⲃⲓ ϫⲉ ϩⲓⲛⲁ
ⲛ̀ⲧⲟⲩⲥⲁⲑⲱⲟⲩ ϩⲁ Ⲫϯ ϧⲉⲛ ⲡⲟⲩϩⲏⲧ ⲧⲏⲣϥ ⲛ̀ⲧⲉϥⲭⲱ ⲛⲱⲟⲩ ⲉⲃⲟⲗ
ⲕⲁⲧⲁ ⲛⲉϥⲙⲉⲧϣⲉⲛϩⲏⲧ ⲉϧⲟⲩⲛ ⲉⲡⲉϥⲑⲁⲙⲓⲟ.

96. ⲓⲥ ϩⲏⲡⲡⲉ ϫⲉ ⲛⲁⲓⲟϯ ⲉ̅ⲑ̅ⲩ̅ ⲓⲥ ⲛⲏⲉⲧⲁⲓⲛⲁⲩ ⲉⲣⲱⲟⲩ ⲛⲉⲙ
ⲛⲏⲉⲧⲁⲓⲥⲟⲙⲟⲩ ⲁⲓⲧⲁⲙⲱⲧⲉⲛ ⲉⲣⲱⲟⲩ. ⲗⲟⲓⲡⲟⲛ ⲁⲛⲁⲩ ⲙ̀ⲡⲉⲛⲑⲣⲉ

ϩⲗⲓ ⲉⲣⲁⲑⲛⲁϩϯ ⲉⲛⲛⲉⲧⲁⲩϫⲟⲧⲟⲩ ⲧⲏⲣⲟⲩ ⲉⲑⲃⲉ ⲛⲁⲓⲁⲅⲓⲟⲥ ⲁⲗⲗⲁ ϣⲱⲡ ⲛ̀ⲛⲉⲧⲁⲓϫⲟⲧⲟⲩ ⲉⲑⲃⲏⲧⲟⲩ ϩⲓⲛⲁ ⲛ̀ⲧⲉⲧⲉⲛϣⲧⲉⲙϭⲓ ⲛ̀ⲟⲩϩⲁⲡ ⲙⲁⲗⲓⲥⲧⲁ ⲛⲏⲉⲧⲁⲩϫⲟⲧⲟⲩ ⲛ̀ϫⲉ ⲡⲉⲛⲓⲱⲧ ⲙ̀ⲡⲓⲡ̅ⲛ̅ⲁ̅ⲧⲟⲫⲟⲣⲟⲥ ⲡⲓⲛⲓϣϯ ⲁⲃⲃⲁ ⲙⲁⲕⲁⲣ ⲡⲓⲣⲱⲙⲓ ⲉⲧⲉⲣⲫⲟⲣⲓⲛ ⲙ̀ⲫϯ ⲟⲩⲟϩ ⲉⲣⲉ ⲫϯ ⲙⲉⲓ ⲙ̀ⲙⲟϥ ⲉⲑⲃⲉ ⲡⲉϥⲧⲟⲩⲃⲟ. ⲥ̀ⲥϧⲏⲟⲩⲧ ⲅⲁⲣ ϫⲉ ⲁⲣⲉϣⲁⲛ ⲛⲓϩⲉⲗⲗⲟⲓ ϩⲓⲕⲟⲕ ⲉⲁⲃⲃⲁ ⲙⲁⲕⲁⲣ ϣⲁⲩϭⲓⲧⲟⲩ ⲉⲡⲟⲩⲥⲡⲏⲗⲉⲟⲛ ⲉϥϫⲱ ⲙ̀ⲙⲟⲥ ϫⲉ ⲁⲙⲱⲓⲛⲓ ⲛ̀ⲧⲉⲛⲛⲁⲩ ⲙ̀ⲡⲓⲙⲁⲣⲧⲩⲣⲓⲟⲛ ⲛ̀ⲧⲉ ⲛⲓⲕⲟⲩϫⲓ ⲛ̀ϣⲉⲙⲙⲱⲟⲩ ϩⲟⲡⲱⲥ ⲛ̀ⲧⲉ ⲛ̀ⲑⲱⲧⲉⲛ ϩⲱⲧⲉⲛ ⲛ̀ⲧⲉⲧⲉⲛⲉⲣⲡⲣⲟⲕⲟⲡⲧⲓⲛ ϧⲉⲛ ⲛⲓⲁⲣⲉⲧⲏ ⲛ̀ⲧⲉ ⲛⲏⲉⲧⲉⲙⲙⲁⲩ ⲛⲁⲓⲁⲅⲓⲟⲥ ⲉⲧⲥⲙⲁⲣⲱⲟⲩⲧ ⲟⲩⲟϩ ⲛ̀ⲧⲉⲧⲉⲛⲉⲣⲡⲉⲙⲡϣⲁ ⲛ̀ϯⲙⲉⲣⲟⲥ ⲛⲉⲙ ⲡⲓⲕⲗⲏⲣⲟⲥ ⲛ̀ⲧⲱⲟⲩ ϧⲉⲛ ⲑⲙⲉⲧⲟⲩⲣⲟ ⲛ̀ⲉⲛⲉϩ ⲙ̀ⲡⲉⲛⲟ̅ⲥ̅ Ⲓⲏ̅ⲥ̅ Ⲡⲭ̅ⲥ̅

97. ⲁⲛⲁⲩ ϫⲉ ⲁⲡⲓⲛⲓϣϯ ⲁⲃⲃⲁ ⲙⲁⲕⲁⲣ ⲭⲛⲁⲩ ⲛ̀ⲧⲟⲧϥ ϩⲱⲥ ⲡ̇ ϧⲉⲛ ⲡ̀ϫⲓⲛⲑⲣⲉϥϩⲱⲗ ⲉⲡⲓⲥⲡⲏⲗⲉⲟⲛ ⲛⲉⲙ ⲛⲓϩⲉⲗⲗⲟⲓ ⲛ̀ⲧⲟⲩϣⲗⲏⲗ ϧⲉⲛ ⲟⲩⲛⲁϩϯ ⲕⲉ ⲅⲁⲣ ⲁⲩⲉⲣⲡ̇ ϧⲉⲛ ⲧⲟⲩⲡⲣⲟϩⲉⲣⲉⲥⲓⲥ ⲁϭⲛⲉ ⲫⲉⲛ ⲥⲛⲟϥ ⲉⲃⲟⲗϧⲉⲛ ⲡ̀ϫⲓⲛⲑⲣⲟⲩⲉⲣⲕⲁⲧⲁⲫⲣⲟⲛⲓⲛ ⲛ̀ⲑⲙⲉⲧⲟⲩⲣⲟ ⲙ̀ⲡⲟⲩⲓⲱⲧ ⲉⲑⲛⲁⲧⲁⲕⲟ ⲉⲑⲃⲉ ϯⲙⲉⲧⲟⲩⲣⲟ ⲛ̀ⲧⲉ ⲛⲓⲫⲏⲟⲩⲓ ⲛⲉⲙ ⲛⲉⲥⲁⲅⲁⲑⲟⲥ ⲟⲩⲟϩ ⲫⲙⲉⲩⲓ ⲙ̀ⲡⲓⲡⲁⲗⲁⲧⲓⲟⲛ ⲉⲧⲁⲩⲉⲣⲡⲉϥϣⲱϣ ⲛⲉⲙ ⲛⲓϫⲓⲛⲟⲩⲱⲙ ⲉⲧⲗⲉⲕⲗⲱⲕ ⲛ̀ⲟⲩⲙⲏϣ ⲛ̀ⲣⲏϯ ⲛⲉⲙ ⲛⲓϩⲟϫϩⲉϫ ϩⲱⲟⲩ ⲉⲧⲁⲩⲉⲣϩⲩⲡⲟⲙⲟⲛⲓⲛ ⲉⲣⲱⲟⲩ ϩⲓ ⲛⲓⲙⲁⲙⲙⲱϣⲓ ⲉⲧϩⲟⲥⲓ ⲛ̀ⲧⲉ ⲫⲓⲟⲙ ⲛⲉⲙ ⲡ̀ⲕⲩⲛⲇⲓⲛⲟⲥ ⲛ̀ⲛⲓϭⲁⲧϥⲓ ⲛ̀ⲧⲉ ⲡⲓⲙⲁ ⲉⲧⲉⲙⲙⲁⲩ ϣⲁⲧⲉ ⲫϯ ϭⲓⲙⲱⲓⲧ ⲛⲱⲟⲩ ϩⲓⲧⲉⲛ ⲧⲉϥⲃⲟⲏⲑⲓⲁ ⲉⲧⲥⲱⲕ ϧⲁϫⲱⲟⲩ ϣⲁⲧⲉϥⲉⲛⲟⲩ ⲉⲡⲓⲧⲱⲟⲩ ⲛ̀ⲧⲉ Ϣⲓϩⲏⲧ ⲉⲫⲙⲁ ⲙ̀ⲡⲉⲑⲟⲩⲁⲃ ⲁⲃⲃⲁ ⲙⲁⲕⲁⲣ ⲛ̀ⲧⲟⲩϫⲱⲕ ⲉⲃⲟⲗ ⲙ̀ⲙⲁⲩ ⲉⲑⲃⲉ ⲫⲁⲓ ⲁⲓϫⲟⲥ ϫⲉ ⲁⲩⲉⲣⲡ̇ ⲁϭⲛⲉ ⲥⲛⲟϥ.

98. ⲁⲛϣⲁⲛⲭⲱ ⲅⲁⲣ ⲛⲁⲛ ⲙ̀ⲡⲉⲣⲫⲙⲉⲩⲓ ⲛ̀ⲧⲁⲛⲁⲥⲧⲣⲟⲫⲏ ⲛ̀ⲛⲉⲛⲓⲟϯ ⲉ̅ⲑ̅ⲩ̅ ⲧⲉⲛⲛⲁϣⲓⲃϯ ϩⲱⲛ ⲉⲃⲟⲗϩⲁ ⲛⲓⲥⲩⲛⲏⲑⲓⲁ ⲛ̀ⲕⲟⲥⲙⲓⲕⲟⲥ ⲟⲩⲟϩ ⲧⲉⲛⲛⲁϭⲓ ϧⲉⲣⲉⲃ ⲛ̀ⲟⲩⲱⲓⲛⲓ ϧⲉⲛ ⲛⲓⲙⲓⲧⲱⲟⲩⲓ ⲛ̀ⲧⲉ ⲛⲉⲛⲓⲟϯ ⲙ̀ⲙⲁⲕⲁⲣⲓⲟⲥ ⲉⲁⲛⲭⲱ ⲛ̀ⲥⲱⲛ ⲛ̀ⲛⲁⲭⲁϩⲟⲩ ⲉⲛⲥⲱⲟⲩⲧⲉⲛ ⲙ̀ⲙⲟⲛ ⲉⲛⲁⲓⲧϩⲏ ϧⲉⲛ ⲟⲩⲑⲉⲃⲓⲟ ⲙ̀ⲙⲏⲓ ⲛⲉⲙ ⲟⲩⲁⲅⲁⲡⲏ ⲉⲛⲙⲟϣⲓ ϩⲓ ⲛⲟⲩϣⲉⲛⲧⲁⲧⲥⲓ ⲛ̀ⲁⲧⲥⲱⲣⲉⲙ ⲉⲛϫⲱⲕ ⲉⲃⲟⲗ ⲛ̀ⲛⲓⲛⲟⲙⲟⲥ ⲛ̀ⲧⲉ Ⲡⲭ̅ⲥ̅ Ⲓⲏ̅ⲥ̅ ⲛⲉⲙ ⲛⲓⲉⲛⲧⲟⲗⲏ ⲛ̀ⲁⲅⲅⲉⲗⲓⲕⲟⲛ ⲛ̀ⲧⲉ ϯⲙⲉⲧⲙⲟⲛⲁⲭⲟⲥ ⲛⲁⲓⲉⲧϭⲓⲙⲱⲓⲧ ⲛⲁⲛ ϣⲁ ⲫϯ ϧⲉⲛ ⲟⲩⲥⲱⲟⲩⲧⲉⲛ ⲛⲉⲙ ϯϫⲓⲛϣⲁϣⲛⲓ ⲉⲛⲓⲁⲅⲁⲑⲟⲛ ϧⲉⲛ ⲡⲓⲡⲁⲣⲁⲇⲓⲥⲟⲥ.

99. ⲕⲉ ⲅⲁⲣ ⲁⲛⲉⲛⲓⲟϯ ⲭⲁ ⲡⲓⲕⲟⲩϫⲓ ⲙ̀ⲙⲁⲛϣⲱⲡⲓ ⲛ̀ⲧⲉ ⲛⲁⲓⲁⲅⲓⲟⲥ ⲛ̀ⲧⲟⲧⲟⲩ ⲙ̀ⲫⲣⲏϯ ⲛ̀ⲟⲩⲉⲕⲕⲗⲏⲥⲓⲁ ⲉⲩϩⲏⲗ ⲉⲙⲁⲩ ⲕⲁⲧⲁ ⲕⲟⲩϫⲓ ⲉⲩϣⲗⲏⲗ ϧⲉⲛ ⲟⲩⲛⲁϩϯ ⲟⲩⲟϩ ϩⲁⲛⲙⲏϣ ⲛ̀ⲧⲉ ⲛⲏⲉⲧϣⲱⲛⲓ ⲉⲧϩⲟⲣϣ ϧⲉⲛ ⲛⲟⲩⲥⲱⲙⲁ ⲛⲉⲙ ⲧⲟⲩⲯⲩⲭⲏ ⲓⲧⲉ ϧⲉⲛ ϣⲓϩⲛⲧ ⲓⲧⲉ ⲛⲁ ⲡⲧⲱⲟⲩ ⲙ̀ⲡⲉⲣⲛⲟⲩϫ ⲓⲧⲉ ⲙⲁⲓ ⲛⲓⲃⲉⲛ ⲁⲩϣⲁⲛⲓ ⲉⲡⲟⲩⲙⲁⲣⲧⲩⲣⲓⲟⲛ ⲛ̀ⲥⲉϣⲗⲏⲗ ϣⲁⲩϭⲓ ⲙ̀ⲡⲓⲧⲁⲗϭⲟ ⲥⲁⲧⲟⲧⲟⲩ ⲉⲃⲟⲗϩⲓⲧⲉⲛ ⲡⲓϩⲙⲟⲧ ⲛ̀ⲧⲉ ⲡⲉⲛⲟ̅ⲥ̅ Ⲓⲏ̅ⲥ̅ Ⲡⲭ̅ⲥ̅ ⲫⲁⲓ ⲉⲧϯ ⲙ̀ⲡⲓⲧⲁⲗϭⲟ ⲛ̀ⲛⲏⲉⲧϣⲱⲛⲓ ⲓⲧⲉ ⲛⲉ ⲡⲓⲥⲱⲙⲁ ⲓⲧⲉ ⲛⲁ ϯⲯⲩⲭⲏ ϩⲓⲧⲉⲛ ⲛⲓⲡⲣⲉⲥⲃⲓⲁ ⲛ̀ⲧⲉ ⲛⲉⲛⲓⲟϯ ⲉ̅ⲑ̅ⲩ̅ ⲛ̀ⲣⲱⲙⲉⲟⲥ Ⲙⲁⲝⲓⲙⲟⲥ ⲛⲉⲙ Ⲇⲟⲙⲉⲧⲓⲟⲥ ⲉⲧⲉ ⲡⲥⲱⲧⲏⲣ ⲛ̀ⲟⲩⲟⲛ ⲛⲓⲃⲉⲛ ⲡⲉ ⲡⲉⲛⲟ̅ⲥ̅ ⲟⲩⲟϩ ⲡⲉⲛⲛⲟⲩϯ ⲟⲩⲟϩ ⲡⲉⲛⲥⲱ̅ⲣ̅ Ⲓⲏ̅ⲥ̅ Ⲡⲭ̅ⲥ̅ ⲫⲁⲓ ⲉⲧⲉ ⲉⲃⲟⲗϩⲓⲧⲟⲧϥ ϣⲟⲩ ⲛⲓⲃⲉⲛ ⲛⲉⲙ ⲧⲁⲓⲟ ⲛⲓⲃⲉⲛ ⲛⲉⲙ ⲡⲣⲟⲥⲕⲩⲛⲉⲥⲓⲥ ⲛⲓⲃⲉⲛ ⲉⲣⲡⲣⲉⲡⲓ ⲙ̀ⲫⲓⲱⲧ ⲛⲉⲙⲁϥ ⲛⲉⲙ ⲡⲓⲡ̅ⲛ̅ⲁ̅ ⲉ̅ⲑ̅ⲩ̅ ⲛ̀ⲣⲉϥⲧⲁⲛϧⲟ ⲟⲩⲟϩ ⲛ̀ⲟⲙⲟⲟⲩⲥⲓⲟⲥ ⲛⲉⲙⲁϥ ϯⲛⲟⲩ ⲛⲉⲙ ϣⲁ ⲉⲛⲉϩ ⲛ̀ⲧⲉ ⲛⲓⲉⲛⲉϩ ⲧⲏⲣⲟⲩ. ⲁⲙⲏⲛ.

BIBLIOGRAPHY

'Abd al- Massīḥ, Yassa. "Doxologies in the Coptic Church", *BSAC* 4 (1938): 97-113.
- "Doxologies of the Coptic Church", *BSAC 5* (1939): 175-191.
- "Doxologies in the Coptic Church, Unedited Bohairic Doxologies II (Tûbahan-Nasî)", *BSAC 11* (1946-1947): 95-158.

al-Maqqārī, Fīlūtā'us, ed. *al-Kitāb al-ibṣaliyat w-al-turuhat al-watos w-al-ādām*. Cairo, 1913.

al-Mas'ūdī, āl-Qummuṣ 'Abd al-Massīḥ Ṣalīb al-Baramūsī, ed. *Kitāb al- ẖulaji al-muqaddas*. Cairo, 1902.

al-Suryānī, Ṣamū'īl. *Tartīb al-bay'ah*. Cairo, undated handwritten text.

al-Suryānī, Ṣamū'īl. *al-ādyurah al-maṣriyah al-'āmerah*. Cairo, 1968.

Amélineau, Emile. *Monuments pour servir à l'histoire de d'Égypte chrétienne: histoire des monastères de la Basse-Égypte; vies des saints Paul, Antoine, Macaire, Maxime et Domèce Jean Le Main, etc. Vol. 25*. E. Leroux, 1894.

Atiya, Aziz Suryal, ed. *Coptic Encyclopedia*. Digitally published by Claremont Graduate University, 1991.

- Aelred Cody, "Doxology", CE 3.
- Archbishop Bassilios, "Coptic Vestments", CE 5.
- Archbishop Bassilios, "Forty-Nine Martyrs of Scetis", CE 4.
- Emile Maher Ishaq, "Difnar", CE 3.
- Emile Maher Ishaq, "Sab›ah Wa-arba›ah", CE 7.

Basset, René. "Mois de Toubeh et d'Amchir". *PO Tome 11* (1915): 609-614.

Browne, Edward Granville. *A hand-list of the Muḥammadan manuscripts: including all those written in the Arabic character, preserved in the library of the University of Cambridge*. University Press, 1900.

Buzi, Paola. "The Life of Maximus and Domitius: Considerations for a Reconstruction of the Cultural Life of Western Lower Egypt in the late Coptic age." In *Augustinianum II* (2001): 521-544.

Chaîne, M. *Le manuscrit de la version copte Apophthegmata Patrum*. Cairo, 1960.

Evelyn White, H.G. *The monasteries of the Wâdi›n Natrûn vol. II the History of the Monasteries of Nitria and Scetis*. Arno Press, 1926.

Forget, Iacobus, ed. *Synaxarium Alexandrinum Tomus I* (1905).

Gabra, Gawdat, and Tim Vivian. *Coptic Monasteries: Egypt's monastic art and architecture*. Oxford University Press, 2002.

Grossmann, Peter, and Hans-Georg Severin. "Zum antiken Bestand der al-Adrâ›kirche des Dair al-Baramûs im Wâdi Natrûn." (1997).

Helmy, Mickel, ed. *al-difnār: al-āntīfūnāriyūn al-ṣaʿīdī*. Cairo: Alexandria School, 2018.

Hyvernat, Henri. *Bybliothecae Pierpont Morgan codices coptici, Photographice Expressi, Codices M584, Tomvs XL.* (Romae, 1922).

Innemée, Karel. "Deir al-Baramūs, excavations at the so-called site of Moses the Black, 1994-1999." *BSAC 39* (2000): 123-135.

Innemee, Karel. "Excavations at Deir el Baramūs". *Grafma Newsletter 1* (1997 & 2 1998).

Labīb, Aqladiyūs, ed. *Pičōm Nte Tipsalmōdia Ethu Nte Piabot Khoiak: Mphrēg Etauthašh Nče Nenioti Ntiekklēsia Nremnkhēmi.* Cairo: ʿain šams.

Munier, Henri. Une relation copte saʾīdique de la vie des saints Maxime et Domèce. *Imprimérie de l'Institut Français d'Archéologie Orientale,* 1917.

OʾLeary, De Lacy. "The Difnar (Antiphonarium) of the Coptic Church/2 Second four months, Tubeh, Amshir, Barmahat and Barmuda/from the Vatican Codex Copt. Borgia 59", (1928).

Papadopulos, Leo, trans. *Saint Paisios the Great.* New York: Holy Trinity Monastery, 1998.

Pasi, Silvia. "The wall paintings of the church of Al-Adra in the monastery of Deir-el-Baramūs (Wadi-el-Natrun)." *Zograf 34* (2010): 37-52.

Pirone, B. "Vita dei Santi Massimo e Domezio nelle Fonti Arabe (Edizione, traduzione e note)." *Studia Orientalia Christiana 29* (1998): 249-388.

Taqī al-Dīn al-Maqrīzī. *al-Mawaiz wa al-I'tibar fi al-Khitat wa al-Athar, vol.2.* Cairo: Government Press, 1892.

Vivian, Tim. "The world is too much with us: The sayings of Arsenius in the Alphabetical Apophthegmata Patrum. A new translation with comments." *The American Benedictine review 70, no. 2* (2019): 163-192.

Vivian, Tim. *Saint Macarius, the spirit-bearer: Coptic texts relating to Saint Macarius the Great*. New York: St Vladimir's Seminary Press, 2004.

Ward, Benedicta. *The sayings of the desert fathers: The alphabetical collection (rev. ed.)*. Kalamazoo: Cistercian Publications, 1984.

INDEX

A

Abū Maqār 73, 93, 95, 97
Agabus 6, 20, 21, 22, 23, 25, 27, 34, 89, 94, 103
Alexandria 11, 34, n.65, n.131
al-Maqrīzī 6, 74
Anastasius 55
Antioch 29, 73
Antiochene 29
Antiphonarium 85, 86, n.109
Apophthegmata Patrum 3, 6, 7, 10
Arabic 1, 3, 5, 6, 10, 13, 55, 63, 74, 81, 86, 87, 93
Arcadius 32, 74
archbishop 11, 32, 33
Arsenius 3, 4, 6, 74, 75, 96
aspasmos 99
Asqelon 22
Athens 28, 29

B

Baramūs 1, 2, 47, 71, 72, 73, 75, 74, 81, 85, 93, 95, 98, 103, 104, 108.
    See also al-Baramūs
Barsoum the Syrian 103
Bitimius 7
Bohairic 1, 3, 4, 7, 12, 13, 53, 55, 81, 113
brothers 3, 5, 6, 31, 63, 64, 68, 75, 77, 81, 91, 94, 103, 104

C

canonical hours 82
Cherub 48, 76, 104
Constantinople 3, 4, 6, 11, 17, 21, 24, 29, 31, 32, 33, 37, 46, 56, 74
construction 72, n.87, 76

D

Daniel n.46, n.48, 36, n.51, 58, 96
difnār 85
diptych 48, 81
doxology 75, 81, 83

E

elder 8, 9, 19, 21, 22, 34, 40, 42, 44, 46, 47, 49
Elijah 22, 35, 38, 43, 59, 88
Elisha 22, 59
Emperor Theodosius I 4, 6, 74. See Theodosius
Emperor Valentinian 3, 4, 5, 8, 13, 17, 19, 30, 55, 56, n.122, 81, 96, 105
empress 13, 31, 63, 64, 68
epilogue 49
epiphany 43
euchologion 83, n. 103
eunuch 31, 33, n. 79

G

Gabala 25, 26
garment/s 21, 34, 38, 39, 41, 59, 92, 96, 103, 104
girdle 8, 9, 39
Greek 2, 7, 9, 10, n.59, 28, 44, 63, 71, 81

H

Habakkuk 36
habit 21, 38, 103, 104. See skema
Honorius 6

I

Iconium 23
iconography 101
Isidoros 11

J

Jacob 13, 32, 65
John Cassian 48, n. 29, n. 68, 82
Jovian 4, 5, 19, n. 35
Judea 36
Julian the Apostate 56, n. 74

Julian (bishop) 73

K

Kīyahk 93

L

Labīb 93
Leontius 29
Lystra 23

M

Macarius 2, 3, 4, 5, 6, 9, 11, 17, 18, 19, 21, 22, 23, 25, 27, 33, 34, 36, 37, 38, 39, 40, 42, 44, 45, 46, 47, 48, 49, 59, 71, 72, 75, 81, 82, 90, 93, 94, 95, 96, 97, 98, 103, 104, 106
madīḥ 93
Magdala 24
Marcellus 31
Monastery of
  al-Baramūs 75
  al-Suryān 71
  of the Romans 11, 17, 71, 74, 75
  St Antony 98, 103, 104, 106, 107
monk 12, 13, 20, 21, 24, 45, 47, 103
Moses the Black 17, 72, 74
Mountain of Scete 94, 95

N

Nicaea 20, 32, 55, 59

P

Palestine 20, 22, 34
Paōni 57
Paphnutius 48, 75, 76
Pisidia 22, 24
prologue 17
psali 86
Psalmodia 93
psalmody 82
Pshoi 3, 11, 17, 24, 46, 73, 93, 96, 109. See also Bishoy

S

Sahidic 1, 5, 10, 12, 13
Samaritan 26
Scete 6, 3, 17, 18, 24, 32, 36, 37, 38, 41, 48, 49, 50, 71, 73, 74, 82, 95, 96
Seleucia 26
Sergius 55
sīrah 13, 63
sister 13, 19, 31, 67
skema 84
Susanna 35

Synaxarium 1, 81, 85
Syria 6, 20, 21, 24, 25, 30, 31, 32, 33, 34, 38, 47, 95
Syrian rite 82

T

tartīb al-bay'ah 98, 99
tasbeḥah 85
Theodosius I 4
Theotokos 57
Tōbi 17, 43, 45, 73, 81, 85, 87, 89, 98
Tune
  adam 85, 86, 93
  batos 85
  watos 85, 86
tutor 74

V

Vatican Library 1, 12, 86

W

Wadī al-Naṭrūn 1, 3, 71, 73, 86
Wadi Habib 149–163
wall painting 85, 104

Z

Zachariah 25

www.ingramcontent.com/pod-product-compliance
Lightning Source LLC
Chambersburg PA
CBHW022133080426
42734CB00006B/349